The Religion of the Apostles: Orthod⟨...⟩
a book by our spiritual son Fr. Step⟨...⟩ ⟨...⟩ ⟨...⟩ to challenge
recent claims by scholars that the teachings of the Holy Church
regarding the Holy Trinity and the divinity of Christ were later developments of the Fathers and Ecumenical Councils. This book delves
into contemporary scholarship on the religious beliefs of the Judaism
of the Second Temple period. It sheds light on the ways that evangelists and the apostles understood the revelation of our Lord Jesus
Christ and how the authors of the New Testament framed their narratives to communicate the very same Faith expressed later in the history of the Church. While challenging at times, this work opens new
ways to read and understand the Old and New Testaments as well
as our liturgical worship. These new ways always point to the wider
Holy Tradition of the Orthodox Church. I welcome this work by Fr.
Stephen and hope that readers will gain a fuller and deeper appreciation of the "faith once and for all delivered to the saints."

—+Joseph
Archbishop of New York and Metropolitan of the Antiochian
Orthodox Christian Archdiocese of North America

In the twenty-fourth chapter of St. Luke's Gospel we are told how
Cleopas and his companion were met by the risen Christ while walking to Emmaus. In the ensuing conversation we are told how Jesus
"explained to them the passages throughout the scriptures that
were about Himself" (Luke 24:27). This passage, together with the
event of the descent of the Holy Spirit at the first Pentecost, has been
taken by the Church to indicate that from those events forward, the
apostles had a complete and coherent Faith to pass on for the conversion of the world. In contrast, much scholarship in recent times
has maintained the view that instead of being whole from the beginning, Church doctrine—particularly Christology—"developed" to

its definitive statements by the Great Councils. In contrast to these claims, Fr. Stephen De Young here presents forceful arguments to show that the Faith of the apostles was indeed complete from the beginning and was simply refined to meet heretical challenges. It is well worth reading.

—+MELCHISEDEK
Archbishop of Pittsburgh and Western Pennsylvania
Orthodox Church in America

With this book, Fr. Stephen De Young is not only leading the charge for Orthodox apologetics in a world of secular biblical scholarship, but he is also doing us all a favor by reviving the cosmic frame of ancient Christians, giving hope to a jaded culture desperately looking for a re-enchanted world in which it can fully participate.

—JONATHAN PAGEAU, *The Symbolic World*

The Religion
of the
APOSTLES

Orthodox Christianity
in the First Century

REV. DR. STEPHEN DE YOUNG

ANCIENT FAITH PUBLISHING
CHESTERTON, INDIANA

The Religion of the Apostles: Orthodox Christianity in the First Century
Copyright ©2021 Stephen De Young

PUBLISHED BY:

Ancient Faith Publishing
A Division of Ancient Faith Ministries
P.O. Box 748
Chesterton, IN 46304

ISBN: 978-1-944967-55-0

Library of Congress Control Number: 2021931259

PRINTED IN THE UNITED STATES OF AMERICA

Table of Contents

Preface

WHEN ASKED TO PICTURE THE earliest churches—the congregations founded and ministered to by the apostles—many today imagine a meager gathering in a small home, likely a bare room. The people would sit on the floor, facing a visiting apostle or teacher, who would lead them in worship, perhaps by singing a hymn or psalm and praying. Then he would teach the group. His message, so it is assumed, would have been simple: Jesus is the Messiah; He had died for their sins. They should put their faith and trust in Him, and they would go to heaven when they died. In the meantime, they ought to set aside their sinful ways and love one another. Simple, unadorned, plain: that is how many people imagine the religion of the apostles to have been.

Yet when these same people find themselves in an Orthodox church, their experience could not be more different from this mental image. An Orthodox church is a space dedicated for worship, not a room in a person's home. It is bedecked with iconography and beautifully furnished. The sharp fragrance of incense fills the air along with chanting, perhaps in a language other than English. The clergy wear colorful robes and move in and out of sight behind a partition that obscures the view of an altar. The service is complicated and confusing in its structure and is difficult to follow even with a service book. The hymns and prayers and preaching are filled with foreign, untranslated words of unclear meaning. It would be counterintuitive to suggest that this seemingly elaborate spectacle bears more in common with the religion practiced by the apostles than does the simpler, more primitive picture our modern imagination conjures up. Yet it is precisely this claim that forms the basis of *The Religion of the Apostles*.

This book is organized systematically, intending to present an orderly account of the religious teachings and practices of the apostles. Nevertheless, it should be noted that it is not possible to construct a fully systematic theology of the religion[1] of the Second Temple period in general nor of the first century after Christ in particular. Not only are the available sources themselves not structured systematically, but the religion of this period was not conceived of in systematic or even theological terms. Ancient religion was inseparable from politics, culture, and every other dimension of life. Because ritual pervaded all aspects of human activity, religion was more lived and experienced than intellectualized or philosophized. As later thinkers began to treat the study of religion as a primarily philosophical or intellectual activity, they withdrew themselves from the traditional religion of their people.

This book is organized topically or thematically rather than chronologically or historically. Part 1 analyzes the way God is described in the Scriptures. It specifically focuses on the way ancient Israel, Second Temple Judeans, and the apostles themselves experienced and understood the multiple Persons—Father, Son, and Holy Spirit—who share the Godhead. Part 2 describes the other beings—angels and demons—who inhabit the spiritual world. It

---

1   A note on terminology: throughout this book I refer to "religion" of the Second Temple period (or even "religion" of the Apostles) rather than the "Judaism" or "Jewish religion." As will become clearer in this book, the religion of Judeans scattered throughout the Roman world in the Second Temple period was varied and diverse, to the point that some scholars have argued that the term "Judaism" is misleading when used in reference to this time period. Second Temple Judaism is not the name of a single religion but a catch-all term for the religious belief and practice of Jewish people.

also describes the ways ancient people interacted, both positively and negatively, with the unseen world populated by those beings. Part 3 describes the Creation and the salvation of the world. This includes, but is not limited to, the salvation of humanity. Finally, part 4 describes the assembled people of God—Israel and the Church—in the Old and New Testaments. Special attention is paid to the way in which the Torah, God's "Law," is interpreted and applied in the life of this community.

The Religion of the Apostles has several purposes. First and foremost, it outlines the contours of Jewish religion in the first century AD. In the religious milieu of Christ's disciples and apostles, religion was not simply a part of life but encompassed all of it. At no point did the apostles consider themselves to be founding a new religion, certainly not one from scratch. Instead, they integrated their first-hand experiences of Jesus Christ into their existing religious understanding and worldview. Certainly their religious life, in all its parts, was transformed, but this transformation was understood by them in terms of fulfillment, not correction, and much less re-creation.

This book can, therefore, serve as an introduction or *prolegomenon* to reading, studying, and understanding the New Testament and the Scriptures as a whole. The present book brings together religious interpretations and understandings from the literature of the Second Temple period (roughly 515 BC—AD 70). Only within the last few decades have scholars begun to grasp that Second Temple literature lends important context to our understanding of the New Testament. Before that, scholarship had long taken for granted that the religion practiced by Judeans in the first century AD was identical to religion as practiced by later Rabbinic Judaism. This is simply not the case. Rabbinic Judaism came to flower only in the fifth century AD with the codification of the Talmud. Christianity had already emerged several centuries before Rabbinic Judaism, which was itself a reaction against Christian faith and praxis.

Jewish scholar Jacob Neusner famously argued that in the Second Temple period, a single, homogenous Judaism did not exist—one must speak of "Judaisms" rather than "Judaism." Indeed, as has been suggested more recently, Rabbinic Judaism as it exists today simply did not exist in this period. The most noticeable difference between the religion of the Second Temple period and later Rabbinic Judaism is that the former revolved around the temple, its sacrificial system, and its priesthood. The destruction of the second temple in Jerusalem required a nearly complete reconstruction of religious practice for Jewish communities that did not embrace the Christian gospel.

Timeline of the Emergence of Christianity from Second Temple Judaism

515 BC—AD 70: Second Temple period

Circa 3 BC—AD 30: Earthly life of Jesus Christ

AD 35: Calling of St. Paul

AD 49: St. Paul writes the Epistle to the Galatians, first New Testament text

AD 69: St. Mark writes his Gospel, the first of the canonical Gospels

AD 95: St. John writes the Apocalypse, the final New Testament text

Circa AD 500: Formation of Rabbinic Judaism

Of what did these "Judaisms" consist? This was a religion divided into many sects, whose borders with one another were often porous, but who defined themselves in terms of distinctive religious calendars, observances, and modes of worship. Despite their differences, however, they shared a common understanding of the created world, its spiritual history, and its ultimate destiny. As a continuation of the religion of this period, Christianity inherited this view of the world. It understood, further, that certain future events had already been fulfilled through the birth, life, death, Resurrection, and Ascension of Jesus Christ.

Likewise, the texts that came to make up the Old Testament, by any understanding of the Christian canon, came into their final form during the Second Temple period. The texts of the New Testament, as well as extrabiblical literature originating both before and after the birth of Christianity, were also written within this milieu. Together, these texts reflect the religious life and experience of religious people around the time that Christianity came into being. Gaining familiarity with their life and experience is, therefore, a necessary requirement for understanding what these texts have to say.

Distorted assumptions about Church history, often originating among scholars, trickle down to misinform the average Christian even after being discarded by the academic circles in which they originated. This book seeks to correct several such presuppositions, in particular the claim that the Church's history and theology can be explained by an evolutionary paradigm. This approach presumed that belief in Christ's divinity must have evolved from an earlier view of Christ as a mere man. Christ's deity, so the claim goes, would have been an affront to the sensibilities of first-century Judeans, who are presumed to be fiercely monotheistic. It followed that the Holy Trinity must have been an even later development. In fact, Trinitarian doctrine and the entire concept of sainthood were wrongly assumed to be a later concession to pagan polytheism.

Scholars are now overturning this evolutionary paradigm, as it fails to fully account for the evidence of Scripture, archaeology, history, and extrabiblical literature. *The Religion of the Apostles* seeks to integrate and explain this evidence, which reveals that these core beliefs and practices of the Church were present from its beginning and, in some cases, even predate Christianity. Although the Second Temple period did witness a transition in response to numerous spiritually and historically significant events, there was not a development—gradual or otherwise—from some sort of primitive spirituality to a more refined religious consciousness.

The other major assumption this book seeks to rectify is the assumed discontinuity between Old and New Testaments, between biblical and extrabiblical literature, and between Scripture and even the earliest apostolic Fathers. In distancing the Old and New Testaments from one another, we tend to assume that prayer, worship, and significant religious practices were simplistic and undeveloped among New Testament Christians. The advanced religious beliefs and practices that had accrued over the preceding centuries are presumed to have been abandoned by the apostles. Placing a similar division between the New Testament and even the earliest patristic writings, it begins to seem that the forms of prayer and worship those early Fathers described were completely disconnected from the practices of the first Christians only a few decades earlier. We infer this discontinuity despite the considerable overlap in time between the composition of the final writings included in the New Testament and the writings by those who came to be known as the apostolic Fathers.

The acceptance of the smaller, rabbinic canon of the Old Testament by most Protestant groups combines with the division between the Testaments to produce a little-understood "intertestamental period." The Old Testament's history abruptly ends, and the New Testament resumes some five hundred years later. The sects of the Pharisees and Sadducees, as well as all manner of other religious traditions, suddenly appear in the New Testament writings without explanation, having not been mentioned in the Old Testament. Yet any reading of history should preclude such easy distinctions between periods, let alone ironclad barriers between the Old Testament, New Testament, and patristic epochs.

Finally, this book serves an apologetic purpose. The Orthodox Christian Church has always professed its Faith to be the faith of the apostles. It does not teach that its Faith somehow *developed* or *evolved* from that of the apostles or their teaching, nor that its teaching began with the apostles and continued from there, nor that its teaching is merely a logical extension of apostolic teaching. Instead, the Church proclaims that its liturgical ritual and way of life are in complete continuity with that of the apostles. This book makes that case. Orthodox Christianity did not materialize from the Fathers of the Church after a disjunction from the living history in which the Scriptures were embedded. It is not an innovation derived from the Church councils that came later. Rather, those councils explained, confirmed, and proclaimed that Faith, which had already existed for centuries preceding them. The life of the Orthodox Christian Church is a direct continuation into the present day of the religious life of the apostles, just as their religious life was a continuation of the life of the people of God since the beginning of creation.

All translations of the Scriptures and other ancient sources are my own. That said, no translation is ever perfect, and that includes the ones I present. Translation is more an art than a science, especially when working with ancient languages that are constructed very differently than the English language. Sometimes, in making a particular point or argument, a translation may need to be very precise about a certain word or explain that the same word is used in two places. For a variety of reasons, however, a standard English translation may lack that precision. For all these reasons it seems best to translate afresh for significant quotations. Old Testament Scripture references are given according to both the Hebrew tradition (which most English Bibles are based on) and the Greek tradition (on which the Orthodox Study Bible and certain other translations are based). When these two systems differ from one another (for example, when the Hebrew tradition numbers a psalm differently than the Greek), the Hebrew tradition references precede the Greek, and a slash (/) separates them.

Saint Paul, Convert?

I T IS EASILY TAKEN FOR granted that Judaism and Christianity represent two separate religious traditions, the latter having grown out of the former during the first few centuries of the Christian era. Implicit in this understanding of Church history is the assumption that the Judaism we would recognize today (which actually has developed from sixth-century Rabbinic Judaism) existed as a single-stranded religious tradition prior to Christianity. In this model, then, Christianity represents an offshoot of Judaism's continuous development from the time of Moses that is regarded as either a transformation or a distortion of Judaic tradition, depending on the sympathies of the commentator.

In recent years, a perfect storm of scholarship from both Jewish and Christian perspectives has begun to capsize these assumptions. This shift began with the work of Jacob Neusner, an American-born (and extraordinarily prolific) scholar of Judaism active throughout the twentieth century. Neusner was the first to contend not only that there were multiple "Judaisms" in the centuries preceding Christ instead of the more uniform Judaism that had long been assumed, but also that these Judaisms were wildly diverse from one another. More recent Jewish scholarship has questioned whether it is correct

1

to speak of "Judaism" at all in that period.[1] Judaism is more properly used to refer to Rabbinic Judaism, a product of the Talmud, which emerged several centuries after the dawn of Christianity.

Just as modern scholars began emphasizing the variegated character of Judaism during this period, their understanding of Christianity's origins also shifted. Instead of seeing Christianity and Rabbinic Judaism as divergent branches of the same tradition, they began to view Christianity as a continuation of the religion that existed before the destruction of the Jerusalem temple. By contrast, Rabbinic Judaism was more accurately understood to originate later, in the fifth and sixth centuries, largely in reaction to Christianity and within Jewish communities that had rejected Jesus of Nazareth as the Messiah.

In all these discussions, St. Paul features as a kind of fulcrum. Since Martin Luther, Western hermeneutics have tended to interpret a fundamental dichotomy between law and gospel into St. Paul's works. This distinction has functioned as a kind of confirmation bias, being read forward into the other New Testament writers and also backward into the Old Testament. According to this understanding, whatever is seen in Scripture to correlate with the "law" (or at least portions of it) is permitted a continuing role in the Church; however, that role is restricted and at any point may be overruled by that which correlates with gospel. Though Luther argued for a more nuanced position, this mode of interpretation often led his theological descendants to marginalize the Old Testament in its entirety.

The problem with this approach is that such a dichotomy is not actually present in St. Paul's treatment of the Torah. In fact, it requires ignoring a wealth of positive statements he makes about the law in his writings (see Rom. 3:31; 1 Cor. 9:8–9; Gal. 5:14). While St. Paul does make certain distinctions regarding the Torah, these do not take the

---

1 Notably, Daniel Boyarin has argued that for the Second Temple period and for some time thereafter, one cannot speak of Judaism but only of the religion of Jewish people at various times and in various places.

form of an opposition between commandment and gospel message. The formulation of this idea by Luther was more directly related to his own personal experience in the sixteenth century than to St. Paul and his writings understood in and of themselves.

This misreading of St. Paul begins with the idea that he is a convert—his experience on the Damascus road is almost universally referred to as his conversion. But on the level of simple logic, for one to "convert," one must leave one religion and join another, and it is a plain fact of history that in AD 35, Judaism and Christianity were not two separate religions. More importantly, Scripture does not present the Damascus road experience as a conversion, nor is that how St. Paul speaks of it after the fact. This event is described twice in the Book of Acts, first in chapter 9 and again in chapter 22 when St. Paul recounts it in a speech. It is also referenced in several Pauline Epistles, notably in 1 Corinthians 15:3–8 and Galatians 1:11–16. Saint Paul's words, as recorded in Acts and his own first-person accounts, describe the event as a vision of the risen Christ, as Christ revealing Himself to him. He moreover cites this experience as the moment he received a call from Christ as God to proclaim the gospel to the Gentiles.

This pattern of vision and calling has parallels in the calling of the prophets in the Old Testament. In Isaiah 6, for example, Isaiah is called to be a prophet during a vision of God seated upon His throne. In the vision, God needs someone to send to His people Israel to pronounce judgment against them, and Isaiah accepts this calling. The verb used by both God and Isaiah here, in the Greek version of Isaiah 6:8, is *apostello*, from which the English noun *apostle* is derived. After his vision, St. Paul identifies his charge as a call to be an apostle— that is, one who is sent—to the nations (the Gentiles) to proclaim the gospel (see Rom. 11:13). Likewise, in the calling of Jeremiah, God proclaims to Jeremiah that He knew him from his mother's womb and had appointed him to be a prophet "unto the nations" or "unto the Gentiles" (in the Greek, *eis ethne*; Jer. 1:5). Saint Paul uses nearly

3

identical language when he describes himself as having been set apart from his mother's womb and called to proclaim the gospel among the nations or among the Gentiles (Gal. 1:15–16).

Clearly St. Paul does not see himself as someone who has left Judaism or the religion of his fathers but as one who was called to a particular service, despite a sinful past persecuting Christ and His Church. His vocation is essentially relayed as a continuation of the role of the prophets in the Old Covenant. Saint Paul perceives himself as persisting in the same religious tradition, one that was being fulfilled in the person and work of Jesus the Messiah. Nowhere in St. Paul's descriptions of his new role does he invalidate the Torah and its commandments. In fact, throughout his life, St. Paul passionately defended himself against the accusation of attempting to do away with the Law, a criticism he faced often (see Acts 21:20–21). Even the typical passages used by proponents of a law/gospel dichotomy to prove St. Paul's antagonism toward the Law often contain evidence to the contrary. In Romans 3:31, for example, St. Paul himself refutes such a dichotomy, declaring that he seeks not to nullify the Law but to establish it.

Saint Paul's personal practices of prayer and piety frame his understanding of his Damascus experience as a prophetic call. The most obvious difference between the experiences of St. Paul and the prophets is that while prophetic calls in the Old Testament involve a vision of Yahweh, St. Paul's is a vision of Jesus Christ. Relatedly, the greatest difference proposed between the religion of the Old Covenant and Christianity is the monotheism of the prophets over against the apostolic proclamation of the deity of Christ. Rather than representing a point of discontinuity, St. Paul's experience reveals to us how he first made the identification of Christ as Yahweh, the God of Israel. The apostolic religion, as presented in the New Testament, is based on an apostolic vision, a vision in which later generations of Christians, particularly ascetics, would seek to share.

Saint Paul lived during the earliest period of development of what would later be called *Merkabah* ("chariot") mysticism within the Second Temple Jewish world.[2] This mystical element of first-century Judaism would later be pruned from the Rabbinic Jewish tradition, surviving only within Christianity. The Merkabah or Chariot tradition refers specifically to Yahweh's throne-chariot in the vision of Ezekiel (see Ezekiel 1), which was carried in flight by four living creatures who bore the faces of an ox, a lion, an eagle, and a human. Because the first temple had already been destroyed by the time the Book of Ezekiel was composed, Ezekiel sees the divine throne in the heavens from which Yahweh governs creation rather than the God of Israel enthroned in the temple with the altar as His footstool, as Isaiah had. In the Second Temple period in which St. Paul lived, when Israel was no longer in exile, this vision became the paradigm by which future visions were interpreted, as a vision of Israel's God insofar as a human person could experience it without losing his or her life.

Merkabah mysticism, then, involved meditating on Ezekiel's vision in the hopes of seeing what he had seen. Although most who practiced this form of mysticism admitted never receiving such a vision, accounts of those who did were recorded in apocalyptic literature of the Second Temple period, in which a common grammar to describe these visionary experiences began to develop.[3] Such narratives often featured a series of heavens, ultimately seven, through which one ascended one by one. Along the way, sojourners were aided by contemplative prayer that centered on the repetition of scriptural texts, most often the Shema (a daily prayer roughly based on Deuteronomy 6:4,

---

2   Merkabah mysticism proper developed parallel to Rabbinic Judaism, though as a spiritual practice it was never embraced by the mainstream of that religion. It formally died out in the tenth century, though elements of its practice persist in the kabbalistic tradition.

3   This happened first and foremost in the Enochic literature, as well as in other apocalypses.

"Hear, O Israel: Yahweh our God, Yahweh is one"). It was also not uncommon to encounter and communicate with angelic beings while ascending through the different levels of heaven. In the highest and purest form of such visions, the ascent culminated in beholding the throne-chariot of the God of Israel, on which would be seated either the Glory of God or the Angel of the Lord figure.

There are several indications in St. Paul's letters that he was familiar with this mystical practice. The most important text in this regard is 2 Corinthians 12:1–6, where St. Paul describes rising first to the third heaven and then into Paradise. Though he frames this vision as one he heard from someone else, the consensus among both the Fathers and scholars is that St. Paul was describing his own experience, as alluded to in verse 6, when he states that were he to boast in such a vision, he would be speaking truth. In any case, the vision and language he uses to describe it strongly correspond to those of early Merkabah sources. The "third heaven" (v. 2) and Paradise (v. 3) he recounts signify a series of ascents. Similarly, he speaks of having heard utterances that cannot be repeated from angelic beings (v. 4).

Accepting, then, that St. Paul was an adherent to this tradition of prayer, new light is shed on his vision of Christ in Acts 9. It is reasonable to believe that on the long journey from Jerusalem to Damascus (it would have taken at minimum several days), St. Paul would have spent much of his time in prayer and meditation, particularly at the hours of prayer. This means that although his vision of Christ was so sudden that it knocked him down, it nonetheless lay within his realm of interpretation. Within the tradition of Merkabah mysticism to which he was accustomed, such a vision would ordinarily have been seen as a gift bestowed on only a few who were blessed to share the experience of Ezekiel and the other prophets. However, when St. Paul receives his vision, it is not an angelic figure he sees, but Jesus Christ, seated on the throne-chariot of Yahweh. Saint Paul's vision on the road to Damascus impresses on him the unshakable reality not merely that Jesus is the Messiah, but also that He is God. It is on this basis St. Paul can proceed in his epistles to speak of Jesus Christ as the incarnate God of Israel.

Further, St. Paul bases his status as an apostle on this vision. What did it mean to be deemed an apostle? An answer one hears often is simply that apostles were those who had personally encountered or seen the risen Christ, but this definition is incomplete. At one point, more than five hundred people beheld the risen Christ before His Ascension into heaven (1 Cor. 15:6), yet while the Twelve and the seventy are numbered as apostles, these five hundred are not given that status. Rather, apostolic authority is vested in those who not only saw Christ, but who received a particular vision of Him, namely of Jesus Christ in His uncreated glory. This is what three of the apostles witnessed on Mount Tabor, this is what all of them witnessed in Christ's death and Resurrection, and finally this is what St. Paul witnessed on the road to Damascus. It is worth noting that this basis of apostolicity is not foreign to the New Testament. The apostles themselves cite such pivotal encounters with Christ in laying claim to their authority to preach:

That which was in the beginning, that which we have heard, that which we have seen with our eyes, that which we have looked on and have touched with our hands, concerning the word of life, the life that was made manifest, and we have seen it and testify to it and proclaim to you the life that is eternal. (1 John 1–2)

For we did not follow cleverly imagined stories when we made known to you the power and coming of our Lord Jesus Christ, but we were eyewitnesses of His majesty. For when He received honor and glory from God the Father, and the voice was carried to Him by the Majestic Glory, "This is My beloved Son, in whom I am well pleased," we ourselves heard this very voice carried from heaven, for we were with Him on the holy mountain. (2 Pet. 1:16–18)

Just as St. Peter had before him, St. Paul saw the light of God's glory and heard a voice from heaven.

From apostolic times, Christ's Ascension into heaven and enthronement were understood within the context of the heavenly ascents and the throne-chariot of God that already had a place in Second Temple religion and mystical practice. It is for this reason, within the Orthodox iconographic tradition, that when Christ is depicted as enthroned, it is on the four living creatures of Ezekiel's vision. These icons serve as a visual means of meditation parallel to the way Second Temple meditation focused on a text, in this case the description in Ezekiel. The God who sat enthroned in the visions of the Old Testament has made Himself known through descending in the Incarnation, before ascending again to His former glory. Rather than repudiating mystical practice, the earliest Christians, as St. Paul exemplifies, continued to pursue contemplative prayer, which for some culminated in the vision of Christ in His uncreated glory. This tradition, renounced in the Talmud, has continued in Orthodox Christianity, blossoming into what would later become known as hesychasm. The Jesus Prayer, with its identification of Christ as Lord and God, has replaced the Shema in this practice.

Saint Paul's vision of Christ enthroned further identifies Him as the lawgiver, the One who issues the Torah. Often, the controversy surrounding St. Paul, especially in Galatians and Romans, stems from the perception that he is proclaiming freedom from the Torah over and against his opponents' insistence that it must still be followed. This is a mischaracterization of the apostle's position. For St. Paul, Christ is not only the giver of the Torah, but also the One by whom and through whom it is properly administered and applied.

Saint Paul's opponents were placing false trust in their identity as the righteous, Abraham's descendants, the children of Israel. Saint Paul points out that Ishmael (Gal. 4:21–25) and Esau (Rom. 9:6–13) were descendants of Abraham as well. Gentiles, obviously, could not change their parentage, but they could become "children of Abraham" by being circumcised. Saint Paul, in contrast, presents Christ as the singular seed, the inheritor of the promises made to Abraham (Gal. 3:16). Through Him, humans of all tribes, peoples, and nations are adopted into the family of God, becoming His sons (Gal. 4:7). As sons, they are coheirs with Christ of the promises (Rom. 8:17).

The contrast established by St. Paul, then, is not one of law versus gospel, but rather what he calls the "law of the Spirit"—which comes through Christ—versus the law of sin and death (Rom. 8:2). The great promise St. Paul sees fulfilled during his ministry is that of the New Covenant. Although this covenant is different than that given at Sinai, it is not one in which the Law ceases completely. Rather, it is one in which the Law is written on a person's heart and exists within him or her (Jer. 31/38:33). It is a time when all will know Yahweh and when sins will be forgiven (Jer. 31/38:34). This would come to pass through the Spirit being poured out on all flesh (Joel 2:28). In this era, it was prophesied that when God placed His Spirit within His people, they would keep His commandments (Ezek. 36:26–32). Saint Paul draws on this language of the Spirit keeping the righteous requirements of the Law within us (Rom. 8:3–4). Keeping the commandments in the New Covenant is not an external obedience but cooperation with the indwelling Spirit.

Since mortal humanity proved too weak and rebellious to follow God's Torah, Christ—having delivered them from condemnation (Rom. 8:1)—works in them to bring about His own righteousness. The Spirit generates fruit in their lives, which even supersedes the demands of the Torah (Gal. 5:22–23). The faithful walk in the Spirit according to God's commandments because God is accomplishing the work of salvation within them (Phil. 2:12–13). It is a work that He will bring to completion (Phil. 1:6). At the end of this age, at Christ's judgment seat, He will look on His works and declare that they are good (Gen. 1:31).

9

To summarize all this, St. Paul understood the religion he practiced (and the gospel he proclaimed) after his encounter with Christ as a continuation of that which he had practiced his entire life. He did not perceive himself to have disembarked from that earlier religion and entered another. Rather, he understood his experience on the road to Damascus in terms of the religion that included the Hebrew Scriptures that had not yet been canonized into the "Bible" as we would recognize it today. He saw the Gentiles he baptized after becoming a servant of Christ to be entering the religion of his youth; worshipping Yahweh, the God of Israel; and becoming children of Abraham. It is therefore completely appropriate to speak of "Old Testament Christianity," the religion that existed under the Old Covenant, as well as the Christianity of the New Covenant. These are, in fact, the same religion. This religion, the religion practiced by the apostles and their successors, is the subject of this book.

PART ONE

The Godhead

✠ ✠ ✠

CHAPTER 1

Divine Father and Son

THERE IS WITHIN THE CHRISTIAN world, even among Orthodox Christian writers and scholars, an assumed narrative regarding the "development" of the doctrine of the Holy Trinity within Christianity. It is presupposed that the people of the Old Testament were unitarian monotheists—in other words, they believed that only one God exists and that God is a single person. It is likewise presumed that through Christ's teaching and deeds, which culminated in His Resurrection and Ascension into heaven, early Christians came to believe that Jesus was also divine in some sense. The development of Christian belief over the next several centuries is then seen in evolutionary terms, in which early "low" or primitive Christology—that regards Christ as vaguely divine, but not necessarily God in the same sense as His Father—is gradually supplanted by the notion that He *is* truly God. The same rationale holds that belief in the Holy Spirit was an even later, albeit similar, development, bringing the Trinitarian doctrine of the fourth-century councils to maturity. Although this narrative is largely taken for granted, it is false.

Far from being unitarian in their monotheism, followers of the Old Covenant believed the God of Israel existed in multiple *hypostases,* the term that would be translated as "persons" in later doctrinal statements. The Greek term *hypostasis* rather literally means "substance." It is, however, used to indicate a concrete being, such as a particular human person. This term was enshrined in the Nicene Creed, which describes three hypostases of the Christian God. In more recent times, it has since been applied by scholars to the understanding of the relationship between a particular presence, encounter, or body of a god over against the conception of that divine being in a general sense. It will here be used interchangeably with "Person" when speaking of the three divine Persons who share the Godhead.

For ancient Israelites and Second Temple Judeans, there was only one Yahweh, but He existed as multiple Persons. Despite a lack of clarity about this in the Hebrew Scriptures, it was believed, discussed, and debated throughout the history of the Second Temple period. There were a variety of teachings regarding the relationships between these hypostases, how they may have come to be, and their nature. It was only beginning in the second century, in reaction to Christianity, that Judaism declared this previously universal view a heresy.

Rather than enacting a new vision of God, the New Testament clarifies and affirms the nature of the God spoken of in the Old. The texts of the New Testament affirm that the God of Israel has eternally existed in three Persons (hypostases)—Father, Son, and Holy Spirit. Further, it teaches that the Son became incarnate in Jesus Christ. Certain Christological and Trinitarian heresies that arose before the Council of Nicaea, such as Arianism and adoptionism, were continuations of strands of thought already existent in pre-Christian Jewish communities.[1] These were seen as incompatible with the teaching of

---

1   Arianism, for example, was in continuity with certain Second Temple writings that identified the Second Person of Yahweh as the Archangel Michael. Eusebius of Caesarea took this position. Adoptionism was in continuity with Second Temple writings that identified the second hypostasis as a deified human person, such as Adam, Abraham, Moses, David, or Enoch. The only

the apostles expressed in the New Testament and in the lived worship and experience of the Church. The writings of early Fathers against heresies, as well as the dogmas codified by the early councils, aimed to summarize and defend the apostolic understanding of the Holy Trinity found within the New Testament, not to introduce entirely new theological concepts or ideas.

The Angel of the Lord

A KEY EXAMPLE OF HOW the Hebrew Scriptures express the multiple persons of the God of Israel is the figure of "the Angel of the Lord" in the Torah.[2] In the text of the Old Testament, this figure is identified as Yahweh, the God of Israel, and yet acts as a Second Person who interacts with both Yahweh and humans. The first such encounter took place in the initial meeting between Moses and the God of Abraham, Isaac, and Jacob, when God revealed His name to Moses. Exodus 3:2 indicates that the "Angel of the Lord" appeared to him in a flame burning within a bush. But in verse 4, when Moses approached, it was "God" who called to him from the midst of the bush. Upon hearing this call, Moses covered his face because he was afraid of seeing God (v. 6). The reference to "the Angel of the Lord"

---

distinguishing factor between these Second Temple views and the Christian heresies that proceeded from them is that the latter were concerned with the nature of Jesus Christ rather than the Second Person of Yahweh as such.

2   Some are troubled by the identification of this figure as an "angel." The word translated "angel" in Hebrew, Aramaic, and Greek simply means "messenger" or "representative." It does not necessarily signify a unique or particularly divine being. Humans, i.e., prophets and apostles, can serve as messengers or representatives of God just as noetic, or spiritual, beings can. The title "Angel of the Lord" can therefore be better translated "Messenger of Yahweh." The "Angel of the Lord" language, however, is so deeply engrained in English biblical culture that it will be used here for ease of reference. "Messenger of Yahweh," however, is sufficiently ambiguous in the text that the question of the identity of this "Messenger" is an open one to be determined from context.

in verse 2 distinguishes this Person from that of Yahweh through the use of Hebrew grammar, but in the subsequent interaction, the Angel identifies Himself as the God of Abraham, Isaac, and Jacob. In this encounter between Moses and God, the Angel is both identified as Yahweh and distinguished from another Person who is Yahweh.

A more complex interaction occurs when God appeared to Gideon in Judges 6. In verse 11, the Angel of the Lord sat under an oak tree and called to Gideon, who was working on the threshing floor, to tell him that the God of Israel is with him. Gideon was skeptical, given the oppression the people of Israel in Canaan were currently facing from Midianites—a sure sign that God had forgotten them. In response, "Yahweh" turned to him and spoke (v. 14). As with Moses' encounter with the burning bush, the God of Israel identified Himself as Gideon's interlocutor. At first glance, it seems the Angel of the Lord is Yahweh Himself.

However, the matter was not that clear cut, at least not for Gideon, who apparently perceived his guest to be a human prophet or messenger, evidenced by his offer of hospitality. Once food was brought out, the Angel of the Lord told him to set it on a rock, at which point He touched it with His staff, and it was consumed by fire as a sacrifice (vv. 20–21). Finally, the Angel of the Lord disappeared. It was only then that Gideon realized to whom he had been speaking and was afraid, since he had seen the Angel of the Lord face to face. In verse 23, Yahweh responded to this concern: although the Angel had departed, Yahweh was still there.

Possibly the most significant appearance of the Angel of the Lord, however, occurs during the Exodus of Israel into the wilderness. In Exodus 23:20, God told Moses He was sending an Angel before Israel to guard them and lead them into the Land of Promise. Israel, so Moses is warned, must listen to this Angel and not rebel, because God was placing His Name in Him. As will be further discussed in chapter 2, this "Name" is itself an Old Testament expression of the

Person of the God of Israel. For example, the temple in Jerusalem is described as the place in which God will place His Name. Thus what God is trying to communicate to Moses is that Israel must obey this Angel because the Presence of God is within Him. If they follow the Angel's commands, their enemies will be God's enemies (v. 23). Incidentally, this language would later form much of the basis of St. John's Christology. In his Gospel, he repeatedly characterizes God the Father as being "in" Christ (see John 14:11, 20; 17:23). Saint John's purpose in doing so, similar to that of the Angel of the Lord in Exodus, is to remind us that to hear and obey Christ is to know the Father; to rebel against what Christ says is to be at enmity with Him (see John 8:19; 10:22–39; 14:7).

This reference to the Angel of the Lord in Exodus is not an anomaly. Throughout God's covenant with Israel, He identified Himself as the One who brought them out of the land of Egypt (Ex. 20:2; Lev. 11:45; Deut. 5:6). After Israel's sojourn ended and the conquest of Canaan was complete, however, in Judges 2:1, the Angel of the Lord said, "I brought you up from Egypt and brought you to the land that I had promised to your fathers." The Angel then revealed that because Israel disobeyed Him, He was now departing and would no longer fight for them against their enemies. When the Angel explained this to the Israelites, they wept bitterly in response (v. 4). That the Angel both conveyed this message to the Israelites and traveled from Gilgal to Bokim reveal that He was a Person who had been physically present with and accompanied Israel throughout the preceding forty-plus years.

This appearance of the Angel of the Lord demonstrates that even the earliest traditions of the Old Testament reveal a second hypostasis of the God of Israel, who both is Israel's God and is Himself a Second Person of Yahweh. When this is taken into account, many New Testament passages considered allegory or reinterpretations of the previous revelation can be seen to be quite literal. The New Testament authors identify this Person as the One who became incarnate as Jesus Christ. It was in this spirit St. Paul believed the Angel of the Lord had been with Israel in the wilderness and that Israel's God had stood on the rock before Moses struck it to produce water (Ex. 17:6). Thus he could proclaim that the rock that followed Israel in the wilderness "was Christ" (1 Cor. 10:3–4). Likewise, Jude, in the earliest and most reliable manuscripts of his epistle, could simply say that Jesus "saved a people out of Egypt" and afterward "destroyed those who did not believe" (1:5).

The Word of the Lord

FAMOUSLY, THE PROLOGUE OF THE first chapter of St. John's Gospel speaks of the Logos, who has existed eternally with God from the beginning and is God. It has become common to read these statements in the prologue philosophically—an attempt by St. John, as a supposed Jewish monotheist, to represent the divinity of Jesus Christ in relationship to the God of Israel. This notion is bolstered by the writings of parallel thinkers such as Philo of Alexandria, a Jewish Middle Platonist in the first century before Christ, who described the divine Logos as an emanation of the one true God.[3] Other scholars have looked to the idea of the logos in Stoic philosophy, an interpretive lens that is prevalent in patristic studies such that the Christology of the Fathers is often read philosophically as well. In this approach, the Fathers are thought to have borrowed the philosophical concept of a logos—a reason or logic that functions as an intermediary between God and the world—and blended it into their understanding of who Christ is, almost as a form of syncretism. This idea, that Jesus Christ is simply the incarnation of a divine intermediary, is often referred to as "Logos Christology." Scholars who opt for a more evolutionary

---

3   Philo describes the Logos as having been begotten of God (Conf. 63). He also identifies the Logos as the same figure as the Angel of the Lord (Somn. 1.228–39; Cher. 1–3).

or developmental interpretation of Church history (explained in the preface of this book) would understand this philosophically based Christology as a stepping-stone between the simple belief in Jesus as a human Messiah on the one hand and the more sophisticated belief in Christ as fully human and divine that supposedly developed later.

Unfortunately, this interpretation rests on a series of misconceptions. From the earliest phases of the Old Testament revelation, the "Word of the Lord" (the *Debar Yahweh* in Hebrew) has been a known—and knowable—entity, a divine Person or hypostasis of Israel's God, not a metaphysical abstraction. It is this knowable figure St. John the Theologian and Philo spoke of. While Philo aimed to integrate this figure into his philosophical system (incidentally, his approach would also be adopted by the later Gnostics), St. John sought to bear witness to the divine Person he had known in his friendship with Jesus Christ.

Several of the misconceptions that cloud understandings of the Word of the Lord arise from misinterpreting not St. John's prologue but the Hebrew Scriptures that came before. When we read in the Old Testament that "the Word of the Lord came to" a particular prophet, we make certain assumptions about what this means. In modern Christian discourse, the phrases "the Word of God" and "the Word of the Lord" are commonly used to refer to the Scriptures. However, in the Scriptures themselves, these phrases are never straightforwardly used this way. Other than a handful of debatable instances, the hundreds of times these terms appear in Scripture unambiguously refer to something, or rather, someone, else. The Scriptures, in contrast, are referred to as "that which is written," from which the word *scripture* derives.

Because of this common misinterpretation, when we read that "the Word of the Lord" came to a prophet "saying" something, we tend to assume that the prophet heard a voice either audibly or in his head. Particularly in modern readings of such passages, it is almost as though the prophet in question was generally "inspired" to speak in some vague spiritual way that in turn gave his words special authority. However, setting these misconceptions aside and examining how "the Word of the Lord" functions in the Hebrew Scriptures themselves paints a different picture.

The first explicit reference to "the Word of the Lord" in the Scriptures comes in Genesis 15:1. The "Word of Yahweh" appeared to Abram in a vision, literally "in a seeing" in the Hebrew. Abram saw something or someone who told him not to be afraid, because "I am your shield." Abram understood the figure he encountered to be "the Lord Yahweh" (v. 2) and pointed out he had no heir to inherit the blessings God had given him. The Word then responded to Abram's difficulty with the promise of a son and identified Himself to be Yahweh, who brought Abram out of Ur of the Chaldeans (vv. 4, 7).

Centuries later, when Israel departed from Egypt and settled in Canaan, they entered a dark period—the time of the Judges—during which much of Israel fell into apostasy and were oppressed by foreigners as a result. In 1 Kingdoms (1 Samuel) 3:1, the situation was so dire that the "Word of Yahweh" was rare, as indicated by a lack of "visions." This was an era in which people did not "see" the Word of the Lord, which coincided with the period following the Angel of the Lord's departure from Israel (Judg. 2:1–5).

The story that follows the above description in 1 Kingdoms (1 Samuel) 3 sheds further light on who or what the prophets actually saw. Yahweh repeatedly called to the young Samuel in the night, who assumed he was hearing the voice of Eli, the priest with whom he lived, since Samuel did not yet know Yahweh—the Word of the Lord had not yet been "revealed" to him (3:7). Once Eli explained to Samuel it must be the God of Israel calling to him, we are told that Yahweh stood next to his bed, as He had at the other times (v. 10). Samuel's vision therefore revolves around a figure that is standing—a person. Yahweh then gave Samuel some dire news for Eli and his family, and the next morning, Samuel was afraid to tell Eli the contents of his "vision" (v. 15). As this event receded into the past and Samuel continued to grow up, Yahweh continued to "appear" to him at Shiloh, revealing Himself by "His Word" (v. 21).

A similar encounter is found in Jeremiah 1. The Word of the Lord came to Jeremiah and spoke (v. 4). When He spoke again, He was identified simply as Yahweh (v. 7). Then He reached out His hand and touched Jeremiah (v. 9). Through his vision of the Word of the Lord, Jeremiah was called forth as "a prophet to the nations" (v. 5). There is a close parallel between Jeremiah's vision and St. Paul's experience on the road to Damascus (Gal. 1:11–16). Saint Paul says that he, like Jeremiah, was set apart from his mother's womb and called to be an apostle "to the nations."

What these various Old Testament visions and events indicate is that in pre-Christian Judaism, the Word of the Lord was perceived and understood as a divine Person who had appeared and spoken to the prophets in bodily form. This Person was both distinguished from and identified as Yahweh, the God of Israel.

Therefore, what St. John seeks in his prologue is not philosophical speculation nor a Christology consistent with some preexisting monotheism. Rather, he is mapping this divine figure of old onto the Person of Jesus Christ by exegeting and integrating the Old Testament Scriptures. He begins by identifying the Word as the agent of Creation in John 1:3, reminiscent of Psalm 33/32:6: "By the Word of Yahweh the heavens were made and by the breath of His mouth all their hosts." The terms for "breath" in Hebrew (*ruach*) and Greek (*pnevma*) are more often translated in Scripture as "Spirit." The Spirit is present in Creation in Genesis 1:2, hovering over the waters. When the Fathers speak of the Father, Son, and Spirit in Creation as mouth, word, and breath, they are not inventing Trinitarian analogies; they are exegeting and interpreting Scripture in the same manner as St. John the Theologian.

In John 1:12–13, St. John speaks of the incarnate Word giving those who believe the authority to become sons of God. This echoes the Word's promise to Abram in Genesis 15 of a son who would inherit the blessings God had given him and offspring like the stars of the heavens (vv. 4–5). Saint John contrasts this with the sons (and therefore heirs) of God who are born not of flesh and blood nor the will of man but of God Himself. In the final verses of his prologue, St. John makes clear that Jesus Christ is the Word made flesh (v. 14). The figure in the visions of Yahweh in the Old Testament was none other than Christ Himself, the Word: "No one has ever seen God, but the unique God who is at the side of the Father, He has made Him known" (v. 18). Here St. John is not invalidating the manifold visions of God throughout the Old Testament by suggesting God is seen only in the Person of Jesus Christ incarnate. Rather, he is identifying Jesus Christ as the God, Yahweh, who was seen by the prophets, incarnate in these latter days.

Saint John's conception of the Word of the Lord as the Second Person of Yahweh who had been seen and experienced in Old Testament accounts was not inconsistent with Jewish mentality well into late antiquity. This notion was so deeply ingrained in the religion of the Jewish people that evidence of it surfaces in Targums, first-century Aramaic translations of the Hebrew Scriptures composed from the beginning of the Second Temple period after the vast majority of Judeans had lost their knowledge of Hebrew (see Is. 36:11). Because these were not strict translations in the modern sense, various traditions of interpretation, theological presuppositions, and sometimes even entire traditional stories were incorporated directly into the Aramaic text.

One such theological tradition centered on appearances of Yahweh to human persons. How could this be, given that the Scriptures repeatedly affirm that no one could see God and live (e.g., Ex. 33:20)?

Wherever the text speaks of a human seeing Yahweh, the translators generally inserted the Aramaic word *Memra*, or "Word" in place of the name "Yahweh." Humans were said to have seen the Memra. Even in contemporary Rabbinic Judaism, it is customary to capitalize, sometimes even entirely capitalize, *Memra* when it refers to the Word of God as the revelation of God's power and presence. This is particularly true when *Memra* occurs in descriptions of God's act of Creation, which is precisely the context in which St. John first speaks of the Logos in his prologue.

The Wisdom of God

IN ADDITION TO IDENTIFYING JESUS Christ as the Second Person of Yahweh in ways that were consistent with appearances of the Word of the Lord in the Hebrew Scriptures, St. John in his prologue also draws on a parallel set of traditions from the same Scriptures that understood the Second Person of the God of Israel to be the Wisdom of God. Understanding this tradition and its import for early Christology links Christian concepts of the relationship between Christ and the Father on the one hand and Christ and creation on the other.

Much of this tradition centers on the personification of Wisdom in Proverbs 8, in which grammatically feminine terms are used.[4] The central portion of this passage features Wisdom proclaiming:

---

4   Here and in other places, feminine pronouns are found in English translations regarding Wisdom. This is because the words for wisdom in both Hebrew (*chakmah*) and Greek (*sophia*) are feminine nouns. Gender as it exists in synthetic languages (those with inflections and grammatical genders, as both Greek and Hebrew have) should not be confused with the human or biological sex of male and female.

Yahweh possessed me at the beginning of His way, from before His works. From eternity, from the beginning, I have been established, from before there was an earth. When there was no abyss I was brought forth, when there were no fountains pouring forth waters. Before the mountains were set in place, before the hills I was brought forth. When He had not yet made the earth or the fields or the first dust of the world, when He prepared the heavens, I was there, when He drew a circle on the face of the abyss, when He established the clouds above, when He strengthened the fountains of the abyss. When He assigned to the sea its limit so that the waters would not trespass his command when He marked out the foundations of the world, then I was beside Him, a master craftsman, and I was His delight, rejoicing before Him day by day, always. (Prov. 8:22–30)

The verbs here translated "possessed" and "brought forth" have a more ambiguous meaning in Greek than in English and can imply creating or making. This argument was used by proponents of Arianism to argue that Christ came into existence at a specific point (albeit before the rest of creation) and therefore was not eternal. This interpretation, heretical though it may be, reveals that by the fourth century, the above passage was firmly connected to the Second Person of Yahweh and to Christ.

The Arian reading of Proverbs 8 was, at best, a misinterpretation. The Hebrew verbs in question do not directly indicate a coming into being of someone who did not previously exist. In verse 22, the Hebrew verb for "possessed" (*qanah*) was used often in regard to commerce, to convey the buying and acquiring of property. It can also refer to possessions already acquired. The Phoenician cognate, *mqna*, refers to property or wealth. Its most important biblical usage, however, is in Genesis 4:1. Eve uses this verb to say that she has acquired a son from Yahweh.

What makes this usage important is the parallel in Proverbs 8 between this verb describing the relationship between Yahweh and Wisdom and the verb used in verses 24 and 25, here translated "brought forth." The verb here, *chul*, literally means to writhe or twist, usually in pain. Its most common application, particularly within the writings of the Prophet Isaiah (23:4; 26:17–18; 45:10; 54:1; 66:7–8), is to childbirth. The parallel of these two verbs in this text reveals a relationship between Yahweh and Wisdom of begotten-ness. The Son is begotten of the Father before any of creation came into being. This text is, in fact, the origin of the teaching of the Church that Christ was begotten of the Father before all worlds. While several texts in the New Testament apply the Greek term *monogenes* to Christ (see John 1:18; 3:16), this Greek term is better translated "unique" or "one and only" rather than the "only-begotten" of the King James Version.

The prologue to St. John's Gospel draws directly on the theme of Christ's involvement in Creation expressed here in Proverbs. His statement that the Word was "in the beginning" not only refers to the opening words of Genesis but also parallels the language of Proverbs 8:22. That the Word was, in the beginning, with or alongside God parallels verse 30. That all things were made by Him and without Him nothing was made that was made (John 1:3) draws on the portrayal of Wisdom as the master craftsman working alongside Yahweh during the days of Creation recounted in Proverbs.

Saint John thereby presents Christ as the Logos-become-flesh in multiple senses. He is not only the figure of the Word of Yahweh seen by the Fathers in the Hebrew Scriptures. He is also the Logos as the plan and structure of all creation. He is the One in whom all created things find their origin, their purpose, and their perfection. Saint Paul can, therefore, call him the Wisdom of God (1 Cor. 1:24) and also say that in Him all things hold together (Col. 1:17). Though He is begotten, He did not come into being from not-being but rather has the status of the Firstborn over all creation (Col. 1:15).

The Son of Man

THE TITLE "SON OF MAN" is best known by most readers of the Scriptures as the title Christ most often applies to Himself, a rare thread running through all four Gospels with utter consistency. In fact, other than references to the Hebrew Scriptures and a single instance in the Acts of the Apostles, this title occurs in the New Testament only as self-references spoken by Christ. When Christ used this term, however, He was drawing on an Old Covenant tradition that had already been well defined by His time. Accordingly, the idea of a particular divine figure known as the Son of Man had formed within the Second Temple period, and many of Christ's references are incontrovertibly to that figure. To understand who, by this title, Christ was claiming to be, we must answer the question the crowds asked of Christ: "Who is this Son of Man?" (John 12:34).

The English translation of the title itself can be somewhat misleading. In its Old Testament uses, including its earliest, it includes the term "man." In this pairing, however, two different Hebrew words are being translated as "man." And so, Numbers 23:19, for example, would better be translated, "God is not a man, that He should lie, or a son of Adam, that He should change His mind." This title refers to one who is a son of Adam, not merely the son of a human father.

The phrase "son of" is itself a Hebrew idiom. A son was seen to be the image of his father—to be someone's son meant a person's character reflected that of his father. For example, the name of the apostle "Bar-nabas" literally means "Son of Encouragement." On the other hand, Judas Iscariot and the Antichrist are at times referred to as "son[s] of perdition" (John 17:12; 2 Thess. 2:3), and Christ rebuked those who opposed Him as sons of their father the devil because they lied and sought to murder Him (John 8:44). The term "Son of Adam," then, means not only that a person is human (calling a person a man or a woman would be sufficient to convey that), but also that the person possesses a trait characteristic of Adam.

Christian readers at least since St. Augustine have tended to see in Adam the archetypal sinner who passes sin on to his physical progeny. This, however, is not the way Adam was seen within the Second Temple period that formed the background for the New Testament texts. Adam was seen rather as the one who brought death to the human race. He is not so much seen as the origin of human sin as the origin of human mortality. Yes, it was his sin that brought about this effect, but the corruption in humanity was seen to be produced by subsequent events in the Book of Genesis and as a result of death and mortality, rather than the reverse. Adam as the source of mortality can be seen in New Testament texts such as John 8:44 cited above, in which the devil is described as having been a murderer at the beginning, and in the contrast between Adam and Christ made by St. Paul in Romans 5:12–17. More importantly, when the phrase "Son of Adam" is used in the Hebrew Scriptures, it serves to remind a human of his mortality, weakness, and fragility, as in Job 25:6; Psalm 8:4; 144/143:3; 146/145:3; and Isaiah 51:12. "Son of Adam" is also the title God consistently bestows on the Prophet Ezekiel, living as he does in exile.

The title is likewise used in reference to the Prophet Daniel in exile (Dan. 8:17), but in addition to references to "sons of Adam," the Book of Daniel also contains the figure who would become known as "the Son of Man" in Second Temple literature. In Daniel 7, Daniel received a vision that predicted a succession of human empires that will dominate the known world in sequence. At the end of the sequence, Daniel beheld a scene of judgment, in which the God of Israel, the Ancient of Days, sits enthroned in the divine council and passes judgment on the wickedness of these empires and all the nations of the world. As one product of that judgment, God takes away the authority (*exousia* in Greek) from these nations but allows them to continue to exist for "a time" (7:12). It is then that Daniel saw one "like a Son of Man" who comes up before the Ancient of Days riding on a cloud, to whom is given all the authority that was taken away from the nations of the earth. This establishes for this Person an eternal Kingdom.

Daniel's description of this Person has two important parts. The first is obvious in Daniel's description: this figure appeared to him as "like a Son of Man," meaning He appeared to Daniel to be a human person. The second factor is less obvious and is contained within the image of this figure riding on the clouds. Among ancient peoples, not only in the ancient Near East but in the surrounding nations as well, riding on the clouds of heaven was a representation of a deity. Deities such as Baal and Zeus rode on the clouds of heaven.[5] For obvious reasons, Israel reserved this language solely for their God, as is the case in Psalm 104/103:3–4, read in every Vespers service, and Isaiah 19:1, to describe the power and glory of Yahweh. This imagery helps to explain why Daniel would describe the human figure he saw as being "like a Son of Man" rather than just declaring Him to be a man. This double depiction would not have been lost on the original Jewish readers of Daniel, who referred to this figure as "the Son of Man." Second Temple literature is filled with identifications of this figure and how He came to be. As a divine figure, He was seen to be a hypostasis of the God of Israel Himself. Some traditions saw this figure as the Messiah to come who would be a divine figure (see, for example, 1 Enoch 48:2–10); others saw this figure as a divinized human from the past, such as Enoch or David himself.

New Testament scholars vehemently debate how Christ uses the title Son of Man to apply to Himself in any given instance. There are, however, several instances that very clearly refer to this apocalyptic

---

5   One of Baal's primary titles is "the cloud-rider" (e.g., *Baal* 2.IV.7–8). Daniel's entire vision in this chapter is a polemic response to the story of the enthronement of Baal, as will be discussed later.

figure from the Book of Daniel as developed in the religious tradition of Christ's time. Christ makes clear reference to the Son of Man coming on the clouds in judgment at the end of time in Matthew 13:41, 24:30, and 25:31; and in Luke 21:27.

Possibly the clearest instance, however, is in Mark 14 (and the parallel passage in Matthew 26:57–68). On trial before Caiaphas and the Sanhedrin, Jesus was asked directly if He is the Messiah (Mark 14:61). Likely, this question was posed to make sense of the lack of evidence against Him so Caiaphas could make the case that Jesus was a dangerous political dissident destined to bring down the wrath of the Romans. His response, however, went further than the questioner had intended, in that Jesus not only answered with "I am," but went on to identify Himself as the Son of Man who will come on the clouds of heaven in judgment (v. 62). Caiaphas's extreme reaction—tearing his clothes and saying that all in attendance had heard Jesus utter blasphemy (v. 63)—shows not only that Jesus' response was not what he had hoped to hear, but also that the Son of Man was considered at this time to be a divine figure. Claiming to be the Messiah descended from David was not blasphemy, but claiming to be God was.

Christ's identifying Himself as "the Son of Man" is important both in a general sense and in its particulars. As we have previously seen, the New Testament writers unambiguously associated the Person of Jesus Christ with the second hypostasis of the God of Israel, described as the Angel of the Lord or the Word of the Lord. In this case, in addition to the New Testament writers (as in Rev. 1:13), it is Christ who identified Himself as that same figure. In its particulars, however, while we have already seen a Second Divine Person embodied in the Old Testament, this figure seen by Daniel is explicitly one like a "son of Adam," meaning that this figure is both divine and human.

Further, Daniel's vision frames the mission of Christ and even establishes the distinction between His First and Second Advents.

The culmination of the mission of the Son of Man is that the authority (exousia) of the nations is taken away from them and given to
Him. Indeed, Christ announced before His Ascension that this has
taken place when He said, "All authority (exousia) in heaven and on
earth has been given to me" (Matt. 28:18). While the nations and, in
particular, Rome, the last of Daniel's beasts, will continue to exist
"for a time," as Daniel prophesied, these nations have been judged,
and the Kingdom of Jesus Christ has been established, which will
endure forever. The mission of the apostles, which they bequeathed
to the Church, will continue through this time, until Christ returns
in the same way that He ascended, on the clouds of heaven, to judge
the living and the dead.

The Body of God

ONE FEATURE OF THE ORTHODOX Jewish synagogue service is
the hymn sung near its dismissal that repeatedly affirms, "God does
not have a body."[6] This particular hymn was added in the fourth or
fifth century as a direct response to, and rejection of, Christianity. On
the surface, far removed as we are from the disputes between Rab-
binical Jewish and nascent Christian communities, we might assume
that the inclusion of this hymn was aimed at rejecting Christian belief
in the Incarnation. In actuality, however, it was intended to deny that
the God of Israel had ever appeared in bodily form, even in the Old
Testament. The primary field of debate in that era concerned how to
interpret the Hebrew Scriptures that would become the Christian
Old Testament. The idea that God's body was not to be sought out or
investigated directly rejected a key element of the Christian interpretation of these Scriptures, namely that the Incarnation of Christ was

---

6   Indeed, one of medieval Rabbi Maimonides's "Thirteen Principles of the
     Faith" states, "I believe with perfect faith that God does not have a body."

a final fulfillment of a long series of bodily appearances by the Second Person of Yahweh.

Even if one were to consider only the Torah, the most uncontroversial part of the Hebrew canon, this affirmation in the synagogue service seems rather strange. Yahweh, the God of Israel, is depicted in bodily form fairly consistently throughout these books—not merely in symbolic references to God's strong right arm, or to His sheltering Israel under His wings, or in other anthropomorphic statements regarding God that are clearly poetic imagery. Rather, the God of Israel stood, walked, interacted with humans face to face, had conversations with them, touched them with His hand, and even ate with them.

The episode at the Oak of Mamre, for example, recorded in Genesis 18, is one of the strangest and most mysterious in the Scriptures. Abraham hosted, and fed, the God of Israel beside his tent. It has long been depicted in Orthodox iconography as the Hospitality of Abraham. Beginning with Andrei Rublev, a detail of this scene has been the only approved Orthodox iconographic depiction of the Holy Trinity. This Trinity icon is used by some local Orthodox churches as the icon for the Feast of Pentecost. The coming of the Holy Spirit at Pentecost marked the conclusion of the revelation of the Holy Trinity to humanity. The Hospitality of Abraham, in many ways, represents the beginning of that revelation.

The revelation of the Holy Trinity does not emerge only when Yahweh's appearance at the Oak of Mamre is compared to other passages, however. It emerges from the text itself. It is important to specify against a common misinterpretation that the three men whom Abraham encountered (Gen. 18:2) are not the three Persons of the Holy Trinity in visible form. In addition to plainly contradicting the other passages already named, when the figures split up, only one of them was identified as Yahweh (18:22). The other two were identified as being angels when they arrived at Sodom (19:1). This is one of several places in which angelic beings are described as having bodies. Indeed, Yahweh and the two angels shared a meal with Abraham (18:8). Saint Jude (1:7–8) compared the attempted crimes of the men of Sodom to the sin of the rebellious angels before the Flood in Genesis 6:1–2.

Yahweh and the two angels did, however, speak with one voice. *Elohim*, generally translated as "God" when used to indicate Yahweh, often takes plural verbs because it is grammatically plural. The name Yahweh, however, is grammatically singular. Nevertheless, throughout the discussion with Abraham, the pronoun "they" is used to introduce Yahweh's speech. The three can, therefore, be seen to be a visible representation, an icon, of the Holy Trinity. Further, within this text, Yahweh spoke to Himself, taking His own counsel (Gen. 18:17–19). We see this dynamic more fully developed in the prayers of Christ to His Father in the Gospels.

Abraham's grandson Jacob, the night before he prepared to be reunited with his brother, Esau, again encountered a "man" who wrestled with him throughout the night (Gen. 32:24). This Person dislocated Jacob's hip during the struggle and gave him the new name of Israel (vv. 25, 28). Afterward, Jacob named the place "the face of God," because he said he had seen God face to face (v. 30). If there is any ambiguity here as to the identity of the wrestler, Yahweh appeared to Jacob again in Genesis 35:9–10 and repeated His blessing of Israel's new name.

To these three examples, dozens could be added from throughout the Hebrew Scriptures. Prophets saw God enthroned and described His physical appearance (Is. 6:1; Ez. 1:26–27). God appeared physically enthroned above the mercy seat on the Day of Atonement (Lev. 16:2). God wrote His covenant on tablets given to Moses with His own finger (Ex. 31:18). At the same time, however, there is a tension present in the text, at least hinted at by the episode with Jacob, in that he commented on having seen the face of God and survived (Gen. 32:30). All these clear statements that Yahweh, the God of Israel, was seen and interacted with human beings in bodily form are tempered by proclamations that no one can see God and live.

The apex of this tension occurs in Exodus 33. We are told at the beginning of the chapter that as Israel sojourned in the wilderness, Moses set up the "tent of meeting" at the edge of the camp. He would enter this tent, the cloud of God's glory would descend on it, and God would speak with Moses (Ex. 33:7–9). We are told that in these meetings, Yahweh and Moses would speak "face to face" as a man speaks to his friend (v. 11). Mere lines later, however, Moses asked God to show him His glory (v. 18), and God told Moses that this is impossible because no man can see His face and live (v. 20). God then passed by Moses, protecting him with His hand, and allowed him to see His back, but not His face, to preserve Moses' life (vv. 21–23). This apparent contradiction was not lost on those who read these texts in the centuries preceding Christ. In the literature they produced, the solution was reached that there were two hypostases of Yahweh, the God of Israel. One of these appeared to human beings in bodily form; the other was unseeable. As mentioned before, there was then a great deal of conjecture as to the identity and origin of this second hypostasis, and He was drawn together with the Word of God, the Angel of the Lord, and the Son of Man as one figure.

When the New Testament authors and the early Fathers spoke of the divinity of Christ, they were identifying the Person of Jesus Christ as this figure from the Old Testament, now incarnate in human flesh. Their emphasis on the Word becoming *flesh* (as in John 1:14 and 1 John 4:2) served to distinguish Christ's Incarnation from appearances of God or angelic beings in bodily or tangible form in the Old Testament. These writers did not need to theorize, invent, or construct what some might call "Binitarian" or Trinitarian doctrine in order to elevate Jesus or explain their worship of Him. The idea of one God existing in multiple hypostases, in this case, three eternally existent hypostases, was not a new idea. When we understand this, we can better understand the teaching of the apostles. In the Person of Jesus Christ, through the Incarnation, we have now come to know the one true God personally and intimately, far more so than the Old Testament saints were ever able to.

And so, the unitarian monotheism of Rabbinic Judaism, not the doctrine of the Holy Trinity, was the innovation in the centuries after Christ. Beginning in the second century, the idea that there was a "second power" in heaven, the second hypostasis of Yahweh, was declared a heresy in Rabbinic Judaism.[7] There is an old rabbinic story of Rabbi Akiva himself needing to be corrected on this matter.[8] This was largely a reaction against Christianity. Likewise, the repeated affirmation in the synagogue that God does not have a body was an even later addition, despite its contradiction of the Hebrew Scriptures, attributable to Christian usage.

Saints Justin Martyr and Basil the Great, as well as Origen,[9] all testify that in their respective eras, Jewish teaching still held that God had a body or a form. Having rejected the Incarnation and repudiated the idea of the second hypostasis of Yahweh, all these bodily appearances would be treated by Rabbinic Judaism as appearances of the singular Yahweh. These Fathers sought to correct this notion among Christian believers lest they think that God the Father had a body. Christianity did not bring in foreign

---

7   Jewish scholar Alan Segal's *Two Powers in Heaven* gives a thorough and detailed account of this tradition of interpretation in the Second Temple period and its ultimate condemnation.

8   As recorded in the tractate of the Babylonian Talmud *Hag.*, 14a. The text here is clearly aimed at revisionist history, as Akiva was known to have been a believer in two powers in heaven, identifying the Second Person of the Godhead as the Messiah.

9   *Dialogue with Trypho*, 1.14; *On the Origin of Man*, 1.5; *Homilies on Genesis*, 1.13, 3.1.

elements, pagan or otherwise, to Judaism in order to create a new religion. Rather, Rabbinic Judaism cut off huge swathes of the belief and practice of the Second Temple period in order to create a deliberately non-Christian religion that relied on a pared-down reading of the Hebrew Scriptures.

Jesus Christ Is Yahweh in the New Testament

THROUGHOUT THE HISTORY OF THE Church, there have been attempts to disfigure the identity of Christ by detaching the Christ whom we encounter in the Gospels from the God of the Old Testament. The first known and perhaps most infamous attempt was made by Marcion, who argued at the beginning of the second century that Yahweh was a different God than the Father of our Lord Jesus Christ, describing the former as violent and wrathful while the latter is loving and compassionate. Views of this sort are most often debunked by demonstrating the love and compassion of Yahweh in the Old Testament. The commands to love God and neighbor are drawn from the Torah, specifically Leviticus and Deuteronomy. His mercy and compassion are continual themes in the Psalms.

It can, however, be equally refuted in the opposite direction. The Christ who walked in the Garden and cursed the serpent, who destroyed Sodom and Gomorrah, who led the people out of Egypt and commanded Joshua's armies is the same Christ whom we encounter in the four Gospels. The Christ of love and compassion and mercy whom we encounter in the Gospels and the teaching of the apostles that make up the rest of the New Testament is the same Christ whom we encounter in the judgment of Revelation as the avenger of innocent blood.

Although true Marcionites are few and far between today, softer forms of this heresy live on, for example, in the tendency to ignore or allegorize away indications of the triune God and the Person of

Jesus Christ in the Old Testament. This is often coupled with one-dimensional, caricatured understandings of the Person of Christ in the New Testament. In other cases, latent Marcionism may express itself through denying that God has any wrath at all, against the consistent testimony of Scripture, the Fathers, and the liturgical tradition of the Church. It sometimes even goes so far as the heresy of universalism, the idea that all humanity finds salvation without reference to free choice.

Against any such view, the Epistle to the Hebrews reminds us that Christ is the same yesterday, today, and forever (13:8). His character has never changed and never will. He is the God who calls us to repentance through the certain knowledge of coming judgment and the God who pours forth His mercy and forgiveness when we turn from our sin to follow Him. He is coming soon, and His reward, for both righteousness and wickedness, is with Him.

The Divine Christ in the Gospels

HAVING EXAMINED HOW CHRIST WOULD have been seen and understood during the Second Temple period in general and vis-à-vis the Hebrew Scriptures in particular, it may seem counterintuitive to then discuss how Christ is seen in the New Testament. Isn't it obvious how New Testament writers perceived Him? This is a particularly pertinent question with regard to the Gospels, which are entirely devoted to the life and saving acts of the Lord Jesus Christ. Nevertheless, exploring the Christology evident in the Gospels within the context of Second Temple religion sharpens our own understanding of Christ and guards against certain modern misinterpretations of these texts. That the faithful of the Second Temple period had come, through careful attention to the text of the Hebrew Bible, to see Yahweh as a Godhead of two or more Persons even before the Incarnation of Christ provided those to whom Christ came with the means to understand His divine identity and relationship to God the Father.

36

As explained at the outset of this chapter, scholars today commonly presume that a form of Rabbinic Judaism that uniformly promoted a form of unitarian monotheism predated Christianity. New Testament scholars who have accepted this incorrect presupposition and marginalized the Old Testament evidence to the contrary have produced all manner of conjectures to explain how a supposed "transition" to belief in the Holy Trinity must have come about. Some, for example, have argued that Trinitarian doctrine was some sort of "compromise" between monotheism and paganism.

Probably the most influential approach, championed by Bart Ehrman[10] (and found even in the writings of many Orthodox scholars), is the idea that the apostles viewed Christ as primarily human or a marginally divinized human. Later generations then gradually came to regard Jesus as more and more divine until He was considered to be fully human and fully divine at the fifth-century councils.

This evolving Christology not only is perceived to have stretched out over the first three centuries of Christian history, it is read retrospectively into the text and historical context of the New Testament itself. So, for example, it is supposed that St. Mark's Gospel, taken almost universally as the earliest of the four Gospels, presents a purely human Jesus. At the same time, proponents of this evolutionary approach are more keen to push the date of composition for St. John's Gospel, widely regarded as the last Gospel to be written, as late as possible, as it clearly teaches a Jesus who is divine.[11] Whether intentional or not, this effectively opens up a larger span of time during which early understandings of Christ presumably shifted and developed, lending the evolutionary thesis more plausibility—or

---

10 Bart Ehrman's book *How Jesus Became God* is a preeminent and broadly read presentation of this view.

11 It was not uncommon to posit the composition of St. John's Gospel in the late second century until the finding of a papyrus fragment of the text in Egypt dating from the first quarter of the second century made this impossible.

at least assuaging some of the doubt as to how such a central belief among Christ's contemporaries could change so quickly (and so drastically). The same happens with the Epistles and other texts of the New Testament—they are arranged according to this evolutionary picture; doctrines (or the understanding thereof) that teach that Jesus is God are assumed to have simply developed over time.

Knowing, however, that the faithful of the Second Temple period had already embraced the idea of a "second power in heaven" or a second hypostasis of the God of Israel and even identified this figure with the coming Messiah (as in 1 Enoch), we should come to the New Testament texts expecting to find something very different. Specifically, we should not expect that the New Testament authors would be arguing for a new theological idea of the nature of God or struggling to understand some reality that has been revealed to them that was beyond their current paradigm. Instead, we should find them presenting Christ as this second hypostasis of Yahweh, the God of Israel, who is become incarnate. Further, we should expect to find this throughout the New Testament literature, not as a product or feature of "development" in early Christian theologizing. As will be seen, this is exactly what is found in the New Testament texts.[12]

As previously mentioned, in St. John's Gospel, Christ is repeatedly and unambiguously identified as Yahweh, the God of Israel, through His own words. As an example, in John 8, Christ stated to His Jewish interlocutors that Abraham had rejoiced to see His day. They replied that Jesus was not even fifty years old, so how could He have known Abraham? He answered, "Truly, truly I say to you, before Abraham was, I am." His meaning was clear to His audience,

---

12   This is historically necessitated by the reality of early Christian persecution. It is hard to imagine thousands of people being quickly convinced of a radically new, humanly produced idea to the point that they were willing to suffer and even die for it.

38

as they immediately picked up stones to execute Him for blasphemy (vv. 56–59). This simple clarity in St. John's Gospel is often then contrasted with the other three Gospels, the Synoptics. As adherents of this paradigm are wont to point out, these texts contain no similarly clear claims by Jesus. This point is sometimes even used to cast doubt on whether such statements could ever have come from Christ's mouth historically. The difference here, however, is not a difference in content. Saint John is not presenting to us a different Jesus than that of St. Matthew, St. Mark, or St. Luke. It is, rather, a difference in approach in the means of communicating that content.

Even a casual reading of St. John's Gospel reveals that it focuses intently on the words of Christ. The vast majority of the text consists of dialogues of Christ with individuals (such as Ss. Nicodemus and Photini), with His disciples, with His opponents, and ultimately with His Father in the chapters immediately preceding His trial and Crucifixion. The text luxuriates in these conversations, allowing them to play out and, in the process, expressing deep and profound theological ideas concerning the identity of Christ. Saint Mark's Gospel, on the other hand, stands in stark contrast, recounting little of what Christ said and focusing almost entirely on His actions. We are told throughout St. Mark's Gospel that Christ is preaching, but the content of that teaching remains unreported. The great teaching sections of St. Matthew's and St. Luke's Gospels, the sermons on the mount and on the plain, are omitted from St. Mark's direct and swiftly moving narrative. This approach, however, is intended to communicate precisely the same Christ. Saint Mark identifies Jesus Christ as the God of Israel in ways more subtle but no less clear to his original readers.

As just one example, in Mark 6:45–52, St. Mark records the miracle of Christ walking across the troubled Sea of Galilee. The disciples had set out in the boat ahead of Him, while Christ remained at the shore to pray. High winds came upon the sea, and the boat was making difficult progress. Christ came to them walking across the water. The disciples initially mistook Christ for a ghost and were frightened, but Jesus entered the boat with them, calming not only them but the sea as well. Saint Mark's conclusion to the story is that the disciples did not understand what this meant, because their hearts were hardened (v. 52). While telling this story, St. Mark included an odd detail, that Christ "went to pass by them" (v. 48). This remark was intended to call to mind a passage in the Book of Job.

Much of the Book of Job is a meditation on a similar theme, on our inability to understand the ways of Yahweh and why He does what He does. Job 9, in particular, describes a similar circumstance. In recounting the many glories of Yahweh, Job describes Yahweh as "walking on the waves of the sea." In Greek, this reads *"peripaton . . . epi thalasses"* (Job 9:8; Mark 6:48). To describe his lack of understanding, Job describes Yahweh as "passing him by." In Greek, the verb "to pass by" is *parelthein* (Job 9:11; Mark 6:48). In the way St. Mark describes these actions, he has put the disciples in the place of Job and Jesus Christ in the place of Yahweh, the God of Israel.

Thus while St. John's Gospel expresses the divinity of Christ via His *words*, St. Mark's Gospel does so through His *deeds*. Rather than reflecting growth, or development, or a variety of competing Christologies, the Gospels present a consistent and coherent picture of Jesus Christ as God Himself, the second hypostasis of the Holy Trinity, incarnate for our salvation. While the Gospels record different words and actions of Christ, this does not imply disagreement, only a different witness describing his own testimony. In the same way that multiple accounts of the same event that describe different details do not imply a multiplicity of events, the Gospel accounts do not imply different "versions" of Christ, particularly when it is seen that what the Gospel writers are doing is identifying the Person of Jesus Christ with a divine figure in whom they already believed.

Saint Paul's Divine Christ

THE CHRISTOLOGY PRESENTED IN THE letters of St. Paul is particularly important to an understanding of the viewpoint of the New Testament as a whole, in that St. Paul's Epistles are the earliest documents, the first written, that discuss who Christ is. Though obviously these letters were written after the events described in the Gospels and, in many cases, the events described in the Acts of the Apostles, St. Paul's written exhortations to the nascent Christian communities that he had established precede the setting down of the Gospel accounts in writing. If there was indeed some sort of "development" of the understanding of the idea of Christ, from a "lower" to a "higher" Christology, one would expect to find in St. Paul's writings a more primitive and lower view of the identity of Christ. In actuality, however, the opposite is true.

Although the question of who authored many of St. Paul's Epistles is a controversial one among scholars, the examples used in the present discussion to illustrate St. Paul's understanding of Christ's divine identity come from epistles that are incontrovertibly Pauline. These texts are also the earliest of St. Paul's writings. Leaving the controversy about authorship aside, these examples are the most important for overturning the idea that Christology underwent a development rather than stemming directly from the Second Temple understanding of Israel's God.

Philippians 2:5–11, sometimes referred to as the Carmen Christi ("hymn to Christ"), is a literary unit that many consider to be an early Christian hymn. Whether it represents a preexisting hymn adapted by St. Paul to his purpose, was composed as a poetic unit by St. Paul, or was adapted into a hymnic form from St. Paul's prose is the subject of discussion. In any event, St. Paul uses it as the theological backbone for his case to the church in Philippi. In it, he proclaims that Christ, while "existing in divine form," also "emptied Himself by taking the form of a servant, by being made in the likeness of men" (vv. 6–7). Christ humbles Himself in the Incarnation and then is exalted back to His divine state. The opening verses of this passage clearly proclaim Christ as divine before His Incarnation, rendering untenable the claim that they could be positing Christ as merely an exalted human.

Saint Paul sees Christ as central to the identity of Yahweh in the Old Testament. He expresses this powerfully by integrating the Person of Jesus Christ into the central confession of the faith of ancient Israel. Though referring to it as a creed would be anachronistic, the central statement of Jewish faith in the first century, used as both an affirmation of doctrine and a meditative prayer by Jewish faithful likely including St. Paul, was the Shema. In his First Epistle to the Corinthians, St. Paul takes the Greek form of this most sacred text and adapts it. The Greek form of the text replaces the name of the God of Israel with the word *Kyrios*, or Lord. It reads, "Hear O Israel, the Lord is our God; He is one Lord." Saint Paul states, "yet for us, there is one God, the Father, from whom are all things, and for whom we exist, and one Lord, Jesus Christ, through whom are all things and through whom we exist" (1 Cor. 8:6).

Saint Paul has inserted Jesus Christ into the Shema by identifying the one God of its confession as the Father and the one Lord as Jesus Christ. In so doing, by modifying the Greek of Deuteronomy, he has presented the one God of Israel, Yahweh, as two hypostases, the Father and Jesus Christ. This serves to identify Jesus Christ as the second hypostasis of the God of Israel and, when united with Philippians, portrays Him as a preexisting divine Person who has become incarnate in these last days.

Saint Paul uses such parallel constructions relatively frequently. In 1 Corinthians 12:4–6, he correlates all three Persons of the Holy Trinity with one another. The pattern "one Spirit, one Lord, and one God" identifies the three as distinct Persons while also bringing them into unity. It likewise emphasizes their shared task, as the three are considered equally. Benedictions such as 2 Corinthians 13:14, "The grace of the Lord Jesus Christ, the love of God, and the communion of the Holy Spirit be with all of you," likewise give the blessing of the God of Israel within the frame of the three Persons.

Far from revealing a primitive stage of Christian belief regarding Christ from which later dogmas regarding the Holy Trinity and Christology would evolve, St. Paul's writings reveal a Christology and Trinitarian belief already fully formed. These earliest of the New Testament writings were able to present such an understanding because St. Paul is interpreting the revelation of Jesus Christ in the flesh and the coming of the Holy Spirit through the lens of existing Jewish understandings of the God of Israel. Rather than struggling to concoct a middle ground between monotheism and polytheism, St. Paul reveals the true nature of the divine figures with whom his readers were already familiar through the tradition in which they had received the Scriptures.

The Divine Christ in the General Epistles

THE "GENERAL" OR "CATHOLIC" EPISTLES of the New Testament consist of the Epistles of James; 1 and 2 Peter; 1, 2, and 3 John; and Jude. These texts are too often neglected in Orthodox circles (as elsewhere) for various reasons. They are relatively short, which means that although they are included in the Orthodox lectionary, they tend to be moved through very quickly and mostly on weekdays. While the Pauline Epistles share a common background and theological purpose, the General Epistles are more eclectic. James, for example, has little in common with the others. Based on biographical information in the Acts of the Apostles and Paul's own autobiographical comments in his epistles, much more information is known about the place, time of origin, and the original recipients of St. Paul's Epistles than can be known for certain about any of the General Epistles.

Despite this diversity and eclecticism, the General Epistles came together as a literary collection, a single unit, quite early in Church history. The Pauline Epistles were compiled and began to circulate as a collection very early, about AD 100. This happened so quickly that every existing manuscript of St. Paul's Epistles is of the collection, not of a single letter. Through the testimony of St. Irenaeus and others, it is known that the four Gospels had been gathered into one unit by the middle of the second century, about AD 150. By roughly the same time in the middle of the second century, these disparate epistles had also been compiled and were circulating together as the General Epistles. Saint Clement of Alexandria wrote a commentary on the collection late in the second century, though this commentary is not still extant.

The General Epistles did not circulate as widely as the other two collections, however, and were not used by every early Christian community. When, through interactions between communities, this collection was discovered by other churches, the clear similarities between 1 John and St. John's Gospel and the clear thematic connections between 1 Peter and other New Testament texts caused them to be quickly adopted by most churches, whereas the understanding and acceptance of the rest of the collection took more time. This is the dynamic that is referred to when they are sometimes described as "disputed books." Adding to this is a series of anomalies in the General Epistles. Much has been made about an apparent contradiction between James and the argument of Galatians and Romans. First and Second Peter are written in a very different Greek style, with 2 Peter being closer to Jude in both style and themes than to 1 Peter. While 1 John has clear connections to St. John's Gospel in both style and content, the connection to 2 and 3 John's brief texts is less clear. For all these reasons, addressing the Christology of the General Epistles necessitates a discussion of the individual epistles and their teaching, from which a consensus can be seen to develop.

Saint James's Epistle is unique on several levels. While the Pauline Epistles speak of Christ primarily theologically, explaining the significance of who Christ is and what Christ has accomplished in the Cross and the Resurrection, St. James teaches in a way that is redolent with the teachings of Christ in His earthly ministry. This is particularly clear when comparing the Epistle of St. James to the teaching sections of St. Matthew's Gospel, such as the Sermon on the Mount. Even so, there is an assumed identity of the Lord Jesus Christ that St. James uses as a presupposition to argue for his case regarding how followers of Christ ought to live.

One example of this comes in James 2:1. The title "Lord" can be argued to be ambiguous. Though the Greek word *kyrios* is used throughout the Greek of the Old Testament to replace the name of the God of Israel, Yahweh, it was also used in the Greek of the time to mean "sir" or "master." However, in James 2:1, St. James describes Jesus Christ not only as "Lord," but as "the Lord of Glory." Saint Paul also uses this phrase in 1 Corinthians 2:8. It is grounded in, among other texts, Psalm 24/23, which describes Yahweh, in the Greek text "the Lord," as the "King of Glory." Saint James is using here the contrast between the life lived by Jesus Christ on the earth and His identity as the Lord of Glory to argue that the wealthy must show similar humility within the Christian community. Another important text is James 5:7–11, in which St. James brings together the God of Israel who rewarded Job for his patience in suffering, the return of God to judge the earth, the identity of Christ as the judge, and the return of Christ as one event with one agent. While St. James does not argue for the divine identity of Christ, his teaching presupposes it.

The Epistles of Peter and Jude represent Christian teaching from the perspective of Second Temple Jewish communities grounded not in Palestinian Pharisaism, but in the larger Second Temple tradition.

These three texts are deeply grounded in the apocalyptic tradition, particularly the visionary literature of the Second Temple period. These epistles understand the glorious appearance of Christ as an imminent reality in which the wicked, both among spirits and among men, will be judged. They understand the world and its systems of power and belief as being fundamental enemies of God and therefore enemies of His people. They see the life of disciples of Christ as a radical call out of the world and into a new reality of the Kingdom within the Church.

All three of these texts draw on the tradition of Enochic literature, which clearly describes a "Son of Man" figure, in line with Daniel's vision, who is the second hypostasis of Yahweh, the God of Israel, and who is identified as the Messiah. It is unsurprising, then, that these texts identify Jesus Christ with this figure. In 1 Peter 1:10–12, St. Peter identifies the Holy Spirit received by followers of Christ in baptism as the same Spirit who indwelt the prophets of old. Rather than merely identifying that Spirit as the Spirit of God, however, St. Peter identifies Him as "the Spirit of Christ" (v. 11). Second Peter 1:1 contains a very direct statement of Christ's divinity, speaking of the righteousness of "our God and Savior Jesus Christ." It is then immediately followed, in 2 Peter 1:2, with a distinction made between "the knowledge of God and of Jesus our Lord."

This follows the pattern observed in the Pauline Epistles of speaking of God the Father and Jesus Christ the Lord while also identifying Christ as God. In verses 16–18, St. Peter further elaborates on a Trinitarian understanding in describing the Transfiguration. In addition to Christ shining with the glory of God the Father, St. Peter speaks of the "Majestic Glory" that carried the voice of the Father, which phrasing he will later parallel in speaking of the Scriptures being produced by men carried by the Holy Spirit (v. 21). The brief Epistle of Jude contains another very clear statement, identifying Jesus Christ as the Angel of the Lord who led Israel out of Egypt and destroyed the disobedient (v. 5; see Ex. 23:20; Judg. 2:1).

Finally, the Johannine Epistles, 1 John in particular, as already mentioned, have clear affinities to St. John's Gospel, which very clearly presents Christ as the God of Israel. First John develops the language of John 8 regarding the unity in faith of the Father and the Son (2:22–24). For St. John, the Person of Jesus Christ is the true image of the Father who brings the knowledge of God and eternal life uniquely (1 John 5:20–21). This understanding of the Father and the Son as two Persons of the one Godhead is also laid out clearly in 2 John. The one who does not remain in the teachings of Christ does not have God. The one who does remain in the teachings of Christ has both the Father and the Son (v. 9). Though the General Epistles represent an eclectic collection of texts expressing apostolic Christianity, regarding their Christology, they are in unity with the Gospels and the Pauline Epistles, teaching that Jesus Christ is the second hypostasis of Yahweh, the God of Israel, incarnate.

Christ in the Apocalypse

THE BOOK OF REVELATION TAKES its name from the first verse, identifying the text as "the Revelation (*Apokalypsis*) of Jesus Christ." This is important to understanding the text. It is not the revelation of "end time" events in the distant future. It is not the revelation of esoteric spiritual secrets about the cosmos. It is a revelation of who Jesus Christ truly is. The Revelation received by St. John is a communication from Christ to seven churches in Asia Minor who are facing persecution, schism, compromise, and heresy. In answer to all these difficulties faced by His people, Revelation proclaims the divine identity of Christ: who He is, what He has done, and what He shortly will do when He returns to judge the living and the dead.

Because Christ is the Lord God, Creator, and ruler of the heavens and the earth, the Christians of these churches can take heart in times of trial, preserve unity in Christ against dissensions, contend for the truth against false doctrines, and maintain themselves pure from a world that is perishing. These struggles were faced not only by Christians at the end of the first century but also by the Church throughout all ages, even to our present day. The answers and the promises of Christ are as important today as they were to the book's original recipients.

The Revelation of St. John repeatedly presents the image of the throne of Yahweh, the God of Israel, reigning in heaven in the midst of His divine council. Revelation 4 describes a scene of heavenly worship before the Lord God of Israel, drawing directly and repeatedly on the language of Ezekiel 1. God the Father is repeatedly described as merely "the One" in Revelation, a reference to the Shema. At the same time, when Christ first appears to St. John (1:12–16), the description of His appearance is a combination of the description of the Son of Man in Daniel 10 and the figure on the throne in Ezekiel 1. Yahweh, the God of Israel, is One, and yet the prophetic descriptions of Him are distributed in St. John's vision between the Person of the Father and the Person of Jesus Christ.

Specifically, there is no description of the Person of the Father, the One on the throne, only the throne itself. The descriptors of the One seated on the throne from the prophetic corpus are used to describe the Person of Jesus Christ. This communicates the same truth expressed in St. John's Gospel, that the God seen and encountered physically in the Old Covenant was God the Son. We see the Father enthroned, holding a text that represents authority and lordship over the earth. The only one who is worthy to take and claim this text is the Lamb, who by being slain has purchased with His blood a people for God from every tribe and tongue and people and nation (5:1–9). The Persons of the Father and the Son are continually distinguished, with Jesus being identified as the Son of Man figure of the Old Testament, and yet the throne is later called the throne of God and of the Lamb (22:1). When St. John falls down in worship before the angel who appears to him, he is corrected (22:8–9). When he does the same before Christ, he is not (1:17–18).

The Nicene doctrine of the Holy Trinity states that the three divine Persons share in one nature, one will, and one energy. This is not a theory or a philosophical conjecture but a description of the Holy Trinity as encountered by the Fathers in the apostolic testimony of Scripture and the power of the Holy Spirit. The Revelation of St. John represents a significant part of this apostolic testimony, as titles and actions are ascribed at the same time to both the Father and the Son. As was already mentioned, the throne of God is both that of the Father and of the Son (22:1), and so the reign and dominion, the Kingdom of God, is ruled by the Triune God. The wrath poured out on the earth at its judgment is the wrath of God (14:10, 19; 15:1; 16:1, 19; 19:15), the wrath of the One seated on the throne (15:7), and the wrath of the Lamb (6:16).

In Revelation 1:8, the Lord God speaks. "The Lord God" as used in Revelation is citing the Greek translation of "Yahweh Elohim," or the God Yahweh, in the Hebrew Old Testament. Here, Yahweh, the God of Israel, identifies Himself as "the Alpha and the Omega, who is and who was and who is coming, the Almighty." We then see Christ identify Himself as "the first and the last" (1:17). The Father, the One seated on the throne, is identified as "the Lord God, the Almighty, who was and who is and who is coming" (4:8–9). And finally, Jesus Christ identifies Himself as "the Alpha and the Omega, the first and the last, the beginning and the end" (22:13–16). The worship of the divine council surrounding the throne is directed first to the Father (4:11), then to the Lamb (5:9–12), and then finally to both the Lamb and the One seated on the throne (5:13). The language is parallel, and sometimes identical, in each case.

49

The texts that make up the New Testament uniformly affirm the divinity of Jesus Christ. This is true of the first written, St. Paul's Epistles, and the last written, the Revelation of St. John, as well as those in between. Although many scholars have presumed that this must have been a belief that evolved over time, setting out the documents in the order they were written belies that point, with no significant difference in content between St. Mark's Gospel and the Pauline Epistles on the one hand, and the Johannine literature on the other, despite differences in genre and style. This is true because the understanding of an at least Binitarian Godhead was present in Second Temple religion before the birth of Jesus Christ. These ideas, gleaned from a close reading of the text of the Old Testament Scriptures, allowed the apostles to understand the revelation of Jesus Christ and the coming of the Holy Spirit in Trinitarian terms. Nicene Trinitarianism and Orthodox Christology as they were later set down by the councils were ways of using the then-contemporary Greek language to express the identity of Jesus Christ as it was revealed to the prophets and apostles who bore witness to that revelation and whose testimony is recorded in the Scriptures.

In his Dialogue with Trypho, St. Justin the Philosopher in the second century lays out the evidence from the Scriptures described above in arguing for the identity of Jesus Christ as Yahweh for his Jewish interlocutor. He summarizes, saying:

> I shall give you another testimony, my friends, from the Scriptures, that God begot before all creatures a Beginning, a certain rational power from Himself, who is called by the Holy Spirit sometimes the Glory of the Lord, others the Son, others Wisdom, others an Angel, then God, and then Lord and Logos; and on another occasion He calls Himself Captain, when He appeared in human form to Joshua the son of Nave. (Dial., 61)

50

Though in St. Justin's day this reading of the Scriptures was being anathematized by the early rabbis, it is to this clear understanding, inherited rather than invented by St. Justin, that he appeals.

Christ's apostles inherited an understanding of Yahweh, the God of Israel whom they worshipped, that was rich and full, not simple or primitive. They saw in the Hebrew Scriptures that Yahweh had not been, indeed could not be, seen by humans. They also read in those same Scriptures that their forefathers had, at various times and places, seen, spoken to, and interacted with God. They even saw places where these two Persons interacted with each other. They understood that their God was not a single Person. As they came to know Jesus of Nazareth by living and traveling with Him, they came to understand that He is the hypostasis of the God of Israel who was seen and spoken with throughout Israel's history, now incarnate as man. They also came to have personal experience of a third divine Person, the Spirit of Yahweh, whom they also found in their Scriptures.

CHAPTER 2

The Spirit, Presence, and Name of God

T HAT YAHWEH, THE GOD OF Israel, had a second hypostasis was firmly entrenched in the religious life and experience of the Jewish people in the Second Temple period, not least because of their familiarity with the Hebrew Scriptures. The Jewish world tended to convey this by speaking of the "two powers in heaven." The identity and origin of this second hypostasis was the subject of much debate and conjecture in Second Temple literature. The New Testament authors identify the Second Person of the Godhead as Jesus Christ, incarnate in their day. In response to this core tenet of the Christian message, the Jewish community that rejected Jesus as the Messiah would also come to repudiate the idea of "two powers in heaven" entirely in the second century.

While the Spirit of God or the Holy Spirit appears in the Hebrew Scriptures, there was far less discussion about His identity and origin. This is likely for several reasons. His identification as the Spirit of God adequately describes His relationship to Yahweh. Yahweh and His Spirit can clearly be distinguished from one another, but it is at the same time clear that His Spirit is not someone other than the God of Israel. His Spirit is not, on the one hand, a second God, nor on the other hand, some kind of inferior created being, because

He is His Spirit. Likewise, it makes no sense to consider the origin of God's Spirit. Someone's spirit exists for as long as they do. In the case of the Holy Spirit, this is forever. Less is said concerning the Holy Spirit in Second Temple literature because His existence was clear and less debated.[1]

The Presence of God among His People

THE HOLY SPIRIT WAS SEEN and experienced in the Old Testament in several ways. The first is directly, as the Spirit, Presence, and Power of Yahweh, the God of Israel. We see Him at the very opening of the Book of Genesis, "hovering" over the waters (Gen. 1:2), a word that in other contexts can refer to a hen brooding over her eggs. This imagery communicates that the Spirit is the One who brings about and nurtures life. Psalm 33/32:6 says, "By the Word of Yahweh the heavens were made, by the Spirit from His mouth all their hosts." The New Testament and the later Nicene characterization of Creation as a Trinitarian act is therefore seen to be based on a reading of the Old Testament Scriptures. This is not the only instance of the three Persons of the Godhead acting in concert in the Pentateuch.

As Israel was led out of Egypt, they were guided by the Presence of Yahweh, who went before them. This Presence is described as a pillar of cloud by day and a fire by night (Ex. 13:21). At different points, Yahweh says that Israel was led out of Egypt by He Himself (Ex. 20:2; Lev. 11:45; Deut. 5:6), by His Angel (Judg. 2:1), and by His Presence (Deut. 4:37). This fiery or shining cloud would be the hallmark

---

1   This being said, "threeness" is found in a number of Jewish sources from the Second Temple period. Philo, for example, argues that there are two powers of God, His Reigning Power and His Creative Power, which He Himself stands between and above. These three are one but are distinguishable in speech and appearance (Cher. 1.27–28).

of Yahweh's Presence throughout the Old Testament. This Presence descends on the tent of meeting when the God of Israel is there to speak with Moses (Ex. 33:7). At the beginning of the worship of the tabernacle, fire comes out from the Presence and consumes Israel's offering (Lev. 9:24) and then soon after consumes Aaron's erring sons (Lev. 10:2).

This same Presence comes and fills Solomon's Temple after its dedication (1 Kin. / 3Kg 8:10), and when Yahweh again appears to Solomon as He had in his childhood, He identifies the temple as the place where He has placed His Name (1 Kin. / 3Kg 9:3). This identifies the shining cloud as the God of Israel Himself. While it is very clear that Yahweh, the God of Israel, is not confined to this building in Jerusalem, He clearly states that He is fully present there in a unique way, in His Presence proper. This is, in essence, the definition of a hypostasis. It is worth noting that the cloud of God's Presence does not return to the temple at its reconsecration under Ezra (Ezra 6:16–18), nor the reconsecration in the Maccabean period (2Mc 10:5–8). When next we see this fire of God's Presence, it is in the Holy Spirit's descent to indwell the disciples of Christ on the day of Pentecost (Acts 2:3–4). This makes every Christian believer a temple of the living God (1 Cor. 6:19).

The Indwelling Spirit

THE DAY OF PENTECOST CONNECTS the cloud of God's Presence to another way the Holy Spirit operates within the Hebrew Scriptures, namely the indwelling of certain individuals. We see this first and foremost in the person of Moses as the preeminent prophet. In the Book of Numbers, God takes the Spirit who indwells Moses and shares Him with the elders of Israel, causing them to prophesy (Num. 11:16–30). Joel 2 prophesies that in the last days, the Spirit would be poured out on all flesh, and all will prophesy, as fulfilled on the day of

Pentecost. This is the primary function of the indwelling of the Spirit in the Old Testament, that the words of the indwelt prophet become the words of God Himself. Saint Peter sees this as programmatic, stating in 2 Peter 1:21, "No prophecy ever came by the will of man, but prophets, though human, spoke from God as they were carried by the Holy Spirit."

The indwelling of the Spirit was not, however, limited to prophets. It was extended to kings and other leaders such as Saul (1 Sam. / 1Kg 10:10) and David (1 Sam. / 1Kg 16:13), who received the Spirit through anointing with oil, which designated them as king. In their lives, we see the Holy Spirit empower not only words from God but divine actions (see Judg. 6:34). It is worth noting that the Holy Spirit would also depart from these leaders if they fell into unrepentant sin. This happened to Saul (1 Sam. 16:14), and David feared it would happen to him after he sinned (Ps. 51/50:11). In all these cases, the indwelling of the Holy Spirit bore the hallmark of imparting authority by transforming the indwelt human person into an agent of and participant in divine action in the world. In order for the words and the works that flow from the indwelling of the Spirit to be of God, the Spirit must Himself be the God of Israel.

The Name of Yahweh

JUST AS THE WORD BECAME the dominant way of referring to the Second Person of Yahweh, so also the Name of Yahweh came to distinguish the Third Person. This understanding of Yahweh's Name would become the basis for understandings of the Holy Spirit among the authors of the New Testament. The second hypostasis of the Godhead had been known and encountered before the Incarnation of Christ, but only in the Incarnation did He walk among men and become identified as Jesus Christ. Likewise, the Spirit of God had been encountered and known before He was poured out on Pentecost, though not as the Holy Spirit in power.

A name is an almost intimate signifier of who a person is, directly related to identity. The name Yahweh is composed of four consonants, the equivalent of YHWH, as Biblical Hebrew was not originally written with vowels. The inflected form *Yahweh* implies causality, literally translated as "He who causes to be."[2] This title indicates that God is the Creator, the One who causes to be those things that are not. This understanding of the name is reinforced by texts in which He says that by means of a future display of creative power, someone will know that He is Yahweh (e.g., Ezek. 20:44; Joel 3:17). The Hebrew Scriptures frequently speak of the Name of Yahweh in a way that does not comport itself with the four consonants that make up the written name. The Name is said, for example, to protect people like a fortress (Prov. 18:10).

This was no less the case with regard to the name of Yahweh in the Hebrew Scriptures, so much so that later Rabbinic Judaism would prohibit speaking or writing the name Yahweh, instead replacing it with the term *ha-shem* ("the Name"). In a Scripture reading, this can serve as a simple pointer to the fact that the Name of Israel's God has appeared in the reading. In more common speech, however, referring to God as "the Name" is a direct pointer to identity and to Person. For Rabbinic Judaism, God is conceived as a single Person, and so it is one title that represents Him. In the Hebrew Scriptures themselves, however, "the Name" is employed to indicate a Person, but one that is distinct from the first and second hypostases (or Persons) of the Godhead.

---

2   The morphology of biblical Hebrew verbs is based on a system of *binyans*, essentially vocalization patterns. These vocalizations nuance the meaning of the verb's action. In this case, the name Yahweh is in the *Hiphil binyan*, causing it to be causative, i.e., "causes to be" rather than simply "is."

At the time of the Exodus, as has already been described, the Angel of the Lord came to accompany the people, leading them through the wilderness and into the land, departing only at the beginning of the time of the Judges owing to Israel's wickedness. When Yahweh identified His Angel to Moses, He stated that the Angel must not be rebelled against. Any rebellion against the Angel would not be forgiven. The seriousness of this warning was due to Yahweh's Name having been placed in the Angel (Ex. 23:20–21).

Israel, of course, did engage in such a rebellion in the wilderness, which was described in later portions of the Hebrew Scriptures. Psalm 78/77 summarizes, "How many times they rebelled against Him in the wilderness and grieved Him in the desert. They tested God again and again and angered the Holy One of Israel" (vv. 40–41). The language of rebellion recurs here along with the language of grieving, both aimed at God Himself. In parallel, Isaiah says, "And they rebelled and grieved His Holy Spirit. Therefore, He turned and became their enemy, and He Himself fought against them" (63:10). Speaking of Israel in the wilderness, Isaiah reuses the language of rebellion and grieving but here describes the rebellion as being against the Holy Spirit, which grieved Him.

All this language plays out in the New Testament writings. When St. John the Forerunner was sent out on his mission of baptism, he was informed that he would recognize the One he had been waiting and preparing for when the Spirit descended and remained on Him (John 1:33). The sign that identified Christ for St. John was the sign that identified the Angel of the Lord for Moses. It is because of this sign that St. John could recognize the incarnate Christ as the Son of God (v. 34). Later in St. John's Gospel, Christ—in the prayer He offers on behalf of His disciples—merges references to the coming of the Holy Spirit with the repeated refrain that He has made the Name manifest (17:6, 12, 26).

Saint Paul uses the language of grieving the Holy Spirit in his Epistle to the Ephesians (4:30). That the Spirit dwelt within the Angel of the Lord and with the people of Israel made their rebellion more dire in consequence. Saint Paul, therefore, teaches that the Presence of the Holy Spirit within the faithful similarly makes the possibility of grieving the Spirit through rebellion against the commandments of Christ possible. The denial of forgiveness for rebellion in the Presence of the Name is likewise attributed to the Holy Spirit by Christ Himself. Every blasphemy will be forgiven except the blasphemy of the Holy Spirit (Matt. 12:31; Mark 3:28–29). Christ gives this warning in response to slander leveled against the Spirit who dwells in Him (Mark 3:30).

God's Presence within the tabernacle and later temple was spoken of in personal terms as the Third Person of the Holy Trinity. This Presence of God was also referred to as His Name. This begins with the altar Moses was directed to build at Sinai, guided by the promise that wherever Yahweh placed His Name to be remembered, there He would make Himself present and bless His people (Ex. 20:24; see Matt. 18:20). As Israel prepared to enter the land of Canaan, Yahweh spoke of the place He would place His Name, a permanent residence for the tabernacle and then the temple (Deut. 12:5–21; 14:23–24; 16:1–11; 26:1–2). When David prepared and then Solomon executed the building of the first temple in Jerusalem, it was referred to as building a house for the Name (1 Kin. / 3Kg 3:2; 5:5; 8:20, 29, 35; 2 Chr. 6:10, 20, 26). Psalm 74/73:7 gave the temple the same description, and Nehemiah employed similar language when the second temple was built (1:9).

Within scholarly circles, there has been considerable debate over Name theology in ancient Israelite religion. There was at one point a consensus that the Name of Yahweh is a hypostasis of Yahweh resident in the tabernacle and temple with whom the

Israelite priesthood interacted. Other scholars have argued that in other texts of the Hebrew Scriptures, the Name is clearly Yahweh Himself. Both of these can be true if we understand the Name of Yahweh as a hypostasis who is also consubstantial with Yahweh, just as is the Second Person of the Godhead, already discussed. The Name is described as a person in numerous instances (see 2 Sam. 6:2; Ps. 20/19:1; Is. 30:27).

Thus, when the New Testament authors speak of the Holy Spirit as God, they are following the Hebrew Scriptures that they inherited. They are not innovating by speaking of a third divine hypostasis any more than they were in identifying Jesus Christ as the second hypostasis of Yahweh, the God of Israel. When, for example, the Holy Trinity was manifest at the Baptism of Christ (Matt. 3:13–17; Mark 1:9–11; Luke 3:21–22), this was not a shocking new revelation to a group of unitarian monotheists but rather a clarification and identification of the Persons of the Godhead already known throughout the Second Temple period. The New Testament writers, in speaking of the agent of the Resurrection of Christ, speak of Him being raised by the Father (Acts 2:24; Rom. 8:11; 2 Cor. 4:14), Christ rising Himself (John 2:19; 10:18), and the Spirit raising Christ from the dead (Rom. 1:4; 1 Pet. 3:18). In doing so, they are not confused or disagreeing but are following the pattern established in the Scriptures by the accounts of the Creation of the world and of the Exodus from Egypt. The Resurrection of Christ is the great Trinitarian action, the fulfillment of both the Triune God's redemption of His people at the Pascha and the beginning of the new creation.

That the Godhead is one and is three hypostases, the Father, the Son, and the Holy Spirit, then, is the testimony of the Hebrew Scriptures. This is not merely a reading backward of later Christian theological categories into those Scriptures. Rather, the distinction of

Persons and the unity of the Godhead were the spiritual experience of the faithful of ancient Israel and of the Second Temple period. This is known through the religious texts of the faithful during these periods, in which they reflect this experience and understanding. The God known and worshipped in Judea in the first century and among the Judeans of the diaspora was and was known to be the Triune God of Christianity.

PART TWO

God's
Divine Council

✠ ✠ ✠

CHAPTER 3

The Powers of the Spiritual World

CONTEMPORARY CULTURE, WITH ITS EMPHASIS on material reality, has dulled our spiritual senses. We have gained a wealth of scientific knowledge and insight that has produced wonders of technology. At the same time, however, we have left behind other aspects of the created world in which we live and have isolated ourselves from the invisible realm in which God and the angelic hosts dwell. At one point in the Prophet Elisha's ministry, his servant was likewise blind. A major detachment of the Syrian army surrounded and laid siege to the city of Dothan, intent on capturing and killing Elisha and all those with him. Seeing the human foes arrayed against himself and his master, Gehazi the servant gave in to doubt and fear. Miraculously, the eyes of his heart were opened to see reality more fully, and he saw a host of angels and archangels surrounding and protecting him on all sides. This was a reality that Elisha, as a prophet, lived in and was aware of every day of his life (2 Kin. / 4Kg 6:11–17).

Unitarian monotheism does not work as a category for understanding the depiction of God in the Holy Scriptures because the Old and New Testaments both bear witness to the three Persons who are Yahweh. It is also a problematic lens to apply when asking

65

whether the Holy Trinity is alone in the heavens. Yahweh, the God of Israel, is not alone—He is surrounded by the spirits who consti-tute the invisible creation. The Scriptures, although English transla-tions tend to obscure it, are not shy about calling these beings gods. There are many of these gods, but none of them is like the God who created them. For Christians of today, angels and demons are an afterthought, perhaps even an embarrassing one. They may be seen as some kind of holdover from paganism or premodern, superstitious cosmologies. Yet the belief systems of ancient Israel, Second Temple Judea, and early Christianity all embraced these beings. They envis-aged the invisible realm and its occupants interacting constantly with the visible world and the people who inhabited it.

In the Scriptures, the hosts of angels, archangels, thrones, domin-ions, virtues, principalities, powers, cherubim, and seraphim are predominantly described using one of two metaphors. The first— already alluded to in the previous sentence—is that of the "heavenly hosts." This reference to the multitude of angelic beings is tied to one of the names of the God of Israel in the Old Testament: Yah-weh Sabaoth, the Lord of Hosts. The Hebrew term *Sabaoth*, often assumed by speakers of English to be related to the Sabbath (*shabat* in Hebrew), comes from the verb *tsavah*, "to give command to." In Genesis 1, this verb conveys how waters and the skies teemed with life brought forth by God. Similarly, at the beginning of Exodus, it connotes how the Israelites had been fruitful and multiplied even in Egypt. The phrase "Lord of Hosts" is not merely pointing to the large number of angelic beings, but to their regimentation. This is properly speaking a martial title for Israel's God and is most often used within military metaphors to describe Yahweh as commander of armies and mighty in battle.[1]

---

1   There is another common usage of the term "heavenly hosts" or "hosts of heaven"
     for angelic beings, which will be described further in a subsequent section.

The second metaphor used to describe noetic beings is that of the divine council. Simply put, the God of Israel is depicted in the Scriptures as a king enthroned, ruling over His creation. The angelic beings, then, are part of His royal court, a divine council, over which He presides. This divine council is both directly depicted and alluded to throughout the Old Testament. In the New Testament, particularly centered on the Incarnation and Ascension of Jesus Christ, the nature of the divine council is transformed. Ultimately, descriptions of God's divine council in Scripture form the framework for understanding the reign and intercessions of the saints in glory, as has been recognized in the Orthodox Church throughout the ages.

The Divine Council in Scripture

IN THE HEBREW SCRIPTURES, TWO key phrases are used to convey God's divine council: the "mountain of assembly" (*har moed* in Hebrew) and the "Most High God" (*el elyon* in Hebrew, *ypsistos theos* in Greek).

The first, the "mountain of assembly," does not pertain to a single mountain where the God of Israel dwelled, à la Mount Olympus in Greek myth, but rather, as the angelic beings are part of the invisible creation, various mountains become the "mountain of assembly." For ancient people, sacred geography overlapped with material geography. The gods of Israel's neighbors were associated with, and sometimes even confined to, particular sacred places. Yahweh is not so restricted and comes to dwell where He pleases, for as long as He pleases. Sinai became the mountain of assembly when God's Presence descended on it, as did Zion when it became the site of divine worship. In the New Testament, Tabor at the time of the Transfiguration of Christ became the mountain. Importantly, in the Book of Revelation, the ultimate battle between Christ and His enemies takes place at *harmageddon* (a Greek transliteration of the Hebrew *har moed*).[2] Saint John's reference in Revelation 16:16 frames the final siege of God's holy mountain in terms reminiscent of the first such siege, when the Amalekites assaulted Israel at the foot of Mount Sinai and dared lay "a hand on the throne of Yahweh" (Ex. 17:16). In whatever place God is, He is surrounded by His divine council and presides. It is because of this mobility that His throne is also depicted as a chariot.

The second term, "God Most High" or "the Most High God," points to the reality that although other spiritual beings exist and are called gods in the pages of the Scriptures, none of them are like Yahweh, the God of Israel. As will be seen, the pagan nations will come to worship some fallen members of the divine council as their gods in place of the Most High. It is not surprising then that in the Scriptures, the title "Most High" is the one that spirits—both angelic and demonic—use to refer to God (see Mark 5:7; Luke 1:32, 35, 76; 8:28; Acts 16:17).

The rebellion of the devil and his fall as they are described in Isaiah 14 and Ezekiel 28 are portrayed as an attempted overthrow of Yahweh's role in the divine council. Isaiah describes the devil's intent to set his throne on high, on the mount of assembly (14:13). He sought to make himself like the Most High (v. 14) but instead was thrown down into Sheol, into the underworld. Ultimately, he was revealed to be the god of nothing but dust and ashes. Ezekiel's description gives even greater detail, recounting the devil's state before his fall, a beautiful creation of God walking in Eden, the Garden of God (28:13). God had created him to hold a position of prestige and honor near His own throne (v. 14), yet the devil became filled with arrogance

---

2   The transliterated "e" in *har moed* represents the Hebrew consonant *ayin*. This consonant was original pronounced at the back of the throat, making a sort of "ng" sound. It was frequently transliterated with a "g" as in the names of the city Gomorrah and the giant Goliath.

over his own beauty and position (v. 17) and committed evil. Therefore, he was cast down from the heavens to the earth and ashes (v. 18).

Ezekiel 28 further connects the devil to the figure of Baal, who was the primary deity worshipped in Tyre, against whom the oracles were directed in Ezekiel 28. This chapter begins by speaking of "the King of Tyre," an ambiguous term that could refer to the human king, whom the Phoenicians perceived as divine, or the god who ruled them. By the end of Ezekiel's prophecy, he is very clearly describing events in the myths associated with Baal. Baal is a title, meaning "lord" or "master," that was applied to many different gods by Phoenicians and other Semitic people groups. There are therefore references in the Old Testament to multiple Baals or to the Baal of a particular place. When used without a geographic or other modifier, and particularly in reference to the Phoenicians and in the life of Elijah, Baal is the god Hadad, who was the principal deity of Aram, ancient Syria, and was seen as the king of their gods. The Baal cycle—a Ugaritic series of myths about the god Baal that became the basis for the festivals and rituals of the Baal cult—recounts how Baal rose up from among the high council of gods to establish a throne over them all.[3] Ezekiel 28, then, can be seen to argue both that the Baal cycle is a false version of the story of the devil's fall in which he achieved his goal and that worshippers of Baal are in fact worshipping the devil.

Baal (sometimes referred to as Beelzebub in New Testament texts)[4] would come to be identified with the devil throughout later

---

3   Much of the religious material surrounding Baal, both ritual texts and the ·
     Baal cycle epic, is preserved in Ugaritic, the West Semitic dialect of the city
     of Ugarit in present-day Lebanon. Ugaritic, though closely related to Hebrew,
     was written in cuneiform on tablets in Mesopotamian fashion.
4   Beelzebub is a corruption of one of Baal's traditional titles. Baal-zebul
     means roughly "high lord Baal." "Baal-zebub" means "lord of the flies." It
     was a term of mockery referring to the place around which flies congregate,
     namely excrement.

Jewish history (see Matt. 10:25; 12:24, 27; Mark 3:22; Luke 11:15, 18, 19). These allusions to the devil's fall, echoing depictions found in the prophetic books, are also important to our understanding of the curse the serpent incurs in Genesis 3. The imagery of being cast to the ground and eating dirt and ashes matches the symbolism found in Isaiah and Ezekiel, and it represents the dead who are seized and swallowed by Sheol or Hades. It is for this reason that in Christian iconography and art, Hades is often depicted as an open-mouthed serpent. It is this imagery that lies behind, for example, St. John Chrysostom's poetic description of the Resurrection of Christ.[5]

The devil, however, was not the only angelic being who fell into sin. The same fate befell similar creatures in the days of Noah (Gen. 6:1–2; 2 Pet. 2:4; Jude 6). The story of the Tower of Babel points to another group who, like the devil, became arrogant and sought to be worshipped as gods by the nations of the world. The Tower of Babel—actually a ziggurat, a step pyramid in the city of Babylon—signified an attempt to erect a mountain of assembly by human effort, a way of drawing God down from heaven in order to manipulate and control Him. The name Babylon (and Babel) is derived from the Akkadian *babilim*, meaning "the gate of the gods."[6]

As punishment and to prevent further such evil, God scattered and disinherited the nations. He then immediately, in the narrative of Genesis, began with Abraham to create a nation for Himself, through which He ultimately planned to reconcile all nations to Himself in

---

5   This imagery is found in St. John's *Paschal Homily* and *Homilies on Matthew*, 26.39. Saint Gregory of Nyssa uses similar imagery in the *Great Catechism*. Parallels are found in St. Gregory the Dialogist, *Moralia*, 33.7.14; St. John of Damascus, *On the Orthodox Faith*, 3.27; St. Cyril of Jerusalem, Catechetical Lectures, 12.15; St. Ambrose, *Commentary on Luke*, 4.11–12; and St. Athanasius, *Life of Anthony*, 24.

6   This Akkadian term is in turn derived from an earlier Sumerian phrase used to describe ziggurats as *kan digirak* or "the god's gate."

Christ. In regard to those other nations, however, Deuteronomy 32:8 reflects on what took place. God reckoned to the nations of the world (numbered in Genesis at seventy) their inheritance; to all the sons of Adam, He set their boundaries according to a certain number. Most English translations at this point reflect the medieval Hebrew text and say, "according to the number of the sons of Israel." In addition to making little to no sense in context, nowhere do the Scriptures number the nations at twelve. The Greek text of Deuteronomy translates an earlier form of the Hebrew, stating that God divided them "according to the number of His angels." Recently, among the Dead Sea Scrolls, the original Hebrew wording has been recovered, which indicates that they had been divided "according to the number of the sons of God" (4QDeut).

Deuteronomy is here recording that when He distanced Himself from them, God assigned these nations to angelic beings in the divine council. These beings became corrupt, however, and were worshipped by the nations they were to govern. This is why all the gods of the nations are demons (see Deut. 32:17; Ps. 96/95:5; 1 Cor. 10:20). This situation is also described in Daniel 10, as Daniel's angelic visitor describes being delayed by a "Prince of Persia," against whom he was aided by St. Michael the Archangel (v. 13), and that he is due for further battle alongside St. Michael against both this "Prince of Persia" and the "Prince of Greece" (vv. 20–21). Psalm 82/81, then, describes the judgment God pronounced against these beings, that they shall perish. The final verse of this psalm is sung in the Orthodox Church on Holy Saturday to celebrate the victory of Christ over the dark powers and the beginning of God's inheritance of all the nations.

The concept of fallen spiritual beings worshipped as gods by the nations under them found in the Hebrew Scriptures resembles the understanding of the nations who were Israel's neighbors. Plato, for example, writes:

Once upon a time the gods were taking over by lot the whole earth according to its regions. . . . So by just allotments they received each one his own, and they settled their countries; and when they had thus settled them, they reared us up, even as herdsmen rear their flocks. . . . Now in other regions others of the gods had their allotments and ordered the affairs, but inasmuch as Hephaestus and Athena were of a like nature, being born of the same father, and agreeing, more-over, in their love of wisdom and of craftsmanship, they both took for their joint portion this land of ours as being naturally congenial and adapted for virtue. (*Critias*, 109b–c)

For Plato, as for Deuteronomy, the nations of the world had been allotted to the various gods, with Athens and its environs being given to Hephaestus and Athena. He describes this ancient era as the age of Chronos, the father of Zeus and previous king of the gods:

Tradition tells us how blissful was the life of men in that age, fur-nished with everything in abundance, and of spontaneous growth. And the cause thereof is said to have been this: Chronos was aware of the fact that no human being (as we have explained) is capable of hav-ing irresponsible control of all human affairs without becoming filled with pride and injustice; so, pondering this fact, he then appointed as kings and rulers for our cities, not men, but beings of a race that was nobler and more divine, namely, demons. . . . In like manner the god, in his love for humanity, set over us at that time the nobler race of demons who, with much comfort to themselves and much to us, took charge of us and furnished peace and modesty and orderliness and justice without stint, and thus made the tribes of men free from feud and happy. (*Laws*, 713c–e)

When referencing the pagan practices among the nations out-side of Israel, St. Paul speaks of their gods as demons just as they do, though with an awareness that these are spirits who are in rebellion against the God of Israel (see 1 Cor. 10:20–22). He admonishes his hearers to heed the call of the Most High God and return to the worship of Him alone, thus recovering that better-ordered time before their idolatrous ways. A prime example of this argument is in St. Paul's words at the Areopagus in Athens (Acts 17:22–31). The apostle presents to the Athenians the Most High God who created mankind and divided the nations, the God who had been lost to their collective memory. He does not live in temples such as the Tower of Babel. He did not scatter the nations out of hatred for them or ill will. The time had now come when He would make Himself known to them and call them to return and repent.

The rebellions of these demonic powers, which will be further discussed in the next chapter, did not destroy the divine council, as it continues to be described in the Scriptures. The role of the spiritual beings who remain a part of the divine council is not purely a passive one. Deliberations take place within the council as God shares His rule over creation with His creatures. The Book of Job features a famous example of the "sons of God" gathering to present themselves to God, including "the Satan." As the angels assemble around the throne of God, Job, though unaware, is being tried. The Satan seeks to test him to see if His faithfulness to God is real (Job 1:6–12).

A less well-known example takes place in 1 Kings or 3 Kingdoms (1 Kin. / 3Kg 22:19–23). God had ordered Ahab to be brought down as king of Israel for his many egregious sins. As the Prophet Micaiah recounted, however, a meeting took place between Yahweh, seated on His throne, and the heavenly hosts gathered about it on all sides. God asked them who would persuade Ahab to venture to Ramoth-Gilead, where he would die (v. 20). After various proposals were brought forth by the angelic beings in attendance, one spirit finally volunteered to speak through Ahab's false prophets and promise him victory in this battle (v. 22). God accepted this plan, and it moved forward, although a true prophet is then sent to Ahab to tell him all this and give him one final chance to repent. Ahab, unfortunately, did not take this final opportunity and perished in battle (v. 35).

While the examples above illustrate the role of angelic beings in implementing God's judgment, in the Second Temple period, their involvement in the divine council was also regarded in a positive light. Certain angelic beings were seen to inspire God's people to offer tears and prayers for mercy before the throne of God. Prayers were made to these angelic beings to represent a person's cause before Yahweh. Angels of mercy were requested to plead for mercy on behalf of God's people. Before the shofar was blown on holy days, a prayer was said requesting the angels presiding over the horn's music to intercede before the throne of Yahweh for atonement for the people. While it is God who reigns from the throne and shows mercy and kindness, in the Old Testament God was seen to involve His angelic creatures in His governance of creation as a grace to them.

The One Who Presides in the Council

IT IS A COMMONPLACE IN St. Paul's theology for the apostle to refer to God the Father and the Lord Jesus Christ as a unified phrase (see, for example, Rom. 1:4, 7; 1 Cor. 8:6; Gal. 1:3; Eph. 1:2–3). This formulation, "One God, the Father, and one Lord, Jesus Christ," ultimately became the basis for the phraseology of the Nicene Creed. The relationship between these two Persons, the Father and Christ, and what this relationship reflects about the divinity of Christ Himself has been the subject of much modern speculation.

Here, too, the fraught evolutionary paradigm of Church history surfaces. At one time, scholars—Christian and otherwise—largely framed St. Paul's language of the two Persons within an evolutionary chain of development in the formation of Christology and the doctrine of the Holy Trinity. As discussed in chapter 1 of this book, however, this presumes that the Second Temple religion the apostles practiced was characterized by unitarian monotheism, which is not an adequate description of the ancient religion of Israel nor that of the Second Temple period.

Ancient religions of the Mediterranean basin and the Levant, including Israelite religion, shared a variety of basic tenets in their vision of the spiritual world. These included the existence of numerous divine beings that existed under the rulership of a Most High God; that some of these powers were malign; that at some point in the past, divine wrath had expressed itself in the form of a flood; that surrounding that event had been a part-human, part-divine race of giant tyrants against whom a war was waged; and many more besides. While many elements of this shared cosmology would be rejected later by Rabbinic Judaism in favor of a simpler unitarian monotheism whose emphasis was more moral than spiritual, that was a historical development that came centuries after the time of Christ. None of the ancient religious conceptions mentioned were denied in the ancient Israelite or Second Temple periods.

Instead, they were accepted as reality by Israelites and later Judeans but reconceptualized within a spiritual and physical created order under the reign of Yahweh, the God of Israel. The other spiritual powers were seen as creations of Yahweh to serve as His divine council, some of whom at various points rebelled. The great heroes and men of renown, part human and part divine, were reconceived as demonic tyrants and their creation seen to be a demonic act of angelic apostasy. The Flood was not enacted out of divine peevishness or rage, but rather out of Yahweh's desire to purify His creation from the corruption brought about by both fallen spiritual powers and fallen humanity.

The relationship between Yahweh and His divine council was among these common elements Hebrew religion shared with surrounding religions and reconceived in its own context. All ancient religions of the Mediterranean and the Levant acknowledged the existence of an assembly of gods. In fact, Yahweh's council consisted of seventy or seventy-two members (see Deut. 32:8 and Gen. 10). This is directly parallel to the general Canaanite conception in which the high god El presided over seventy or seventy-two assembled sons. Another common element was the conception that beneath the authority of the Most High God, the council was presided over by another person who was conceived of as a unique or special son of the Most High God. In Canaanite religion, these figures were El and his son Baal. In Greek religion, these figures were Chronos and Zeus. Parallels exist within all the ancient belief systems of the region. The stories of the ascent of Baal, Zeus, and their parallels to this exalted position presiding over the divine council are formative stories for the religions of their respective cultures.

A recurring motif across the myths of ancient religions that surrounded Israel was that the being who presided over the council had not always been in that position. Not only had they been elevated to that status, they ascended to it through violence or rebellion. Zeus attacked his father and imprisoned him, along with the other Titans, in Tartarus. Baal slayed Yam and Mot and was enthroned at the head of the council after leading a successful rebellion to overthrow its previous leadership. Within the pages of the Scriptures, these rebellions in the divine council are acknowledged, though once again reconceived. First and foremost, the rebellious members of the council did not succeed in overthrowing the rule of Yahweh and were instead crushed. Ezekiel directly parallels the story of Baal's divine rebellion with the defeat and throwing down of the devil in Eden (Ezek. 28:12–19). By the New Testament writings, Second Temple understandings firmly correlated these divine usurpers with the devil. The New Testament contains numerous instances where Beelzebub, a slightly corrupted form of one of Baal's titles, is used as a name for the prince of demons (Matt. 10:25; 12:24, 27; Mark 3:22; Luke 11:15, 18–19). Saint John associates Zeus with Satan when he refers to the high altar of Zeus's triumph at Pergamon as "Satan's throne" (Rev. 2:13). Saint Peter identifies the location where the rebel angels were imprisoned from the time of Noah as Tartarus (2 Pet. 2:4).

The second major distinguishing feature in the religious conceptions of ancient Israel and Judea was that in addition to Yahweh serving as the Most High God, He also presided over the divine council. Israel still understood that there are two different divine roles. A second hypostasis, a Second Person who is also Yahweh, presides over the council as the divine Son. He appears in several significant passages of the Hebrew Scriptures in this role as governing the council. It is this figure whom the New Testament writers teach has become incarnate as the Person of Jesus Christ.

One of these texts is Psalm 82/81. This psalm prophetically describes a scene in which Yahweh takes His stand among the gods of the council. He issues judgment against the sons of God to whom the nations had been assigned in Deuteronomy 32:8. They have not served Yahweh, nor have they governed justly. Rather, they have brought about wickedness on the earth and sought to be worshipped themselves as gods by the nations that Yahweh, the God of Israel, had assigned them to govern. They will die like men; they will be defeated and destroyed. All this will happen when God arises to judge the earth,[7] at which point, His inheritance will be not only Israel but all the nations (82/81:8).

Christ quoted this passage in John 10:35–36 after the Judeans had accused Him of blasphemy and nearly stoned Him for calling Himself the Son of God. This term—Son of God—can have several meanings, including Messiah. In this instance, however, what occasioned

---

7   The word here translated "arise" is *anasta* in Greek. This is the same root as the Greek *anastasis*, "resurrection."

the charge of blasphemy was Christ's statement that He and the Father are one. It is clear that the Judean leaders understood Jesus to be claiming to be the Son of God who commands the divine council, and He reaffirmed this by quoting Psalm 82/81. He pointed out that in the psalm, those beings are called gods to whom the Word of God came. This is St. John's favored term for the preincarnate Christ as seen in his Gospel's prologue. Christ's response was therefore clear: if the members of the divine council are called gods and sons of the Most High, then why would it be blasphemy for the Word Himself to call Himself the Son of God? His opponents clearly understood exactly who Christ was claiming to be, as they again sought to seize and kill Him for blasphemy.

Another of these texts is Daniel 7:9–14. Daniel's vision in this passage reworks a scene from the Baal cycle in which Baal, after he had rebelled against the former leader of the divine council, was brought before his father El to be crowned. He was enthroned and proceeded to rule over the whole world. The understanding of the Judean people, however, was of course that the devil's attempted revolt had been a failure, causing him to be cast down into the underworld with the dead. In this context, the enthroned Yahweh is described using tropes common to portrayals of the Most High God in all religions. Then a second figure is introduced, who looked to Daniel like a human person. This human person was riding on clouds. This vision, therefore, depicts the second hypostasis of Yahweh, who will be manifest as a human. This vision, as it was interpreted to Daniel, concerns the latter days as this figure is enthroned and given a Kingdom that will have no end. In Mark 14:61–63, Christ cited this text as He stood trial before the high priest. It is not a coincidence that Christ ascended into heaven accompanied by clouds and that this event was interpreted as His enthronement (see Acts 1:9; 2:34–36).

The religious narratives of the nations can thereby be seen to be false gospels. They are triumphal stories that never took place and that were, rather, defeats. They ascribe victory over the ruling spiritual powers to rebellious spiritual beings who in truth were judged and thrown down rather than emerging triumphant. The true gospel, the story of Christ's victory, begins with Yahweh, God the Son, descending from the glory He shared with the Father eternally (John 17:5) to be made man. The incarnate Son of God then waged war against the hostile spiritual powers oppressing humanity, against the power of sin, and against death itself. Arising victorious, He ascended back to His former estate, bearing with Him our shared humanity, and is enthroned in the heavens over a Kingdom without end. "'He ascended': what does it mean if not that He had also descended into the lower regions, that is, the earth? The one who had descended is also the one who has ascended above all the heavens so that He might fill all things" (Eph. 4:10).

Angels and Stars

AS MODERN PEOPLE, WHEN WE think of the sun and stars, we imagine masses of incandescent gas, gigantic nuclear furnaces in which hydrogen is transformed into helium at, literally, astronomical temperatures. When we think of the moon, we picture a large, dusty rock orbiting around the earth every twenty-seven days. We are at least vaguely aware that ancient people did not understand the luminaries this way, but we believe our modern understanding is superior because it is based on mathematics and scientific observation. Ancient explanations and descriptions are regarded as quaint folktales and myths now supplanted by real knowledge. This creates a difficulty for modern readers of the Scriptures, as those Scriptures are quickly judged to be incongruent with the modern worldview.

Modernity has had two typical responses to this dilemma. On one hand, biblical references to bodies such as the sun and stars are dismissed as some sort of condescension by God in His revelation to primitive people or outright fairy tales. On the other, a modern understanding of these things is read back into the biblical stories. For example, certain passages in Scripture may be interpreted to be talking about clouds of gas undergoing nuclear fusion in the depths of space. Both approaches represent a failure of modern people to listen to and properly hear the biblical text and what it is attempting to tell us. When the Scriptures speak about the stars of heaven, they are actually helping us understand our destiny as human persons in Christ.

In Scripture, stars are consistently connected with angelic beings. The term "heavenly host" or "the host of heaven" is used throughout to refer to both astronomical bodies visible in the sky (see Gen. 2:1; Ps. 33/32:6; Jer. 33:22) and the angelic beings as a group (1 Kin. / 3Kg 22:19; Is. 24:21; 34:4; Dan. 4:35; Luke 2:13). In most cases, it is not clear which of these two is in view in a particular reference. It appears most likely that the reference is to both (Deut. 4:19; 17:3; Dan. 8:10; Acts 7:42). As already described, the title of the God of Israel, Yahweh Sabaoth, is directly related. Yahweh Sabaoth proclaims His powers as the God of gods, worshipped by all the heavenly powers. This same interplay can be seen in references in the Scriptures to the stars and to angels (Job 38:7; Mark 13:25; Rev. 1:20).

This is not, however, a primitive confusion. Ancient people did not believe that the lights in the sky were angels, whereas now we moderns understand that they are balls of gases. Rather, all ancient people, both inside and outside of Israel, understood that there were spiritual powers associated with the governance of every aspect of the created order. Nature spirits and gods were associated with all the elements of the natural world, including those objects in the heavens above, those on the earth beneath, and those in the abyss beneath the earth (Ex. 20:4; Deut. 5:8). The Scriptures do not dispute that these beings exist. Rather, they describe these beings as spiritual beings created by God who act either in service to or in rebellion against Him. In speech, ancient people often did not distinguish between a person or an object and the spiritual powers who stood behind it and animated it. This represents a particular view of the sovereignty of God as He governs His creation through the members of His divine council. At the Creation, a share in that governance was also given to humanity (Gen. 1:26).

Philo of Alexandria describes the Jewish understanding of the heavenly bodies in the first century AD in the following way:

> Some have supposed that the sun and moon and the other stars were gods with absolute powers and ascribed to them the causation of all events. But Moses held that the universe was created and is in a sense the greatest of commonwealths, having magistrates and subjects. . . . These magistrates, however, in his view do not have unconditional powers but are lieutenants of the one Father of all. . . . So all the gods that the senses know in the heavens must not be supposed to possess absolute power but to have received the rank of subordinate rulers. . . . Let us proceed to give honor to the immaterial, invisible, understood by the intellect alone, who is not only the God of gods, whether perceived by sense or by mind, but also the maker of all. (*Special Laws*, 1.3)

Philo is not shy about calling the sun, moon, and stars gods. Rather than being independent powers to be worshipped in their own right, they are lesser officials in God's divine administration over his creation who preside with relative, delegated authority.

Philo's discussion of the sun, moon, and stars is not philosophical speculation or a point of popular piety. It is a portion of his commentary on Deuteronomy 4:19–20 and describes his understanding of the Torah's teaching on the subject.

> Beware if you should lift your eyes to the heavens and seeing the sun and the moon and the stars and all the host of heaven be led away and bow down to them and serve them. These are things that Yahweh your God has allotted to all the nations under all the heavens. But Yahweh

has taken you and brought you out of Egypt, the furnace of iron, in order to make you a nation to be his inheritance, as you are today.

After the Tower of Babel event, Yahweh had given over all the nations to the governance of spiritual powers who, rather than imitating his governance, had become corrupt and had begun to be worshipped by those nations (Deut. 32:8, 17). But He had chosen Israel for His inheritance and had revealed Himself to them so that they might know Him and worship the true God (Ps. 117:27 in the Greek).

When St. Paul decried the nations for having worshipped creating beings rather than the Creator, he was not speaking of the material stuff from which idols were made, but rather of the spiritual powers who were being worshipped instead of God Most High (Rom. 1:25; 1 Cor. 10:20). Saint Andrew of Caesarea described this as also being the view of the Fathers in his interpretation of the devil as the "prince and power of the air" (Eph. 2:2).[8]

The relationship of these spiritual beings as patrons and governors of various elements of creation remains, however, and continues into the present age. Just as Israel had St. Michael as its prince (Dan. 10:21; 12:1), churches have angelic patrons (Rev. 1:20). The rebellious gods of the nations were judged at the Resurrection of Christ and are being thrown down (Ps. 82/81). God's sovereignty, however, remains the same, and so these fallen, former holy ones are being replaced with new holy ones. And so, in the Church, we now have not only angelic beings but glorified humans as patrons of churches, cities, and nations.

The destiny of human persons not only is described as coming to share in the governance of God over His creation. Our actual physical destiny, the destiny of our material bodies and their glorification, is associated with angelic beings. Daniel, speaking of the resurrection, says that the righteous will shine forever like the stars of heaven

---

8   *Commentary on the Apocalypse*, 12.34.

(Dan. 12:3). Christ says that in the resurrection, human persons will be "like the angels" (Mark 12:25; Matt. 22:30). Saint Paul speaks at length of the resurrection of the body in light of the bodily Resurrection of our Lord Jesus Christ. He directly utilizes the language of Deuteronomy 4 when he states:

> There are celestial bodies, and there are earthen bodies. There is one glory indeed of the celestial, and another now of the earthen. There is one glory of the sun and another glory of the moon and another glory of the stars because a star is different from another star in its glory. So also is the resurrection of the dead. The body is sown in corruption. It is raised in immortality. It is sown in dishonor. It is raised in glory. It is sown in weakness. It is raised in power. It is sown an ensouled body. It is raised a Spirit-filled body. If there is an ensouled body, there is also a Spirit-filled body. Just as it has been written, "Into the first man, Adam, came a living soul," into the last Adam came the Spirit who gives life. (1 Cor. 15:40–45)

For St. Paul, one consequence of the Resurrection of Christ and the pouring out of the Holy Spirit is the glorification of humanity, and this includes not only the soul but the physical body (Rom. 8:17, 30). Saint Paul never questions but always affirms the physical, bodily resurrection. The transfiguring Presence of God Himself, however, transforms the human body from an earthen one to a celestial one as the angels possess. But this is not all. In Christ's Incarnation, death, Resurrection, and Ascension, He raised our shared human nature with Himself, such that our humanity now sits enthroned in the heavens in His person. Christ shares with us His own glory, the glory He shared with the Father before the world was created (John 17:5). We are now, like the holy angels, rightly called "sons of God," but in the resurrection, mankind has an even greater destiny: to be conformed to the likeness of Christ Himself (1 John 3:2).

CHAPTER 4

Spiritual Powers of Evil and Human Rebellion

T HE FIRST ELEVEN CHAPTERS OF Genesis have long been seen as a sort of prologue to the rest of Genesis, the Torah (or Penta- teuch), and the whole of the Hebrew Scriptures. Within these chapters, we read of the Creation of the world and of humanity, the expulsion from Paradise, the descent of man, the Flood of Noah, the descent of the nations, and the Tower of Babel. Theologically, particularly in the late antique West, Genesis 3—the expulsion from Paradise—became a site of major theological focus, often touted as the chronicle of "the Fall" of man. The debates that emerged in that context concerned what precisely this fall entailed and represented. It was interpreted as the first and pivotal act of human disobedience to the law of God and per- ceived increasingly in strictly legal terms. This singular event, as under- stood by the theological anthropology of the Christian West, brought the entire human race under God's punishment.

Likewise, much of the scruples that eventually brought about the Protestant Reformation revolved around which components of human nature remained free, that is, not touched by the deprav- ity that has supposedly infected humanity as a result of Adam's sin. Further debate questioned the degree to which Adam's descendants carried guilt from his trespass. In the last century, the focus of this inquiry has shifted to even earlier events in salvific history, namely the Creation of the world and of humankind. Once again, the evolutionary approach to the salvific past has prompted modern thinkers to reevaluate biblical narratives.

While these later foci engage legitimate and timely questions, the conclusions they led to do not reflect the way Genesis 1–11 were read by the ancients nor the way they were understood in the apostolic era, when they were read through the lens of the Person of Jesus Christ. These early chapters of Genesis recount a threefold problem in God's creation. How God seeks to manage this problem through bringing about Israel forms the content for the rest of Genesis and the Torah. Finally, the New Testament describes how Jesus Christ has definitively and finally defeated all three of these problems in order to bring about a new, resurrected, restored, and glorified creation in the new heavens and the new earth.

The Three "Falls"

BECAUSE THEOLOGICAL DISCUSSION OF GENESIS has been preoccupied for centuries with the curses handed down in chapter 3, contemporary examinations of this book have paid less attention to the other two events of Genesis 1—11 that can likewise be described as "falls" of humanity. In addition to humanity's expulsion from Paradise in chapter 3, Genesis 4—9 describes the sinful corruption of humanity at the instigation of demonic powers, culminating in the Flood in the days of Noah. Finally, Genesis 10 and 11 describe the sin of humanity at the Tower of Babel and the division of the nations. Each of these "falls" produced a problem for and within humanity that God would address throughout the remainder of the Scripture and ultimately, definitively, in Christ.

Indeed, few of the later theological constructs associated with "the Fall" are actually present within the Genesis 3 narrative. The warning given by God to Adam was that on the day he ate of the fruit of the tree of the knowledge of good and evil, he would certainly die (Gen. 2:17). The deceptive serpent enticed Eve with knowledge she was not prepared or mature enough for and was punished by being cursed to eat the dust of the earth. Here the serpent is cast down and is given the power of death. The ashes he eats are the ashes Adam shall return to (Gen. 3:14). Death makes its claim through sin (1 Cor. 15:55–56). The curse placed on humanity is one of toil and struggle in this life, ending in death (Gen. 3:19). Accordingly the story of Genesis 3 is the story of how mortality came to the human race, a narrative that plays out first through Cain's murder of Abel then through the genealogies that follow. Repeated again and again, after each individual's long life comes to an end, is the ubiquitous phrase "he died." Such a commonplace detail can easily be taken for granted when we read these passages, but its repetition underscores the point that "death reigned from Adam to Moses" (Rom. 5:14). This is the first problem: death.

Death, having penetrated the human race, then gave purchase to sin and corruption. Sin crouches at Cain's door, seeking to master him, and Cain yields to it (Gen. 4:7). In the ensuing genealogies, the line of Cain becomes increasingly corrupt, culminating in the murderous Lamech, but also manages to advance civilization and culture. By the sixth chapter of Genesis, humanity has become so corrupt that everyone's desires are always evil (Gen. 6:5). Here again, spiritual beings are involved, seducing human women (6:1–2). The text echoes the historical literature and genealogies of other cultures in the ancient Near East. Texts such as 1 Enoch bring these ideas together more explicitly, preserving the ancient tradition that spirits, like the serpent, led people to knowledge they were not prepared to bear in order to corrupt and destroy humanity, culminating in demonic sexual immorality. These are the spirits "who sinned in the days of Noah" (1 Pet. 3:18–20). This is how the second problem entered the creation: sin.

The final chapters of Genesis 1—11 are sometimes neglected but are no less important. The genealogies following the Flood describe the descent (literally and figuratively) of the seventy nations that made up the known world. While the genealogies describe their familial ancestry, the story of the Tower of Babel chronicles their fall. Here, Babylon is explained as the capital of a world empire in which a grand ziggurat was being built, a structure intended to stretch up to heaven and bring God down so that He could be coerced into serving man. In response, God did indeed descend but only to drive them away, confusing their languages and separating them. This event is further recounted in Deuteronomy 32:8, which affirms that God assigned the various nations to the sons of God. The nations of the world began to worship these angelic beings as gods and became enslaved to them. This is the third problem afflicting God's world: the dark principalities and powers.

God deals with these three events and the three problems they created in myriad ways throughout the Scriptures. With the patriarchs, the early fathers of Israel whose stories are told in the remaining chapters of Genesis, we see the beginnings of God's provision to manage these three problems. Death is managed through human fertility, through the promise that Abraham's descendants would be more numerous than the sands of the seashore. Sin is managed through the priestly role of sacrificial offering and intercession undertaken by Abraham, Isaac, Jacob, and Job. The principalities and powers and their domination of the nations of the Earth are dealt with through God's formation of a nation, Israel, for Himself, His own peculiar people, who will be separate and apart from the nations dominated by wickedness.

Genesis as a whole serves as the prologue to the remainder of the Torah, which goes on to codify these resolutions to the three problems of Genesis. The Torah regulates human reproduction and sexual morality, as well as inheritance, to ensure the continuation and flourishing of humanity on the earth. The Torah establishes the sacrificial system, centering around the Day of Atonement, to manage sin and uncleanness within God's people, to prevent their destruction. The Torah strictly forbids the idolatry of the nations and other actions and relationships that might render Israel or her people subject to the principalities and powers that govern the nations and seek Israel's destruction. Israel is to be maintained holy and set apart, to serve as a light to the nations that lay under darkness, until the time comes when Yahweh will visit His people and deal with these problems once and for all.

The entirety of the New Testament, then, is the apostolic record of that visitation that took place in the Person of Jesus Christ. Through His death and Resurrection, Christ has dealt once and for all with death, having defeated and disarmed it (see 1 Cor. 15). Christ has accomplished and made possible complete purification and cleansing from sin and corruption through His blood, applied through baptism (in the likeness of the Flood, 1 Pet. 3:20–21). Christ has once and for all defeated and disarmed the powers and principalities that once governed this world and the nations (John 12:31; 16:11; Col. 2:15).

Just as the events of the Tower of Babel are too often neglected, so also is the fact that now the nations, the Gentiles, are reconciled to God in Jesus Christ through His defeat of the powers who ruled the nations. The work accomplished by St. Paul and the other apostles in the Book of Acts is not a sort of afterthought or epilogue to St. Luke's Gospel but represents the completion of Christ's reversal of Genesis 1—11. Solving this third problem is the completion of Christ's work (Acts 1:1). Saint Paul's concern for the reconciliation of Jew and Gentile in his epistles is not an organizational issue of who was to make up the early Church. It was rather part and parcel of the gospel of Jesus Christ.

For St. Paul, the rebellions of Genesis 1—11 are resolved eschatologically in reverse order. The reconciliation of the nations to God began on the day of Pentecost and was completed in the apostolic era. Christ at His Ascension was enthroned, and all authority in heaven and on earth resides with Him. Sin is now being remedied through baptism for the forgiveness of sins, through repentance, and through the sanctification and glorification of Christ's Church. The last enemy to be defeated will be death in the resurrection, which will produce a new creation, which will be the realm of eternal life (1 Cor. 15:20–27).

Giants on the Earth

IN RECENT TIMES, THE REDISCOVERY of the original ancient context of Genesis 6:1–4 has led to a fascination with the subject of the "Nephilim," who were borne of sexual immorality involving angelic beings and human women.[1] In some quarters, this has been developed into full-fledged conspiracy theories regarding these Nephilim still existing in our world today. Those fascinated by crypto-archaeology produce doctored photos of what they hold to be gigantic human skeletons, the remains of these people. This near obsession has exploded as a reaction to a reading of Genesis and later texts, championed by St. Augustine and other later writers, that reads these texts in a demythologized way, seeing all involved parties as human.[2] The interpretation of these few verses in Genesis leading into the Flood of Noah seems to be primarily a subject of literary curiosity. Understanding this text and the traditions that lie behind it, however, is critical to understanding later narratives

---

1   This took place in a ritual context in which a king, seen as divine, would engage sexually with a temple prostitute. Within the ritual, one or the other party would be seen to be embodying a particular pagan god. This resulted in the next generation of kings and "mighty men" with two divine and one human parent.

2   The only earlier father to take this position was St. Ephrem the Syrian, whose understanding closely parallels the position taken by later Rabbinic Judaism.

within the Torah, the entire arc of the Book of Joshua and Joshua's conquest, and even the early history of monarchic Israel in the Books of Samuel/Kingdoms.

The word *Nephilim*, sometimes left untranslated in English translations of 6:4, refers to "giants." Some have sought its origin in the Hebrew word *naphal*, arguing for a translation of "fallen ones," connected to the fall of the angelic beings involved. The verb, however, would be the wrong conjugation and would be something closer to "those fallen on." Some have advanced that translation, arguing that it is referring to the fact that the descendants of these being were attacked and slain by Israel. All this is seen to be special pleading, however, in light of the fact that the Aramaic word *nephilin* means "giants." This is certainly the understanding taken by the Septuagint translators, who rendered the word *gigantes*.

Like the English "giant," this is often a reference to physical size, but it is important to note that it can also be used to describe a tyrant or what we in modern times would call a bully or a thug. Its usage is similar to the phrase "strong man," an English idiom for a dictator, though not necessarily a statement about a person's physical stature. It includes both size and demeanor. By placing this word in parallel in the text with a reference to the *gibborim*, the mighty men, the heroes, the men of great renown, Genesis 6 recasts these figures from ancient traditions in the Near East as something darker, more wicked, and more brutal.

Later Second Temple Jewish literature such as 1 Enoch and the Book of the Giants discovered among the Dead Sea Scrolls at Qumran preserve the ancient Babylonian traditions that formed the background for the genealogies and narratives of Genesis 4—6. In Babylonian tradition, there was a group of seven gods called the *apkallu*. In king lists tracing the succession of dynasties, each of the six kings who reigned before the Flood was listed with the name of the apkallu who served as his advisor. These gods were considered by the Mesopotamians to have communicated various advances of technology, art, and culture to humanity through these kings, which is what enabled them to rule. It is not a coincidence that these are the same advances described in the genealogy of Cain in Genesis 4:17–24. Genesis is actively engaging with and correcting the pagan version of the story.

The first post-Flood king likewise has an apkallu listed as his advisor, and then the following kings, such as the hero Gilgamesh, are said to be "two-thirds apkallu," or the product of divine and human coupling. The Sumerian king list, which lists Gilgamesh among the kings of Uruk, identifies him as "the son of a spirit" or a "ghost." The Book of the Giants from the Dead Sea Scrolls identifies Gilgamesh as one of the Nephilim. Genesis can, therefore, be seen to be interpreting what was, for its original hearers, the historical record of gods and kings through a very different theological lens. Similar elements are found in cultures throughout the ancient world, including, for example, the Greek story of the "gigantomachy," or war with the giants, and the stories of heroes such as Herakles or Achilles with divine and human parents.

The writers of biblical texts, as well as later Jewish and Christian interpreters, saw these so-called gods as demonic spirits (Deut. 32:16–17). The "wisdom" they taught was actually depravity and corruption. These heroes were petty tyrants, polluted by-products of demonic fornication. As Genesis 6 communicates, these "giants" were present on the earth not only in the time of the Flood of Noah but also after (Gen. 6:4). They continue to appear in the early history of Israel as recounted in the latter part of the Torah, the Book of Joshua, and Samuel in the form of multiple tribes. Just as at the time of the Flood, these demonically wicked "heroes" of the nations were under God's judgment, and it would be Israel that served as the means by which that judgment was brought to bear. Israel would expressly be sent by God to annihilate the giants, and only the giants, as a distinction was made between these and Canaanite foreigners per se.

Likely the most famous of these giants in Israel's early history is Og, the king of Bashan. The narrative of the Og's defeat is decidedly spare, representing only five verses (Num. 21:31–35), and recounted in eleven verses in Deuteronomy (3:1–11), much of this consisting of descriptions of the land rather than the battle against Og. Deuteronomy 3:11 identifies Og as a giant and describes his gigantic iron bed. It is not just the size of the bed that is suggestive of Og being one of the Nephilim, but also that this bed matches the dimensions and description of a ritual bed found in excavations of the ziggurat at Etemenanki, which was used for pagan sexual rituals. Deuteronomy, then, indicates by this that Og was the product of demonic fornication.

Like his neighboring king Sihon, Og was not given a chance to make peace with Israel. The result of war with Israel was not merely the loss of land. Rather Og and his people were completely eradicated from the land because of his origins. Despite the brevity with which the Scriptures chronicle Og's defeat, it is cited later in the Old Testament as a particularly triumphant moment in the history of Israel (see Ps. 135/134 and 136/135, sung as the Polyeleos in the Orthodox Church; and Amos 2:9). Alongside reference to Og's bed and likewise his demonic origins, we are told in Deuteronomy 3:11 that he was the last of the "Rephaim," which in this context pertained to a line of kings who were ethnic Rephaites. Bashan, the territory over which Og ruled, located in the Golan Heights, is the site of many megalithic tombs that would have been hundreds and in some cases even thousands of years old by the time the Israelites encountered Og. *Rephaim* seems to be derived from an Ugaritic root, *rph*, which refers to ancient (dead) kings in several funerary and religious texts. It signifies that Og is therefore presented not only as a giant but as the last of a race of these kings who were extinguished once Og and all his sons were slain.

Though the "Rephaim" as a line of kings met their end with Og, this is not the last time that they are seen in the Scriptures. In Isaiah 14:9, as Babylon's destruction was prophesied, it is said that as Babylon sinks down to Sheol, the realm of the dead, the Rephaim rise up to meet them. In Isaiah 26:14, the false gods Judah had sinfully worshiped are now Rephaim in the grave. In Psalm 88/87:10, the psalmist questions whether God works wonders for the dead, and whether the Rephaim rise up to praise him? This is paralleled in verse 11, placing the Rephaim in the place of destruction. In many other passages, the Rephaim are described as the denizens of Sheol or Hades (see Prov. 2:18; 9:18; 21:16; Job 26:5–6). To dwell among them would not bode well—not only would this imply sharing in their disastrous fate by proximity, but simply being among them was a threat in and of itself, whether in Hades or elsewhere.

The other major biblical clan group of giants is the *Anakim*, sometimes called the "Sons of Anak" in English translations. In Arabic traditions, Og himself is referred to as *Uj ibn-Anaq*. In Numbers 13, twelve spies were sent to scout out the land as the people of Israel drew near to Canaan. The spies returned and reported that they had seen the "Anakim" in the land, in the south, near Hebron, and that the Anakim were Nephilim (Num. 13:22, 28, 33). This news caused most of the spies, and the majority of the people, to refuse to enter the land for fear of the Anakim. This rebellion was punished by forty years of wandering in the wilderness. Deuteronomy identifies the Anakim as related to the Rephaim and with a third group of giants whom the Moabites referred to as the *Emim*, or "feared ones" (Deut. 2:10–11).

Throughout the narratives of the conquest beginning in Numbers and Deuteronomy and continuing in Joshua, it has been noted that, in some cities and locations, God commanded complete and total destruction of the residents. In others, the people in the land were merely dispossessed and their land given by God to Israel. A careful reading of the text reveals that those places where total destruction was mandated were the places in which the Anakim dwelt, while those where the Anakim have not been cited were spared total annihilation. This is made especially clear by the summary of Joshua's conquest in Joshua 11, which culminates with the statement that the mission was accomplished because Joshua had cut off all the Anakim from the land and had devoted their cities to destruction (v. 21).

We are told in verse 22 that the only Anakim who survived judgment at the hands of Israel had done so by fleeing to three Philistine cities: Gaza, Gath, and Ashdod. Goliath, the giant slain by the Prophet David, came to oppose Israel from Gath (1 Sam. 17), marking him out as one of these surviving Anakim. David, as king of Israel, completed the task of the conquest and unification of the land, conquering the city that would become Jerusalem, for example. One of these tasks that fell to David and his military lieutenants was the final eradication of the giants who had escaped to the Philistine lands. These battles are described, with details concerning the size and power of these giants, in 2 Samuel 21:15–22.

The texts of Numbers, Deuteronomy, and Joshua do not describe a holy war or genocide directed at a particular ethnicity of human beings but a war waged by the worshippers of Yahweh, the God of Israel, against His spiritual enemies, demonic powers that had come to dominate the region of Canaan and the Transjordan. It is important to remember, as we read these texts as modern people, that ancient peoples did not have a concept of secular space. People, places, and even objects were not spiritually neutral. Either people, places, and objects existed within a sphere that had been consecrated to Yahweh, the God of Israel, or they existed outside of that space, under the control of dark spiritual powers.

At Christ's Ascension and enthronement in heaven, His Kingdom was established and breaks in to expand on the earth. The Church's ministry brings people, territories, and the things of this world into the Kingdom, purifying and restoring them through the sacramental blessing of people, places, times, and objects. Outside the Church, however, ancient people made no distinction between persons of great temporal authority—such as a king or Caesar—and the spiritual power(s) who invested rulers with that authority, which Jews, Christians, and pagans alike recognized. While the pagans regarded these powers—such as the genius of the emperor—as gods to be worshipped, Jews and Christians considered them demons, in continuity with the ancient kings described in the Scriptures. It is for this reason that St. Paul can say that "our struggle is not with blood and flesh, but with the rulers, with the powers, with the cosmic powers of the darkness of this age, with the evil spirits in the heavens" (Eph. 6:12).

Spiritual Forces of Evil: The Devil

THE FIGURE OF THE DEVIL or Satan as a personal spiritual being appears at a few distinct points in the Scriptures, in which his origin and identity are described. The biblical picture of this entity, however, is very often distorted by later popular Christian literature and modern popular culture. In John Milton's famous Puritan epic *Paradise Lost,* he recast the devil as a principled revolutionary, an almost romantic rebel. There is far more of Milton than of Scripture in the average Christian of today's understanding of the devil, what his goals and purposes are, and how he came to be who he is today. The various demons and devils of Scripture are often merged together or arranged into some kind of hierarchy (or more recently a bureaucracy) in a way that is not grounded in the Scriptures or the early Fathers of the Church. The Scriptures, on the other hand, associate these creatures in their present state with chaos and destruction rather than order of any sort. The devil is the first of these rebellious spiritual powers whom we encounter in the Scriptures, though he is not initially known by the title "the devil" (which is a rough transliteration of the Greek *diabolos,* "the Slanderer").

The devil first appears in Scripture in Eden in Genesis 3. There are parallel accounts, however, regarding the fall of Satan in Isaiah 14 and Ezekiel 28 that must be taken into account in order to fully understand what transpires. In these latter two passages, the discussion of the devil's fall is fused to oracles against the kings of Babylon and Tyre respectively for two important reasons. The first is that, as stated above, ancient Israelites did not differentiate between temporal powers or rulers on the one hand and the spiritual powers that stood behind them on the other. The second reason is that what is here being prophesied is a fall from the pinnacle of the world's power down to the grave, which has no greater exemplar than the story of what became of the devil.

In most English translations of Genesis, the devil is referred to as "the serpent." This sometimes gives the impression that he was literally a talking snake or that the curse later placed on him was something on the order of a fable to explain why snakes have no legs. The Hebrew word used, however, connotes not only a snake or serpent but also the quality of being deceptive or cunning. This is also borne out in the way he is introduced (Gen. 3:1). The serpent is said to be shrewder than any of the land creatures that God created on the sixth day, which includes human beings.

This description is embroidered into Ezekiel's account of what the devil was like before his fall in Eden (Ezek. 28:12–14). Here he is described as an angelic being, clothed in precious gems and dwelling in God's Presence. In the ancient Near East, the dwelling place of the gods was conceived of as a garden or a mountain of assembly; here those images are merged to describe the dwelling place of the true God of Israel.

The devil is identified as a "guardian cherub" (28:14). While Satan is often reckoned as having been an archangel, it bears repeating that ranks of angels are not various species but rather offices held or roles performed. Angels do not mate and reproduce in order to produce

different lines or tribes of angels. Rather, they hold different offices
or jobs. These offices are distinguished in the functions they perform. The angels receive the grace of God commensurate with that
office to allow them to accomplish their purpose. Saint Dionysius the
Areopagite directly parallels the celestial hierarchy with that of the
Church. The laity, deacons, priests, and bishops are not different species of human but rather human persons granted different offices by
the grace of God.

The term *cherub* (plural *cherubim*) literally means "living creature." The "living creatures" of Ezekiel and Revelation—who each
had four faces and surrounded the throne of Yahweh in flight—are
to be understood as cherubim. These creatures were, in Babylonian
understandings, sphinx-like spiritual beings who protected the
thrones of the gods.[3] In Egyptian thought, the parallel creature was
a *seraph* (plural *seraphim*). *Seraph* was the Egyptian word for serpent.
Consequently, seraphim were serpentine beings who protected the
royal throne. The Pharaonic headdress, which resembles a cobra's
hood and features a cobra protruding from the brow of that headdress, is a representation of a seraph. Thus, the identification of the
devil as a serpent in Genesis 3 and a cherub in Ezekiel 28 are actually
commensurate with each other. In Greek translation, made after the
return from Babylon, the translators chose a word from Babylonian
mythology used to describe the primordial gods, "dragon," and used
it to replace the Egyptian-influenced "serpent" imagery. The devil as
a dragon is an identification then picked up by St. John in the Book
of Revelation.

---

3   It is worth noting that both angelic beings as described by the Scriptures and
    pagan gods as depicted by their worshippers are theriomorph, i.e., they pres-
    ent a mixture of human and animal forms. This included, originally, the gods
    of the Greeks, the residue of which produces, for example, Homer's reference
    to "cow-eyed Hera."

What then made the devil wicked? In Isaiah 14:13–14, which chronicles his sin in the context of the divine council, the devil before his fall is compared to the morning star (the planet Venus, 14:12), drawing on the common identification of angelic beings with stars. It is from the Latin translation of this verse that the name "Lucifer" is derived. The devil wanted to ascend above all the other angelic beings in the council and supplant God Most High. In Genesis 3, we see the dragon convincing the first humans to pursue knowledge that was at that point forbidden them by God for their own protection.

Second Temple literature and the early Fathers saw these as descriptions of the same event and reconciled them together. Man, though created later and with the land animals, was created for a glorious destiny in Christ (Ps. 8:4–8). Satan's pride took on the character of envy, and he sought to supplant God in the lives of His creations by becoming the one who teaches them and brings them knowledge. He sought to become their god. Because he was unable to create, he sought to destroy them. This will become a pattern that will be seen in the actions of all the demonic powers. It is not possible for any created being literally to overthrow the Triune God's reign over His own creation. The most these evil spiritual beings can hope to accomplish is to usurp God's role among other creatures, thereby sowing chaos and destruction.

As already mentioned, the curse placed on the devil in Genesis 3:14–15 is not the story of how snakes lost their legs. The reference to the land animals in verse 14 is parallel to the introduction of the dragon in verse 1. He had been superior in his cleverness to all God's creatures on the earth and had sought in that pride to elevate himself even higher; instead he is driven down below them. He does not lie just on the ground as humans did but rather beneath the earth and in the underworld. Ancient people were well aware that snakes do not literally eat dust (v. 15). Rather, they swallow things whole. The "dust" here is a reference to the dust from which man was made and the dust to which he would return (v. 19). The devil becomes a ruler but a ruler of the dead.

The gravity of this fall is further described in the parallel passages in the prophets. Isaiah 14:11 says, "Your pomp is brought down to Sheol with the sound of your harps. Maggots are spread out as a bed under you, and worms cover you over." Verses 13–15 say:

> You said in your heart, "I will go up to the heavens above the stars of God. I will place my throne on high. I will sit on the Mountain of the Council in the far reaches of the north. I will go up above the peaks of the clouds. I will make myself like the Most High." But you are taken down to Sheol, to the far reaches of the abyss.

Sheol literally means "the grave" but was the word across early West Semitic languages for the underworld, the realm of the dead. In Ezekiel 28:16–18 his fall is described as being consumed by fire that came out from God's holiness, leaving him only a heap of ashes.

The devil receives a kingdom of ashes and dust in Genesis 3, while human persons become mortal, subject to corruption and death. Through humanity, the entire creation becomes subjected to death and futility, under which they still labor (Rom. 8:19–21). The ultimate solution to this, for the creation and for humanity, will be found in the resurrection at Christ's glorious appearing, as St. Paul sees (Rom. 8:22–25). This has already begun, however, in the Resurrection of Jesus Christ, through which the devil has been deprived of his kingdom. In St. Mark's Gospel, Christ speaks of the end of the devil's kingdom, pointing out that for the strong man's goods to be taken away, he must first be bound (Mark 3:23–27). Hebrews 2:14 states that Christ partook of human flesh and blood so that, "through death, He might destroy the one who has the power of death, that being the devil."

It is for this reason that the celebration of Pascha has always revolved around the harrowing of Hades, or Sheol. Through death and Resurrection, Christ has bound Satan and left his kingdom empty and void. This conception undergirds the many liturgical proclamations issued during Pascha that not a single one of the dead remains in Sheol, that Christ has raised up all those who have fallen asleep, and that He has emptied the tombs. These are not declarations of universal salvation but rather of the purging of the kingdom of death that had once been presided over by the devil. The understanding of the devil as the ruler of death's dominion is likewise implied in countless other Orthodox Christian hymns, from the Troparia for Sundays to the statement in the Trisagion for the Departed that proclaims Christ has "trampled down death and made powerless the devil." Christ will return to judge the dead as well as the living; they are now under His dominion, as He has reclaimed the narrow authority the devil had possessed and left him with nothing. The devil will not, in the age to come, rule over the wicked, who are condemned to the lake of fire, but will suffer the same condemnation there as all the other wicked, both angelic and human.

That the devil has *already* been defeated and his kingdom laid waste—in the past tense for the New Testament authors—exposes him as little more than a raging beast, one with decidedly more bark than bite. Because he has been starved of even the dead to consume, he "prowls about like a roaring lion, seeking someone to devour" (1 Pet. 5:8). His defeat has led to his great wrath on the earth as he seeks to destroy humanity because he knows that he has only a short time left before his final judgment and condemnation (Rev. 12:12). Despite his vitriol, however, the devil lacks any real power or authority and is therefore left only to scheme, laying traps and snares for human persons to fall into, in the hopes that they may come to share in his eventual condemnation (2 Cor. 2:11; Eph. 4:27; 6:11; 1 Tim. 3:6–7; 5:15; 2 Tim. 2:26). The time is quickly coming when he will be finally, and definitively, crushed beneath the feet of the saints (Gen. 3:15; Rom. 16:20).

Spiritual Forces of Evil: The Angels Who Left Their Former Estate

THE GIANTS OF THE OLD Testament, who owe their existence to demonic sexual immorality, are described as having angelic "parents." These angelic beings play an important role in the unfolding of the Old Testament and in New Testament theology. They were the spiritual participants in the second of the three events of spiritual and human rebellion described in the early chapters of Genesis, the descent of humanity into sin and corruption. It was commonplace in the Fathers and other early Christian writers to speak about the sinful state of humanity remedied by Christ in terms of one of the three events or "falls" enumerated at the outset of this chapter—death, sin, and the domination of the world by fallen principalities and powers.

Typically one event took precedence over the others, depending on who was writing, while the other two were subordinated. Saint Irenaeus sees the key event as the sinful corruption of humanity begun by these angelic beings.

> And for a very long time, wickedness extended and spread and reached and laid hold upon the whole race of mankind, until only a very small seed of righteousness remained among them. Illicit unions took place on the earth, when angels were united with the daughters of the race of humanity; and they bore to them sons who for their exceeding greatness were called giants. And the angels brought as presents to their wives' teachings of wickedness. They brought them the knowledge of roots and herbs, dyeing in colors and cosmetics, the discovery of rare substances, love potions, aversions, amours, concupiscence, constraints of love, spells of bewitchment, and all sorcery and idolatry, which are hateful to God. Through the entry of these things into the world evil extended and spread, while righteousness was diminished and enfeebled. (*On the Apostolic Preaching*, 18)

Eusebius of Caesarea, on the other hand, considers the Babel event and the consignment of the nations to angelic beings, who came to be worshipped as gods, to be the critical "fall."

> Then surely the All-Good, the King of kings, the Supreme, God Almighty, so that the men on earth might not be like brute beasts without rulers and guardians, set over them the holy angels to be their leaders and governors like herdsmen and shepherds. He set over them all, and made the head of all His Only-begotten and Firstborn Word. He gave Him for His own inheritance the angels and archangels and the divine powers and the immaterial and transcendent spirits. Even also, from those things on earth the souls among men beloved by God, called by the names of the Hebrews, Jacob and Israel. . . . But the angel-guardians and shepherds of the other nations allowed them, because they were not able with their mind to see the invisible or to ascend so high because of their own weakness, to worship things seen in the heavens, the sun and moon and stars. For these, indeed, being the most wonderful of the things of the material world, invited upward the eyes of those who see. . . . And this again the great Moses mystically says. For in exhorting the inheritance of the Lord to grasp with a clear mind and pure soul that which is only known to the mind and is immaterial, he prohibits all terror of the things seen in heaven, adding that "the Lord your God has divided them for all the nations." And it is worth realizing why he says that they were divided. Because unseen by us, they that bear the earthy and demonic nature are everywhere wanderers, flying through the air around the earth unknown and unacknowledged by men. The good spirits and powers and, indeed, the divine angels themselves are ever at odds with the bad. (*Demonstration of the Gospel*, 4.6–8)

Finally, St. Augustine saw the most important of the "falls" as the curse of Genesis 3. His understanding, coupled with his rejection of

103

what was then the traditional understanding of the identity of the Nephilim, became paradigmatic for Western theology from the late antique period until the present day. Saint Augustine rejected the idea of an angelic rebellion described in Genesis 4–6 and saw the expulsion from Paradise in Genesis 3 as the source of both sin and death. In Scripture and the Fathers, however, mortality and sinful corruption are seen to have different, albeit related, origins. Sinful corruption entered humanity, who were already weakened and mortal by having been cut off from the source of life, through the efforts of these angelic beings, resulting in their own fall and imprisonment.

The story that unfolds from Genesis 4—6 is a deliberate parallel to a Mesopotamian story, and both are conveyed through genealogical chronicles. The Mesopotamian story in question, exemplified in the Sumerian kings list, describes the greatness of Babylonian civilization and its divine origins. As mentioned above, each of the kings before the Great Flood is paired with a divine being called an apkallu, which the Mesopotamians worshipped as gods. These beings are also sometimes referred to as the "seven sages" and were believed to serve at the behest of the high god and assist in his governance and maintenance of the universe. They were said to have taught the kings with whom they are paired various wisdom regarding metallurgy, astrology, and other forms of ancient wisdom. These secrets made them powerful and great.

After the Flood, the kings, described as being part man and part apkallu, are the reason for Babylon's greatness. It has preserved this divine knowledge from before the Flood, centered around the person of its king. In later Mesopotamian material, these apkallu were portrayed as having given these secrets over to human beings without permission. For this misdeed, they were imprisoned by the high god in the depths of the river, the abyss. In the third century BC, a certain Berossus, who was a priest of Bel (Baal) serving in the court of the Seleucid king in Syria, presented the basic mythology of his religion in Greek. In addition to recounting the information above and including a story parallel to that of the Tower of Babel, he parallels these stories to the Greek story of the defeat of the Titans and their imprisonment by Zeus in Tartarus.[4]

Genesis 4—6 tells nearly the same story, but instead of portraying the greatness of the world's kingdoms that culminated in the city of Babylon, it narrates the corruption, sin, and wickedness of humanity under the influence of rebellious angelic powers. It begins with Cain becoming a murderer under the influence of the power of sin, which is portrayed as a creature that masters him (4:7). The line of Cain's descendants brings about innovations in culture and technology but culminates in the kingly figure of Lamech, who hymns his own greatness and superiority to God in a song sung to his two wives (4:23–24).

The genealogy of Seth, the third son of Adam and Eve, in Genesis 5, contains none of the great achievements of his brother Cain, merely reiterating over and over again that—despite how long his descendants' lives may have been—each one of them (other than Enoch) died through the mortality inherited from Adam. Likewise, the giants, the great men of renown, the great kings and heroes of Mesopotamian religion, are here cast not as the preservers of ancient wisdom but as the illegitimate and unclean offspring of rebellious angelic beings and their interactions with humans (6:1–4). By the end of the story, God has looked on the world and seen that mankind had become so corrupt that every thought of his heart was always evil all the time (6:5). He, therefore, determined to save His creation through Noah by using the waters of the Flood to cleanse the taint of humanity's sin from the earth (5:29).

---

4   There are also, it should be noted, clear connections between the story of the seven sages and that of Prometheus in Greek religious traditions.

These chapters of Genesis interact polemically with Mesopotamian religious belief, but they do not themselves preserve the traditions on which Genesis comments. These traditions were, however, preserved in a multitude of Second Temple texts, most famously in 1 Enoch, but also in a multitude of other texts such as the Book of the Giants from among the Dead Sea Scrolls. These connect the two opposing traditions in a way that makes the original context and interpretation plain. Cain's descendants produce these cultural and technological innovations because they are receiving these secrets from angelic beings who are giving them over not in order to assist mankind but in order to aggrandize themselves and be worshipped by humanity. Ultimately, they seek to destroy humanity by giving over secrets for which humans are not ready. Their sin is therefore directly parallel to the sin of the dragon in Genesis 3. They follow after his example. And so it is that God punishes these angelic beings by imprisoning them in the abyss, in the underworld beneath the earth until the Last Day, when they will find their judgment in the lake of fire (see 1 Enoch 21:6–7).

This understanding of the identity of these beings is referenced repeatedly in the text of the New Testament. Second Peter 2:4 reads, "For God did not pardon angels when they sinned but rather threw them into Tartarus and committed them to chains of gloomy darkness to be kept until the judgment." Here St. Peter makes plain the connection between these wicked angels and the Titans of Greco-Roman religion through reference to Tartarus in addition to paralleling the language of 1 Enoch and other related literature. In his list of examples, St. Peter places this example immediately before the Flood. Saint Jude, likewise, refers to the angels who did not remain in their original estate and are now kept in eternal chains beneath gloomy darkness until the Day of Judgment (v. 6). Saint Jude parallels this with those of Sodom who chased after "strange flesh," seeking to fornicate with the two angels sent to Lot's home (v. 7). Revelation 9 presents part of the final judgment as the abyss is opened, with smoke rising from it as from a furnace, and demonic beings emerge therefrom (9:1–3). They are ultimately all thrown into the lake of fire (Rev. 20:10), which Christ Himself says was prepared for "the devil and his angels" (Matt. 25:41).

It is these rebellious angels who are responsible for the spread of sin and corruption in the world, and this is brought out in Second Temple literature through the identification of their leader. Texts such as 1 Enoch and the Apocalypse of Abraham identify the leader of these rebellious angels as Azazel. Azazel functions as a devil figure in this literature and is sometimes blamed for the whole of the evil of these fallen and imprisoned angels. First Enoch 9:6 states that Azazel had taken the secrets reserved in heaven and taught them to men and women who were striving to learn them. As a result, 1 Enoch 10:8 says, "The whole earth has been corrupted through the works taught by Azazel; to him credit all sin" (compare 1 John 3:8; 5:19).

The Orthodox Church is clear that salvation embraces the whole human person in transformation into the likeness of God. Through theosis, human persons participate in God's work in creation and are transformed by Him. This is paralleled in a negative way by a proper understanding of sinfulness. Saint Dionysius the Areopagite makes it clear that the reason angels differ from one another in glory (1 Cor. 15:40–41) is that, because of their different offices, they participate to different degrees in the grace of God. The loss of this participation and the subsequent diminution and corruption of their being is what it means for an angelic being to fall. The same is true for human persons. To be corrupted by sin means that the body and soul of a human person lose their connection with the life of God, and they become subhuman and unliving. Condemnation on the Last Day consists in the permanence of this state. In our current age, salvation takes the form of repentance, and repentance is purification, healing, and transformation in being conformed to the likeness of Christ (Rom. 8:29).

Spiritual Forces of Evil: Demons

THE DEVIL WAS CAST DOWN into Sheol or Hades to devour and rule over the dead. The angels who sinned were confined in chains in the abyss for their crimes until the end of the world. Other angelic beings, to whom the nations were assigned at the Tower of Babel, later became corrupt and sought the worship of the nations they were to govern. These last beings did not fall like the others and remain in the heavenly places according to St. Paul (Eph. 6:12), though they are judged at the Resurrection of Christ (Ps. 82/81) and their reign is undone as the gospel proceeds to all the nations (1 Cor. 2:6). All authority in heaven and on earth is now given to Christ following His victory, and so all the nations are called to become His disciples (Matt. 28:18–20). Saint Gregory the Dialogist says that this is why the angels of God, His divine council, are said to stand on His right and His left.[5] Those on the right are the elect angels (1 Tim. 5:21), and those on the left are the wicked angelic beings who will receive their full judgment on the Last Day by Christ through the saints (1 Cor. 6:3).

None of these wicked angelic figures, except for the devil himself, are described as roaming the earth. Further, as was common ancient belief, confirmed by St. Paul (1 Cor. 15:40–41), angelic beings have bodies, albeit bodies of an entirely different sort than the earthly, terrestrial bodies of humans. In early Jewish thinking, anything created has, or at least had, a body. At a few points in the Old Testament, however, we are confronted by "unclean spirits," which are bodiless and come to dwell in the bodies of others. Likewise, the Gospels and the Acts of the Apostles are replete with references to demons who take possession of the bodies of humans, animals, and idols. Despite the major part that demonic possession and exorcism play in the

---

5   *Moralia*, 1.2.35.

ministry of Christ and His apostles, the origin of these demons and the phenomenon of possession are never in the New Testament narrated or described. The phenomenon is merely presumed by the New Testament writers as something about which readers would have common knowledge. What, then, was the understanding of these demons in the Greco-Roman pagan and the Jewish worlds of the first century AD?

The word from which "demon" is transliterated into English, *daimonion*, was used flexibly in classical Greek sources. It generally referred to divine beings of a lower tier or, more recently, the object of worship. The word is therefore frequently used of figures whom we would refer to as Greek and Roman gods, including occasionally Zeus. The word was also used to refer to the spirits of deceased ancestors, particularly notable ancestors such as heroes and kings. The connective tissue of these usages comes on two sides.

First, both these divinities and the ancestral spirits were objects of worship in the Greek and Roman worlds. This crossover can also be observed in Canaanite religion, for example, in the witch of Endor's identification of the spirit of Samuel as a "god" (1 Sam. 28:13). Second, within certain classical authors was still retained the knowledge that the spirits now worshipped as gods had once been ancient figures of renown. Zeus is still occasionally identified with an ancient king on the island of Crete: Asterion, the father of Minos. Though "demon" has obviously become a pejorative term for a specifically evil spirit in modern usage, in ancient usage outside of Jewish and Christian sources, it carries no such association.

Plato describes the origin of demons in the *Cratylus*:

> It is principally because demons are wise and knowing, I think, that
> Hesiod says they are named "demons." In our older Attic dialect, we
> actually find the word *daemones*. So, Hesiod and many other poets
> speak well when they say that when a great man dies, he has a great

destiny and a great honor and becomes a "demon," which is a name given to him because it accords with wisdom. And I myself assert, indeed, that every great man, whether alive or dead, is demonic and is correctly called a "demon." (397c–398c)

Because these spirits were, at least currently, without bodies, in order to interact they needed to be provided with bodies. This took place in two primary ways. The first was through the crafting of images that the spirit could possess in order to receive worship and offerings. It is for this reason that an image of a god or goddess was the centerpiece of Greek and Roman temples. The spirit was believed to inhabit the image as a new body. For this reason, it is common in Jewish literature in the Greek language from this period to refer to the idol itself as daimonion.

The second mode of interaction with these spirits was through their possession of a human body. In the Greek and Roman worlds, the most prominent form of this was the institution of oracles, human priests or priestesses who would be possessed by a daimonion who would speak wisdom through them. The most prominent of these was the famed oracle of Delphi, where the Pythia was believed to be possessed by Apollo. This was seen as a positive and beneficial phenomenon in the Roman world despite the counter-understanding by Jewish and Christian communities (see Acts 16:16–24).

Another mode of demonic possession understood in the Greco-Roman world was more subtle. It was believed that great men, rulers and those of great accomplishment in various cultural fields, were possessed by these divine spirits who inspired and animated them. The Latin term for one of these beings is *genius*, and it is ultimately from this that our modern usage of that term is derived. So, when early Christians were commanded to participate in the worship of the Roman emperor, it was actually to the genius of the emperor that they were commanded to offer incense or sacrifice. Likely the most famous ancient figure who actively claimed to be demon possessed as part of his defense of himself, however, is Socrates. In Plato's *Republic*, Socrates states, "Finally, my own case is hardly worth mentioning, my demonic sign, because it has happened to no one before me, or to only a very few" (496c). In the *Apology*, he describes his experience further: "I have a divine or spiritual sign which Meletus has ridiculed in his deposition. This began when I was a child. It is a voice, and whenever it speaks it turns me away from something I am about to do, but it never encourages me to do anything" (31d).

This phenomenon was also known within the ancient Jewish world but was interpreted very differently. Ancient Judaism understood the great heroes and kings of the surrounding pagan nations as being not heroes but giants, tyrants, thugs, and bullies. They understood the proposed mixture of human and divine parentage of these heroes as being their origin in demonic fornication for which the offending spirits were punished and the progeny of which were eradicated by God. It was therefore natural for their religious outlook to similarly interpret the phenomenon of demons, that they were the disembodied spirits of dead giants. This understanding is reflected in a variety of Second Temple sources, such as 1 Enoch 15:8–9.

First Enoch and many of the Dead Sea Scrolls refer to these spirits as being of illegitimate birth, referring back to their origin. This is in harmony with the identification of these beings as "unclean spirits," unclean by their mixture. The Torah distinguishes clearly between evil and unclean as separate categories, and so to call something unclean is not to indicate that it is evil per se, though these spirits are also called "evil spirits" in other places. Uncleanness is commonly associated with being of a mixed origin, and the Torah contains countless examples, from sewing a garment from two different kinds of cloth to sowing multiple types of seed in the same field (Lev. 19:19; 22:9–11).

This understanding created a certain logical difficulty, however, in that the spirits of the slain giants were seen to have been punished along with their parents. The spirits of the Rephaim, the giant line that included Og of Bashan, for example, are inhabitants of Sheol, according to the Scriptures (Is. 14:9; 26:14; Ps. 88/87:10; Prov. 2:18; 9:18; 21:16; Job 26:5–6). How then are there still these demonic spirits present in the world? The Book of Jubilees is a Jewish text that enjoyed immense popularity in the first century after Christ and retells the stories of Genesis, including many Jewish traditions surrounding the text. It answers this question through the figure of Mastema, a leader among the giants, who at the time of their impending destruction bargained with God to allow himself and one-tenth of the demonic spirits to remain in the world in order to test humanity and afflict those in whom wickedness is found (10:8). God consents to allow this because He intends to use the evil spirits, who had been a part of the corruption of humanity, to bring human persons to repentance. This is how the evil spirit who came "from God" to afflict Saul is understood (1 Sam. 16:14–16, 23; 18:10; 19:9). This understanding of demonic activity also lies behind St. Paul's references to handing someone over to Satan through excommunication for the purpose of bringing repentance (1 Cor. 5:5; 1 Tim. 1:20).

The bargain struck by Mastema with God, however, has an expiration date when, at the Last Judgment, these spirits will be punished for eternity in the abyss. This idea underlies many of the confrontations that take place in the Gospels between Christ and various demonic entities. In Mark 1:23–26, the demon's recognition of who Jesus Christ is leads to the immediate question as to whether Christ has come to destroy the demons (i.e., they associate the arrival of Christ with the time of the end). In Christ's confrontation with the Gerasene demoniac, St. Matthew records the demons asking if He had come to torment them "before the time" (Matt. 8:29). Saint Mark records that the demons pleaded with Christ not to send them out of the land (Mark 5:10). Saint Luke makes clear that the alternative to them continuing to dwell in the land is confinement in the abyss

(Luke 8:31). The abyss was seen to be in the depths of the sea, and although the demons were cast into the swine, this is where they met their end (Matt. 8:32; Mark 5:13; Luke 8:33). Because the activity of these demonic spirits was seen as being strictly limited by God Himself, the fact that Christ is able to command and punish them is prominent in the Gospels precisely as evidence of His identity as Yahweh, the God of Israel.

Spiritual Forces of Evil: The Satan

IN A CONFUSION OF TERMS that has a long history, the devil and Satan are generally considered to be the same demonic being. Yet there are two different strands of tradition, one regarding the devil, one regarding Satan. These two streams often merge but also sometimes diverge in the Scriptures, Second Temple writings, and early Christian tradition. The figure of the devil and his fall from a place in God's divine council has already been discussed. Having served as a cherub or seraph, a guardian of God's throne, he sought to supplant God in the lives of newly created human beings out of envy, resulting in his being cast down to Sheol to reign over the dead in a kingdom of dust and ashes in Genesis 3.

This figure—though clearly seen in the understanding of death and Christ's victory over it in the New Testament and in the liturgical tradition of the Orthodox Church—lacks many of the common features and characteristics of Satan. He was not, per se, an archangel, certainly not one of the seven. And St. Michael was not directly involved in his fall. Job presents a figure, "the Satan," who remains a member of the divine council long after Genesis 3. There are clear references in the New Testament to the fall of Satan that seem not to refer to events in Eden. These discontinuities in the presentations of the devil and Satan are often papered over. Merely smudging the contradictions obscures the details of both traditions in favor of making them fit together more neatly. Examining the two separately allows these details to emerge.

The reason for these inconsistencies is that at the earliest layer of Jewish tradition, these elements referred to different demonic beings, two different devil figures. These are the devil, or dragon, and the Satan. While these figures are distinguished in Second Temple sources and many of the early Fathers, as time passed they began to be merged together in certain later Fathers. By the end of the sixth and the beginning of the seventh centuries, Fathers such as St. Andrew of Caesarea were openly discussing the conflicting evidence they had received from previous Fathers regarding whether these beings are two or one.[6] They commented on, for example, the fact that there seem to be two different falls of Satan described in Scripture. The Quran, written after this period, merges these two figures together by name self-consciously.

This second figure is the Archangel Samael. His name, in Hebrew, means "the venom of God." Samael regularly appears in lists of the seven original archangels up to and including that of St. Gregory the Dialogist at the end of the sixth century. In Jewish tradition, Samael plays several roles, none of them very positive. He is primarily identified as the angel of death. This is not in the sense in which the dragon, when cast down to Sheol, was made lord of the dead. Rather, Samael is the angel whom God sent to take lives and claim souls. Though not directly mentioned in the text of Exodus, traditionally he was responsible for the slaying of the firstborn at the Passover. He was likewise traditionally understood to be the angelic being seen in 2 Samuel / 2 Kingdoms 24:15 and in the parallel passage 1 Chronicles 21:15, killing the people of Jerusalem. He is also identified as the angel in 2 Kings / 4 Kingdoms 19:35 who in one night killed 185,000 members of the Assyrian army during their siege of Jerusalem.

---

6   *Commentary on the Apocalypse*, 12.34.

As mentioned, Samael's duties included not only bringing about physical death in many cases, but also the claiming of souls and their delivery to Sheol, the underworld. God's preservation of the souls of the righteous from Sheol, therefore, took the form of preserving that soul from the hands of Samael. Here the role of Samael as the adversary (in Hebrew, *Satan*) begins to be seen. Jude 1:9 refers to a contest between St. Michael and Satan over the body of Moses. Saint Jude's reference here seems clearly grounded in the traditions of the Assumption of Moses, which describes the body of Moses being taken into heaven. In this text, it is precisely Samael who is playing this role, of seeking to claim the life of Moses, while God sends St. Michael to claim his soul and body so that he can partake of the resurrection. This tradition is also referenced more subtly at the Transfiguration of Christ when Moses appeared resurrected alongside the Prophet Elijah, who had not ever physically died, with no distinction made regarding the embodied state of the two.

In the Book of Job, we are presented with the figure of "the Satan." The definite article is here important because the Hebrew language does not use the definite article before proper names. In the Greek language, the article during the biblical period was still not a definite article per se, but rather a pronoun, and so is found frequently before proper names. This, however, was not the case in Hebrew or Aramaic. This figure being identified as "the Adversary" therefore describes an office or role played by this angelic being, rather than giving his name. When he first appears in Job 1:6–8 he comes along with the rest of the divine council of Yahweh, the God of Israel, to present himself, and this begins the dialogue between himself and God. When God speaks of the faithfulness and righteousness of Job, it is the Satan who makes accusations against him and desires to test him (Job 1:9–11). This angelic being is then allowed to kill all of Job's children, servants, and livestock (Job 1:13–19). In the second chapter, the Satan is allowed to afflict Job further but not to kill him.

Though we are never told this being's name, it fits the profile within Jewish tradition of Samael.

Saint Michael is presented in Scripture as the angelic being to whom the care and protection of God's people Israel were assigned (Dan. 10:20–21; 12:1).[7] This was seen to have developed from St. Michael's role as the guardian angel of Israel himself, the Patriarch Jacob. As their protector, it fell to St. Michael to defend the souls of the righteous among God's people from Samael. Likely because of this adversarial relationship between the two archangels, some Jewish traditions identify Samael as the guardian angel of Esau, Jacob's brother and early rival, and then his descendants in the nation of Edom. This creates a dynamic within Jewish literature of Samael, the Satan, accusing those of the nation of Israel while St. Michael defends them before the throne of God. It is also why, in both ancient and later Rabbinic Jewish literature, the figure of Satan is seen as a morally ambivalent one. He is both an angelic member of God's divine council and the one who accuses the brethren and carries out other dark tasks.

The New Testament, however, describes the fall of this being as well, understanding it as impelled by the Incarnation of Christ, in particular His death on the Cross. In Luke 10:18, Christ says that through the ministry of His disciples, He has seen the Satan fall from heaven like lightning. This brief phrase is further developed in the teaching of St. John's Gospel, in which the Satan is referred to as "the prince of this world" in comparison to Daniel's identification of St. Michael as "your prince." In John 14:30, Christ states that this archangel prince is coming for Him but has no hold over him, meaning that he can make no accusation against Christ. In John 12:31 and 16:11, Christ says that at the Cross, this prince will be

---

7   *The Testament of Dan* 6:1–2, as preserved at Mount Athos, reveals that by the second century BC, St. Michael carried out this role in part by serving as an intercessor in prayer for the people.

judged. Revelation 12:7–12 places this event after the birth of Christ (12:5). This is distinguished by, for example, St. Andrew of Caesarea in his commentary on this passage as a second fall: as he says, "The fathers thought, after the Creation of the physical world, the devil was thrown down because of his arrogance and envy" (12.34).

Saint Michael is described as the angel of this fall, finally defeating his adversary (Rev. 12:7). Though it is not often brought out in modern English translations, 12:9 reads, "And that great dragon was cast down, that ancient serpent, that one who is called the devil. And the Satan, the deceiver of the whole world, was thrown down to the earth. And his angels were thrown down." A voice from heaven describes the Satan here as "the accuser of our brethren . . . who accuses them day and night before our God" (12:10). He has finally been defeated by two things. First, by the blood of the Lamb who was slain, because, that blood having cleansed the brethren, the Satan can no longer make any accusation against them. Second, because they have gone to their death without rejecting Christ and so like Job have passed all his tests, he is unable to touch them (12:11). There is, therefore, no role left for him in the heavenly places; and after his defeat through the life of Christ, his fall, and his knowledge that he will at the judgment be confined to Gehenna, he is no longer morally ambiguous but has become an open blasphemer of God. Saint Justin Martyr testifies to this effect, according to St. Irenaeus (*Adv. Haer.*, 5.26.2) and Eusebius (Hist. 4.18.9).

There are many separate traditions regarding the devil and demonic powers underlying the descriptions of these evil spiritual beings in the Scriptures. Within the Fathers, some clearly differentiate these figures while, in others, elements of the various figures are seemingly blended together. Already by the time of St. Andrew of Caesarea, he could read the preceding Fathers, including works no longer available to us, and see that some saw the devil and the Satan as separate figures while others seemed to see them as one. Later in

Church history, even elements of Azazel, Mastema, and other traditions that have been discussed are blended into this single figure. The exact details, while they may be the subject of morbid curiosity, are less important than an awareness by Christians of the types of demonic activity, temptation, accusation, and opposition experienced in the spiritual life in Christ.

Understanding these traditions also reaffirms that every aspect of salvation presented in the Scriptures is grounded in Christ's defeat of these powers. Human persons are saved from the rebellion into which they've been led by these powers through the defeat of those powers, the purification and healing of the person, and their union with God in Christ. Through this union, human persons come to displace and replace these fallen powers as heavenly sons of God who participate in the reign of the Lord Jesus Christ over the whole of creation.

CHAPTER 5

The Saints in Glory

IN THE OLD TESTAMENT, BEFORE the Incarnation of Christ, only certain human beings had limited direct encounters with God and the unseen world of angels and demons. Humanity's repeated falls into sinful rebellion separated them from God and His divine council while also subjecting them to the power of demons through sin. Nevertheless, the prophets on select occasions had visions and other experiences that allowed them to stand before God and be privy to the deliberations of angelic beings. A few individuals, Enoch, Moses, and Elijah, either when they died or beforehand, were even taken up to permanently join the divine council.

In the Person of Jesus Christ, our humanity was joined forever to God, and everything changed. What previously only a select few had experienced became a possibility offered to everyone. The work of Christ meant not merely the defeat and doom of the demons but also the salvation of humankind. Along with redeeming humanity from the depths of sin, He also exalted them to the heights of heaven. In glory, the saints alongside the angels are granted the gift of participating in Christ's rule over creation for all eternity. While their reign with Christ will reach its fullness in the life of the age to come, it is already a reality in this present age.

The removal of the barrier of sin and wickedness also means that death does not present an obstacle to human connections in Christ. The life of the saints in the heavenly places is a life of intercession in prayer and participation in the works of God in the world. While the saints are now unseen, they are no less present than Christ Himself. Wherever He is, the angels and saints are there with Him. Their ministry not only is directed toward God but is directed toward God on behalf of His creation, most of all humans working out their own salvation just as the saints who preceded them.

Humans in the Divine Council

THERE ARE SEVERAL WAYS HUMAN persons in the Old Testament encountered and interacted with God's divine council. These modes of interaction laid the groundwork for a transformed relationship in the New Covenant. Simply put, every encounter with God the Father in the Old Testament was mediated either through God the Son, as described in chapter 1, or by angelic beings, as will be discussed here.

Although these encounters are far from common, the usual mode of interaction between a human person and the divine council in the Old Testament is for a human person to be brought into a gathering of the council. The vision in which Isaiah received his prophetic calling is recorded in Isaiah 6. Isaiah saw the Lord enthroned, "high and lifted up." Closest to the throne are the seraphim, whom he beheld worshipping Yahweh perpetually. When Yahweh spoke, however, it was not to command Isaiah. Rather it was to pose a deliberative question to the council gathering in which Isaiah was now present. The question—"Whom shall I send, and who will go for us?"—is not dissimilar to the scene in 1 Kings / 3 Kingdoms 22:19–20, where the question is posed to the council as to who will persuade Ahab. In that case, a spirit volunteered to go; in this case, Isaiah volunteered to bring the message of judgment to Israel.

Though it is not detailed as such in the Torah, Moses' meeting with God on Mount Sinai is described by later Judaism, including in the New Testament, as his entering into such a meeting. The New Testament repeatedly says that the Torah was given by, or through, angels. Saint Stephen referred to the Judean authorities as those who had "received the law delivered by angels" and not kept it (Acts 7:53). Saint Paul, in Galatians, describing the addition of the Torah to the Old Covenant, noted that it was "delivered by angels in the hand of a mediator" (Gal. 3:19). Saint Paul's subsequent comment in verse 20 makes clear that this mediator is Christ.[1] Hebrews describes the seriousness of the commandments of the Torah by pointing out that "the message declared by angels proved to be reliable, and every transgression or disobedience received a just retribution" (2:2). Beyond the New Testament, this was the common understanding of the giving of the Torah in Second Temple Judaism, as seen for example in Josephus: "We have learned the noblest of our doctrines and the holiest of laws from the angels sent by God" (*Antiquities* 15.136).

Further, the tabernacle was constructed according to the pattern of the place of meeting that Moses beheld on the mountain (Heb. 8:5). As seen in Isaiah's vision, the constant focus of the divine council is on giving glory, honor, and worship to the One who sits on the throne. The place of worship and the shape of worship are then earthly icons of the divine assembly into which human persons enter in worship. The tabernacle's curtains and veils were adorned with images of angelic beings in worship, culminating in the cherubim atop the ark of the covenant in the most holy place. Likewise, in the

---

1   For St. Irenaeus, this is the basis for the unity of the Old and New Covenants, that they have the same mediator, namely Christ. "And Jeremiah says: 'Behold, I will make a new covenant, not as I made with your fathers in Mount Horeb.' But one and the same householder produced both covenants, the Word of God, our Lord Jesus Christ, who spoke with both Abraham and Moses, and who has restored us anew to liberty, and has multiplied that grace which is from Himself" (*Adv. Haeresies*, 4.9.1).

worship itself, as maintained in the Orthodox Divine Liturgy, there is a conscious awareness and invocation of the fact that worship is a participation in the continual and eternal worship enacted by the divine council in heaven. A handful of cases in the Old Testament involve people who became members of the divine council either without experiencing physical death or shortly thereafter as their bodies were taken up. The first of these was Enoch, listed seventh from Adam in the genealogies of Genesis 5:21. What exactly happened is not entirely clear in Genesis, which states only that "Enoch walked with God, and he was not, for God took him" (v. 24). Sirach says little more, only that "Enoch pleased the Lord and was taken up into heaven. He became an inspiration for repentance for all time to come" (44:16). For Sirach, Enoch is a model of salvation in the midst of a sinful world, a human who chose the difficult path of righteousness and repentance. Likewise, the Book of Wisdom understands Enoch to have been taken out of a world full of wickedness before it could corrupt his innocence (4:10–15).

Beyond these brief mentions in Scripture, however, the memory of Enoch was perpetuated in a wealth of Second Temple literature. The most well-known text in this regard is 1 Enoch, though there is a great body of other material and 1 Enoch itself consists of multiple collections of material brought together into one text. The New Testament references material from 1 Enoch, although minimally, in 1 and 2 Peter and in Jude; and the Fathers universally accepted and referenced the book's basic message until the beginning of the fifth century. In 1 Enoch, Enoch was brought into the divine council and received a vision of the history of the world and the nature of the cosmos, culminating in his receipt of a special place within God's divine council.

These and similar events discussed in the Hebrew Scriptures are often obscured by today's "pop eschatology," whereby people who die either "go up to heaven" or "go down to hell." This is not, of course, the teaching of the Scriptures, which proclaim that bodily resurrection in the world to come follows the judgment of the living and the dead. Particularly in the Old Testament, there is no distinction made regarding the fate of individuals who die—both the righteous and the wicked go to the grave (*Sheol* in Hebrew or *Hades* in Greek). The Patriarchs Abraham, Isaac, and Jacob, and a wicked king such as Omri, were said to "rest with their fathers" after their deaths. This is a situation that will be fundamentally transformed at the Resurrection of Christ, and that transformation forms the basis of many of the hymns of Pascha.

Therefore the notion that Enoch "went to heaven without dying" is misleading, because those who died in the Old Covenant were not seen to "go to heaven" at all. Enoch, rather, was chosen by God to join the divine council as the Prophet Elijah (also known in the Orthodox Church as St. Elias) later would. At his introduction in Genesis, Enoch's ascent is not described in detail. Elijah, however, was taken to heaven in a chariot of fire. While Ezekiel's vision of God's throne as a throne-chariot has already been discussed, it is worth repeating that the reason God's throne serves as a chariot is because His reign is not limited to one particular location, but rather ranges throughout the creation. This is likewise true of the divine council, for wherever Yahweh is, there are the angelic hosts surrounding His throne and serving Him.

And so, as Daniel described his vision of the divine council, he saw thrones (plural), then the Ancient of Days took his throne while the council surrounded Him on lesser thrones (Dan. 7:9). That Elijah was taken to heaven in a fiery chariot is, therefore, a way of describing that he has been made a member of the divine council alongside the angelic beings. It became a commonplace of Second Temple literature that Enoch and Elijah would someday return with an angelic mission related to the coming of the Messiah. This tradition may well be the referent of Revelation 11:1–14. Likewise, the iconography of St. John the Forerunner combines both the imagery of the returning Elijah, as referenced in the Gospels (Matt. 11:13–14; 17:12–13; Mark 9:13; Luke 1:11–17) and angelic imagery. When Elijah and Moses appeared on Mount Tabor with Christ, they were engaged with Him in discussion as councilors to the king.

The final major figure of the Old Testament to be raised to membership in the divine council is Moses. Unlike Enoch and Elijah, the Prophet Moses experienced physical death as described in Deuteronomy 34:5, but then the God of Israel buried the body so no one knew where it was (v. 6). Though it is not described in the Old Testament, traditions within early Judaism described the fate of Moses' body and why it was not found. The Scriptures do not elevate the soul over the body, as though the soul were somehow the "real" person and the body merely a husk to contain it. Rather, they teach that a human person is a union of body and soul and that the separation of the two at death is unnatural.

Because of human sin and rebelliousness, the devil has the ability to lay claim to the dead. This was the narrow authority he received when he was cursed in Eden (Gen. 3:14). Because Moses had repented of his sin and led a life that pleased God, his body was not subject to the devil's authority. As we are told in Jude 1:9, the Archangel Michael came and contested Satan's claim to Moses' body. This understanding of the human body forms the basis for St. John Chrysostom's *Paschal Homily*, in which the devil and Hades "seized a body" but encountered God and were embittered. This also forms the basis for the Church's understanding of the disappearance of the body of the Theotokos after her burial, as celebrated at the feast of her Dormition. As with Moses, Satan had no claim on the body of Christ's mother, and so tradition tells that when the apostles returned to her tomb after her burial, her body was likewise not found.

The Saints of God

THE WORD "SAINT" OR "SAINTS," in standard English translations of the Bible, is derived from the Latin *sanctus*, a translation of
the Greek term *agios* (plural *agiois*), and appears constantly in the
inscriptions of iconography. In the New Testament, this word is used
to describe both the worshipping community of the Church in its
sojourn on earth and the "dead in Christ" (see Acts 9:13, 32, 41; Rom.
1:7; 12:13; 1 Cor. 14:33; 2 Cor. 9:12; Eph. 2:19). This Greek term is
actually the substantive form of the adjective "holy." It could be translated simply as "holy one" or "holy ones." The term *saint* already had
a specific usage in the Hebrew Scriptures, in the Greek translation
of those Scriptures, and in the religious literature of Second Temple
Judaism that preceded the New Testament. The usage of this term as
a reference to Christians serves as an indicator of a change in the cosmic state of affairs, the fulfillment of Old Testament prophecies, and
the destiny of humanity transformed in union with Christ.

In the Old Testament, the holy ones of God are, first and foremost,
the angelic beings who make up the divine council. This is seen, for
example, in Psalm 89/88:5–7, "Let the heavens praise Your wonders,
O Yahweh, Your faithfulness in the assembly of the holy ones. For
who in the heavens can be compared to Yahweh? Who among the
sons of God is like Yahweh? A God greatly to be feared in the council of the holy ones, and awesome above all who surround him." The
angelic beings of the divine council surround Yahweh, and while
some of them fell and came to be worshipped as gods by the nations,
none of them is like the only true God, Yahweh, the God of Israel.
"Who is like You among the gods, O Yahweh? Who is like You in majesty among the holy ones?" (Ex 15:11 in the Greek).

Israel, when gathered in worship, participates in the divine council, and so they too, in these moments, are described as "holy ones"
(see Lev. 11:44–45; 19:2; 20:7, 26; 21:6; Num. 15:40; 16:3). When

Yahweh is depicted as coming in judgment, it is with His holy ones, as in Zechariah 14:3, "Then Yahweh my God will come, and all the holy ones with him." This parallels New Testament texts such as Matthew 16:27, "the Son of Man is about to come in His Father's glory, with His angels." In describing how Yahweh came to Israel, Moses says, "Yahweh came from Sinai and dawned from Seir on us. He shone forth from Mount Paran. He came from the ten thousands of holy ones with flaming fire at His right hand. Yes, He loved His people. All His holy ones were in His hand" (Deut. 33:2–3). The holy ones of God are here depicted as "flaming fire," an image also found in Psalm 104/103:4, "He makes His angels spirits, His ministers flaming fire," and quoted in Hebrews 1:7.

The importance of this imagery in Hebrews is explained by St. Dionysius the Areopagite in his *Celestial Hierarchies*. The fire in which the angelic hosts share, to varying degrees in their orders, are the divine energies, that is, the grace and glory of God. Hebrews 1 contrasts the participation of the angels to Christ's glory. While the angels graciously partake in the glory of God, that glory belongs to Christ Himself as God (Heb. 1:8–12). In Hebrews 2, however, the argument continues to describe the Incarnation of Christ, who was "made for a little while lower than the angels" but was then "crowned with glory and honor," after which all things were made subject to Him (2:7–8). While we do not yet see all things as subject to Christ, we nonetheless bear witness to Christ, who was incarnate so that He might taste death for all mankind, now crowned with honor and glory (vv. 8–9).

This discussion in Hebrews has an important frame. It begins with the statement that "it was not to angels that God subjected the world to come" (2:5). This stands in contrast to the previous age of the Old Covenant, in which the nations had been given over to angelic dominion. Important to note, however, is that Hebrews is not merely pointing to Christ's reign over all creation but also to those who are saved through Him. Those who find salvation in Christ are here called His sons (2:10, 13), parallel to the sons of God of the Old Covenant. They are called His brothers (vv. 11–12), concerning whom He testifies in the congregation. Through the Incarnation, Christ has delivered those who share in His human nature from death and the devil (v. 14), and through the Ascension, He has elevated that nature even above the angelic nature. In Christ, human persons become partakers of the divine nature beyond any of the ranks of angels and come to be rightly numbered among the holy ones.

The Governance of Creation

IN THE OLD TESTAMENT, GOD'S authority on earth was imaged and represented by human authority within Israel. Moses, the judges from Joshua through Samuel, and the king represented the rule of God over His people. The seventy elders in Israel equaled in number the angelic beings of the divine council who had been assigned rule over the nations. The Davidic line of God's chosen king over Judah, in particular, was a representation of God's authority on earth, its court representative of the divine council. David and his line, however, represented the rule of God in a preliminary and provisional way, such that the fulfillment of God's reign over His people was ultimately seen to be the Christ, the Messiah, who would actualize God's rule over His people in the age to come.

It is for this reason that the prophecy of 2 Samuel 7:16, that David's house and the kingdom will be forever, is transformed in view of the coming Messiah in 1 Chronicles 17:14 to the promise that David's descendant will live in God's house and that God's Kingdom will be forever. These prophetic themes are fulfilled in the Person of Jesus Christ, such that before His Ascension into heaven to be reenthroned, He stated, "All authority in heaven and on earth has been given to Me. Therefore, go and make disciples of all nations" (Matt.

28:18–19). God's rule over Israel has found its fulfillment in Jesus as the Christ, and Christ has also reclaimed authority over all the nations through the defeat of the fallen spiritual powers who had controlled them (Col. 2:15).

The New Testament is clear that this authority is no more isolated in the New Covenant than it was in the Old Covenant. Quite the opposite. Now, through Christ, human persons have entered into glory and joined the divine council as part of the family of God. The promises of the Scriptures regarding Christ's saints are not merely promises of passive rest but promises of participation in the rule and reign of Christ. Christ tells His disciples that when all is made new and He sits on His throne after the Ascension, they will "sit on twelve thrones judging the twelve tribes of Israel" (Matt. 19:28). Saint Paul says that the saints will judge the world (1 Cor. 6:2) and that the saints will judge even angels (v. 3). For him, we are already seated with Christ in the heavenly places through Christ's Ascension (Eph. 2:6). The Revelation of St. John characterizes the present age—during which Christ will reign over His enemies before His glorious appearing—as the time when the saints will be raised to rule and reign with Christ in the heavens (Rev. 20:4–5). Revelation then goes on to describe the role of the saints in glory as that of priests (v. 6) who will intercede before the throne of Christ.[2]

The saints in glory, therefore, are filling not only the places within the divine council that fallen angels once occupied but also the role they abdicated. Since the angelic beings who were formerly part of the divine council had been called "gods" and "sons of the Most

---

2   It should be noted that the Greek noun used in Revelation 20:6 translated as "priest" is not *presbyteros*, which is commonly translated in the same way in English parlance. *Presbyteros*, shortened to *prester* and then *prest* in English, forms the origin of the term "priest." St. John, however, uses the word *ieros* here. This is the term used not of the elders of the people in the Old Covenant, but of the sacrificial priesthood.

High" (Ps. 82/81:6), the New Testament authors and the Fathers—most famously St. Athanasius—speak of our becoming sons of God. When St. John bears witness to the worship of heaven near the end of his life, in addition to the angelic hosts seen in similar previous apocalyptic visions, there are glorified human members of the divine council. These are represented by the twenty-four elders (Rev. 4:4, 10; 5:5–14; 7:11–13; 11:16; 14:3; 19:4). These elders are seated and wearing crowns, sharing in Christ's rule over the creation (4:4).

That there are twenty-four elders in the divine council is significant for two reasons. First, these are two groups of twelve constituted of the twelve patriarchs, with Manasseh replacing Dan, and the apostles, with St. Paul replacing Judas, fulfilling Christ's prophecy concerning the apostles (Matt. 19:28). Second, the divine council is composed of seventy/seventy-two members. This means that human saints in glory constitute one-third of the divine council. This is the precise proportion of the heavenly host that had joined the devil in rebellion by the time of the birth of Christ, according to St. John (Rev. 12:4). Saint John is not saying that there are only twenty-four demons or twenty-four saints. Rather, he is using these numbers symbolically to indicate the replacement of the fallen members of the angelic host with the saints in glory.

It is for this reason that, since the very beginning of the Church, nations, cities, churches, families, and individuals who once were entrusted to "gods" as their benefactors have instead found heavenly patrons in the saints.[3] This is not, as some would suggest, some sort of concession to popular polytheism. Quite the opposite. It is a function of the gospel of Jesus Christ, which declares that the malign demonic powers who once enslaved the nations have been cast down

---

3   To give a very specific example, ancient Thessalonica had been devoted to the worship of Aphrodite, a spiritual power cast down and supplanted by St. Demetrios.

(Gal. 4:8–9; Col. 2:8, 20) and that the saints now rule and reign with Christ, judging the nations as He promised.

Just as in the Old Covenant believers sought the intercession of the holy ones before Yahweh (see Job 5:1), so also, as the saints in glory serve as priests before the throne of Christ, they intercede for the faithful (Rev. 20:6). Just as the ranks of angels had different roles and participated differently in the grace and glory of God, so also the saints have their unique roles (1 Cor. 15:40–41). The royal priesthood of the saints in glory is part and parcel of, and inseparable from, the authentic gospel of Jesus Christ.

The Theotokos, Queen and Mother

WITHIN THE MEDIATORY ROLE OF the saints and their patronage, the Theotokos, Mary, the Mother of Jesus Christ, has a special role, as has been recognized within the Christian Faith from the very beginning. Saint Irenaeus, the bishop of Lyons in the mid-second century, was a disciple of St. Polycarp, who had himself been a disciple of St. John the Theologian, one of Christ's twelve apostles. As the spiritual grandson of St. John, who had himself lived with the Theotokos in Ephesus, he writes about her in a way that reflects an already developed theological vision. Saint Irenaeus develops the idea of Christ as the new Adam (Rom. 5:12–21), including describing the Theotokos as a new Eve.[4] He contrasts the devil's temptation with the angel's announcement and Eve's disobedience with Mary's faithfulness. In a parallel way to Eve's sin having helped bring about humanity's death, through the Theotokos, the Life of all came into the world.

The veneration of the Theotokos in the West developed in ways that ultimately produced Marian dogmas, the Immaculate Conception and the Assumption, that the Orthodox Church does not

---

4   *Adv. Haeresies*, 3.22.4.

recognize. In response to these developments, the heirs of the Protestant Reformers, though not those Reformers themselves, reacted
by seeking to minimize the importance of the Theotokos to the point
of rejecting details of her personal history and life that had been held
universally since our earliest sources. Once the role of the Theotokos
within the divine economy had been repudiated, Protestant scholars had the need to explain how these teachings came into being and
came to be universally held. It has become common for those scholars
to suggest some connection between the veneration of St. Mary and
pagan goddess worship, related to their suggestion that the veneration
of the saints, in general, contained some connection to polytheism.
As was seen in the case of the role of the saints, however, it will be
seen that the veneration of the Theotokos as experienced within the
Church has existed from the beginnings of the Faith, being grounded
firmly in the Scriptures and in the religion of the Second Temple
period and its anticipation regarding the mother of the Messiah.

The earthly authorities of the Old Covenant were a direct reflection of the divine council, through which the God of Israel exercised
His rulership and authority over His creation. The earliest institution
of the Torah was the seventy elders surrounding the one appointed
to judge Israel, seventy in number because that was the number of
the divine council assigned to govern the nations (Deut. 32:8). This
remained when there came to be a divinely appointed king. The earliest kings, Saul and David, as they made war to secure the land given
them by God, were surrounded by their mighty men (*geburim*), who
led their armies, in parallel to the heavenly hosts surrounding Yahweh Sabaoth. The Archangel Gabriel's name identifies him as the
gebur or "mighty man" of God.

With the kingdom established under David, this council took
the form of the elders of the people and the royal court surrounding
David as he ruled and administered that kingdom. In all these cases,
the earthly authority served as an image of God's heavenly authority

and was commanded to serve in the administration of God's own rule. Kings were then judged based on how well they imaged the righteous rule of God on earth in their role. The king, surrounded by his royal council, was not only an image and earthly reflection of God's heavenly rule but was also a prophecy of a day when the earthly and heavenly rule would be united as one in the Messiah.

The Southern Kingdom of Judah was ruled by the line and house of David from the division of the kingdoms until the exile in Babylon. Within the Davidic monarchy, an important institution grew up within the king's court. The first and second chapters of Chronicles go to great pains to emphasize that after the destruction of Judah, David's line still will one day produce the messianic king. The genealogies in St. Matthew and St. Luke's Gospels and the accounts of Jesus' birth serve as reminders that he is of this line according to the flesh.

Typically, when we consider the king and queen of a nation, we assume the queen of a nation is the wife of the king. This, however, is because the medieval paradigm of monarchy had been so deeply affected by Christianity that it had to make at least a pretense of monogamy. Yet in the ancient world, as is reflected, for example, in 1 and 2 Kings and 1 and 2 Chronicles, polygamy was widely practiced by the nobility, which of course included kings. This practice was never sanctioned by God; in fact, the Torah explicitly forbids kings from acquiring many wives (Deut. 17:17). Nonetheless, polygamy was the reality. When references appear in the history of Judah's monarchy to a "queen mother," it is often presumed that this is merely a function of a polygamous monarchy. Kings could have many wives, but they could have only one mother. The reality of polygamy, however, does not fully explain the institution of queen mother within Judah because there is no parallel institution in the Northern Kingdom of Israel, let alone in many other monarchies of the ancient world that were equally polygamous. It is unique to David's line within Judah.

The origin of this practice is described in 1 Kings 2:19. Shortly after Solomon's succession to the throne, he had a second throne placed on his right hand for his mother, Bathsheba, to sit beside him as queen. The king's right hand has always had a significant meaning throughout the Scriptures, culminating in New Testament references to Christ's throne being located at the right hand of the Father. This is the preeminent position within any king's council; by situating his mother beside him, Solomon established her as his foremost advisor. From this point on, throughout 1 and 2 Kings and 1 and 2 Chronicles, as the succession of each descendant of David to the throne is announced, the name of his mother is also announced because she holds this role.[5]

In a particularly dark period of Judah's history, Athaliah used the authority of this role as queen mother to attempt to wipe out the Davidic line (2 Kin. / 4Kg 8:26; 11:1–20). This institution is referred to elsewhere in the Old Testament, a chief example being Psalm 45/44. This psalm is an ode to the king, and as the king is the icon of the God of Israel, it moves easily from the praise of the king himself (v. 2) to praise of God (v. 6), with the lines sometimes blurring between the two. This, too, is prophetic of the messianic king, who will someday unite the two. Within the imagery of this ode to divine kingship is the statement that at the king's right is the queen in glorious array (v. 9). This psalm concludes with a prophecy of the future role of the saints in governing the nations (v. 16).

The most basic claim of the entire New Testament is that Jesus is the Christ, the Messiah of Israel. Because Christ is also proclaimed to be the incarnate second hypostasis of the Holy Trinity, in Him heaven and earth, the divine and the human, are united. This includes, at His enthronement at His Ascension, the union of the throne of God and

---

5   See 1 Kin. / 3Kg 14:21; 15:2; 15:10; 22:42; 2 Kin. / 4Kg 8:26; 12:1; 14:2; 15:2; 15:13; 15:30; 15:33; 18:2; 21:1; 21:19; 22:1; 23:31; 23:36; 24:8; 24:18 and parallel passages in 1 and 2 Chronicles.

the throne of David. Already, as we have seen, these were prophetically linked in their institution. The reign of Jesus Christ over His Kingdom not only is the bringing together of Davidic and divine rule but is the fulfillment of the former. The words of Psalm 2:7 stating "Today You are My son; today I have begotten you" are a critical part of this royal psalm, read at the succession to the throne of a new Davidic king. Within the idea of adopted sonship is the idea that the son now has the obligation to serve as an image of the Father. This is fulfilled in Jesus Christ, who is the express image of God the Father (Heb. 1:3), of whom He is begotten. But it is also fulfilled at the Baptism of Christ, in which Christ is anointed at the hand of the prophet, not with oil but with the Holy Spirit, and the words of succession are spoken (Luke 3:22; Acts 13:33; Heb. 5:5). Christ is the true Son of God, begotten, not adopted.

For a faithful believer in the God of Israel in the first century AD, religious expectation was focused on the coming of the Messiah and the beginning of the messianic age.[6] It would, therefore, have been natural that when such a person heard the apostolic proclamation that Jesus of Nazareth is the Christ who has come, that person would ask the name of His mother. It would have been a natural expectation, based in the Scriptures and traditions of the Jewish people, to expect that His mother would have this role, at His right hand, as closest advisor and queen. The New Testament authors take great pains to correct popular misunderstandings related to the Messiah, particularly the idea that he would be a political leader in this world and would come to establish a national Israel in this world free from Roman domination. At no point, however, do these authors seek to correct this expectation as it pertains to Christ's mother.

---

6   In response to Christianity, Rabbinic Judaism would later divorce these two ideas, minimizing the role of the Messiah himself in favor of speaking merely of a coming age of peace and prosperity.

Repeatedly, the Scriptures of the New Testament reinforce these expectations by highlighting the importance of the Theotokos not only in the ministry of Christ but also, as described in the opening chapters of the Acts of the Apostles, in the community of the early Church. As just one example, there is a clear parallel between the interaction between Bathsheba and Solomon in 1 Kings 2 and that between the Theotokos and Christ at the wedding at Cana (John 2), though the Theotokos shows herself a wiser and holier woman than her ancient ancestor. In both cases, the mother of the king brings a request for aid to the king and then follows the judgment of the king. Bathsheba's request is denied because it would have been a disastrous mistake (1 Kin. / 3 Kg 2:13–25). The Theotokos's request for aid at the wedding feast is honored, and through it, new wine and joy are brought to the feast.

It is this understanding that has led, since the beginning of the Christian Faith, to the special role given to the Theotokos among the saints in glory. For example, Celsus, a second-century pagan and enemy of Christianity, devoted a portion of his refutation of Christianity to disparaging the understanding of the Theotokos as queen and mother. Specifically, he attacked the gospel of Christ by arguing that St. Mary, as a common peasant, was not worthy to be the mother of a king.[7] Contrary to Celsus, however, it is she who stands at the right hand of Christ the king, and among the intercessors with whom Christ shares His rule and reign, she has a special status of honor. She signifies the fulfillment not only of queen motherhood, but of motherhood itself (Gen. 3:15), and even, we may see, of womanhood.

---

7   Origen, *Contra Celsum*, I.28, 39.

Christ's Forerunner and Baptist John

THE FIGURE OF ST. JOHN the Forerunner looms large in the Gospels and the Acts of the Apostles, even long after his death had been recorded. This reflects his great historical importance in first-century Judea, as reflected in the writings of Josephus, among other places. His coming as the forerunner of or precursor to the Messiah had been prophesied in the Hebrew Scriptures, which spoke of the return of the Prophet Elijah. The reappearance of this hallowed prophet was understood to be a harbinger of the expected Christ (literally the "anointed one" or Messiah), well known to Jewish communities of the era. Elijah's prominence among the prophets is reflected in the Orthodox iconographic tradition, which depicts him standing at the left hand of Christ enthroned. He serves as the link between the Old Testament prophets and the New Testament saints. Despite all this, basic aspects of his identity, his way of life, and his mission are little investigated in the Scriptures and therefore not well known or understood.

Saint John's life is frequently described as being "angelic"—he was an "angelic man." In iconography, he is frequently depicted with large wings, the typical mark of an angel or archangel. Traditionally, after he and his mother, St. Elizabeth, fled into the desert following the murder of his father, St. John was raised by angels into adulthood (Luke 1:80). These angelic connections are variously parsed but often understood in a shallow way just to indicate that St. John was somehow like an angel in his way of life, usually because of his celibacy and fasting, hallmarks of an ascetical lifestyle. Saint John, however, signified a continuation of the prophetic way of life, not simply the beginning of the monastic. Many prophets were married, with their wives receiving the title of "prophetess" based on that union (see Is. 8:3–4).

Saint John's "angelic" nature conveys something far deeper about the lives of the prophets of the Old Covenant and the saints of the New Covenant. In the context of the contest between the Prophet

Jeremiah and the false prophets, Yahweh, the God of Israel, gives the paradigmatic criteria for a true prophet: the true prophet has stood in God's divine council and heard its deliberations and is serving as its messenger to the earth (Jer. 23:18–22). This is the pattern seen in the prophetic call of Isaiah as he begins his ministry (Is. 6:1–13). Humanity belongs to both elements of creation—the visible and the invisible—and was created to inhabit and integrate both before sin obscured humanity's ability to perceive the spiritual realm. The gift of the prophets of the Old Covenant and many of the saints of the New Covenant is that, through the purification of their spiritual senses, they are given to live in both and serve as a messenger (the literal meaning of the words for "angel" in Hebrew, Aramaic, and Greek) of the invisible to the visible. When Elisha's servant sees the heavenly host arrayed to protect the prophet from the armies of Syria, he is being granted to see what the prophet already clearly saw (2 Kin. / 4Kg 6:15–17). The angelic associations surrounding St. John the Forerunner reflect his participation in the life of the invisible creation, the spiritual realm, from which he was commissioned to begin his ministry of baptism and to identify Jesus as the Christ (John 1:29–34).

This angelic life is the key to understanding the connection between St. John and the Prophet Elijah. As previously discussed, at the end of his earthly life, St. Elias was taken up to join God's divine council. Christ took counsel with Elijah and the Prophet Moses, who had also been taken into the divine council at his death, on Mount Tabor at the Transfiguration. By the first century, it was firmly embedded in Second Temple Jewish tradition that Elijah would return before the coming of the Messiah and the Day of the Lord. This was directly prophesied by the Prophet Malachi (3:1; 4:5–6). Though the emphasis on Messianism would later fade from Rabbinic Judaism, even in contemporary Jewish practice, a seat is left open at the Passover meal for the Prophet Elijah, should he choose that night to return.

Saint John the Forerunner is clearly presented by the Gospel writers as the fulfillment of this prophecy. This begins at the level of appearance (compare 2 Kin. / 4Kg 1:8 and Matt. 3:4). More directly, Christ twice identified St. John as the Elijah who was to come before Him (Matt. 11:7–15; 17:10–13; Mark 9:11–13). On the other hand, in St. John's Gospel, when directly questioned as to whether he is Elijah or "the prophet," St. John the Forerunner responded that he is not (John 1:19–22). Somewhere in between lies the prophecy concerning St. John received by his father, that he would come "in the spirit and power of Elijah" (Luke 1:13–17). The perceived ambiguity regarding the connection between the two prophets has led to suggestions as bizarre as that St. John was a "reincarnation" of Elijah.

To understand how St. John can both be and not be Elijah, it is helpful to examine the concept of heavenly patronage in the Second Temple period. After Job had lost everything, his friend Eliphaz asked him, "To which of the *holy ones* will you turn?" (Job 5:1, emphasis added). In the context of Job, however, and much of the rest of the Old Testament, this term is used to refer to the angelic beings of the divine council. Eliphaz's question, therefore, presumes that angelic beings play an intercessory role before the throne of God. Later in the Book of Job, Job himself indicated that he had such a representative, referred to as his "witness" (Job 16:18–22). This understanding becomes the basis for what are today called "guardian angels," angelic patrons who represent righteous individuals in the council of God. This tradition is directly referred to by Christ Himself in Matthew 18:10. Through Christ, resurrected human persons are now likewise members of the divine council and fulfill this same role (Heb. 11:39—12:2; Rev. 4:9–11; 6:9–11; 8:4).

As St. Elias is taken up in his fiery throne-chariot, he performs his first action as a member of the divine council, which is passing on his prophetic role and ability to his disciple Elisha. This takes the form of Elisha requesting and receiving a "double amount of his spirit"

(2 Kin. / 4Kg 2:9). Elisha received this request from Elijah, and it is manifested at the Jordan near Jericho, the place of the beginning of Joshua's conquest (Josh. 3:15–17). Afterward, one of the communities of prophets, the forerunners of monastic communities in the New Covenant, recognized that "the spirit of Elijah rests on Elisha" (2 Kin. / 4Kg 2:15). Elijah commissions and is the heavenly patron of Elisha, whom he has known personally. Likewise, St. John the Forerunner, who has been privy to the divine council, knows St. Elias, who has sent him forth under his patronage to continue his prophetic mission. Saint John, therefore, is the Elijah who was to come in being his representative but at the same time is not Elijah in that he is a different human person who comes in St. Elias's spirit and power.

Saint John's mission as the forerunner of Christ was not only to identify Him before the multitudes but also to "prepare His way." This is not merely a vague statement that St. John's ministry began first in temporal sequence but refers to something very particular. The great promise of all the Old Testament prophets was that the exile that Israel had been forced to endure would one day come to an end. At one level, the Babylonian exile had ended under Cyrus when the tribes of Judah and Benjamin and portions of Levi were allowed to return to the province of Judea at the end of the sixth century BC. This return of a group of exiles was not the promise of the prophets, however. Many of the members of these tribes had not returned but remained in Babylon or in Egypt.

Further, however, the promises of the prophets were regarding the restoration of the entire nation, all twelve tribes, ten of which had been dispersed by the Assyrians among the nations with seemingly little hope of return. Most pointedly, the promise that Yahweh, the God of Israel, would return to Zion, to His temple, had not been fulfilled. The dedication of the second temple had been accompanied by none of the signs of God's Presence that had accompanied the dedications of the tabernacle or that of Solomon. Malachi's promise of the coming of Elijah had promised precisely this (3:1). Saint John's rhetoric regarding the coming of judgment and of fire that will consume all Israel if they do not repent mirrors Malachi's language regarding his mission directly (4:5–6).

The Old Testament prophecy most associated with St. John and his ministry is Isaiah 40:3 (see Matt. 3:1–3; Mark 1:2–4; Luke 3:2–6; John 1:23). In the last of these references, St. John the Forerunner identifies himself with the voice crying, "In the wilderness prepare the way of the Lord." At the time the Gospels were written, there were no chapter and verse divisions in the Scriptures. When the beginning of a prophecy such as this one from Isaiah is cited, it is a way of alluding to the entire text, not only the single verse quoted. Isaiah in 40:3–31 prophesies the end of the exile when Yahweh, the God of Israel, will Himself return to defeat His enemies and lead Israel back into the land where He will dwell with them. The reconstituted Israel whom Yahweh will reclaim as His people begins with a remnant that is purified by and survives God's judgment at the Day of the Lord (see Mic. 2:12; Jer. 23:3; Joel 3:5; Obad. 17; Is. 6:13; 7:3; 10:22). The mission of Elijah, according to Malachi (4:5–6), is precisely to gather this remnant and prepare it for Yahweh when He comes. This mission is entrusted to St. Elias based on his interaction with God in 1 Kings / 3 Kingdoms 19:9–18, which immediately preceded the calling of Elisha.

Saint John the Forerunner fulfilled his mission by purifying a repentant people, a faithful remnant of Israel at the shore of the Jordan. When the Lord came to the Jordan to be baptized and begin his mission of conquest, St. John gave to Him this people to form the basis of the reconstituted Israel who will receive God's New Covenant. His life exemplifies what human life was created to be in this world and the world to come. He is the epitome of the mission and message of the prophets who came before him, both proclaiming the fulfillment of their prophetic word in Jesus Christ and accomplishing finally the mission for which they were all sent: the purification of a remnant of God's people Israel through repentance and a return to faithful obedience to Israel's God.

Heavenly Patronage

FIRST CORINTHIANS 15 IS THE chapter out of St. Paul's entire corpus that most fully expresses the apostle's understanding of the resurrection of the dead. The first half of the chapter discusses the importance of Christ's Resurrection and how it is inviolably linked to the resurrection not only of human persons but of all things. In the second half of the chapter, St. Paul describes, insofar as he can, what the resurrection of humanity and ultimately of the entire creation means. The chapter closes with St. Paul reveling in a hymn of victory over death. Amid this discussion, St. Paul gives a series of rhetorical examples as evidence of the centrality of the resurrection of the dead to the Christian religion. This was necessary because not all the Jewish faithful—the core of the communities St. Paul planted—had believed in the resurrection of the dead previously. Some first-century Jewish sects did; others did not—the same is true of different Jewish groups today. The acceptance of the Resurrection of Christ, however, St. Paul argues in 1 Corinthians 15:12–19, entails the belief in the general resurrection of the dead.

One example St. Paul gives, in particular, has been the subject of much speculation throughout Christian history. In 1 Corinthians 15:29, he refers to "those who are baptized for the dead." If the dead are not raised to life, then this practice makes no sense. The exact practice St. Paul was referring to, however, has not had a single, unified history of interpretation. There are very few comments from early Christian sources on the text, and those that do exist do not agree with each other. A close reading of the text, however, gives an idea of what this practice was. It is, in fact, a practice that still occurs today within the Orthodox Church and, ironically, was practiced even by the patristic commentators who did not make this particular connection.

In 1 Corinthians, St. Paul inquires: "Otherwise, what will they do, those who are baptized for the dead? If the dead are not raised at all, why then were they baptized for them?" (15:29). Many modern understandings of this verse are shaped more by ambiguous English translations than by careful analysis of the original language. Nor do many of these modern interpretations take into account the overall context of St. Paul's discussion in this chapter and throughout 1 Corinthians.

Saint Paul refers to "those who are baptized for the dead," meaning that he is referring to a particular group. There are some who are baptized for the dead, and others who are baptized, but not "for the dead." It is important to notice that the word "baptized" is passive in both uses in this verse. It is not "those who baptize for the dead," but "those who are baptized for the dead." The action here being described is something done by those who are being baptized, not by the baptizer. So, the fact that St. Paul refers to "those who" does not mean that it is some other sect outside of what would be recognized as Christianity. This verse isn't speaking of people who perform some type of baptism other than Christian baptism, but rather to a group of people who receive Christian baptism in a certain way.

Baptism, for St. Paul, is not merely an action that conveys certain benefits on an individual who receives it. Rather, baptism creates a series of relationships into which the recipient is brought by the action. So, for example, the apostle can speak of those who passed through the Red Sea as having been "baptized into Moses" (1 Cor. 10:2). Being baptized into Moses in the cloud and the sea, the Holy Spirit and water, brought them into a relationship with Yahweh, the God of Israel, and that relationship was mediated through Moses and through the covenant that was given through Him. Likewise, St. Paul speaks of those who have received Christian baptism as those who have been baptized into Christ and so have put on Christ (Gal. 3:27). Elsewhere in the New Testament, the baptism of repentance for the forgiveness of sins is referred to as "the baptism of John" for this same reason (Matt. 21:25; Mark 11:30; Luke 7:29; 20:4; Acts 18:25).

In the Church of Jesus Christ of Latter-day Saints, living persons are baptized as a proxy for deceased, unbaptized persons. This verse is often cited as a witness to their practice. This is based on the assumption, among others, that "the dead" to whom St. Paul here refers are deceased non-Christians who are in some way made Christians by virtue of a currently living person being baptized. There are any number of problems with this. First and foremost, it is unclear at best how a dead person receiving the Mystery of Baptism would benefit from it, any more than a deceased person receiving any other mystery of the Church. A deceased person receiving the Eucharist or monastic tonsure, or being married, makes no more sense than a deceased person receiving the Holy Spirit into the temple of his or her dead body.

Saint Paul goes to great pains in 1 Corinthians 10 to argue that baptism does not necessarily entail salvation (1 Cor. 10:1–6). Further, 1 Corinthians was written to the Church in Corinth, at the latest, in AD 57. This means that there were only twenty-four years between the writing of this epistle and the first Christian baptisms. Hypothetically, then, the baptism of people on behalf of the people who died during those twenty-four years would have had to become a practice widespread enough in the early Christian communities that St. Paul could reference it during that window. This suggestion, therefore, makes neither theological nor historical sense.

The key to understanding the identity of "the dead" in the first half of 15:29 is obscured by the English translation. Even though it is translated in both halves of the verse as "the dead," St. Paul uses the Greek article only in the first case. This is common for St. Paul. When he is speaking about all deceased persons in the world, he does not use the definite article. He is referring to dead people in general. This is the case in the second half of the verse, "if the dead are not raised at all." When he uses the Greek article, which would most correctly be translated "these dead," he is nearly always referring to deceased Christians in particular. Hence the article separates "these dead (Christians)" from "the dead" in general. If the people to whom St. Paul refers are being baptized for dead Christians who would themselves already have received Christian baptism during their lives, then our understanding of the baptism "for" them must change.

The Greek preposition here, *uper*, is the source of the English prefix "hyper" and is related to *super* in Latin. It is the origin of English words "up" and "over" and the German *uber*. In this context, with a noun referring to persons, it can mean "for the benefit of," "instead of," "as a representative of," or "in the name of." This range is roughly paralleled in the English word "for," hence the translation. If I say that I went to the store "for" someone, it could mean that I went because they could not. It could also mean that I went on their behalf. Or it could mean that I went in order to be of assistance to them. If "the dead" is here understood to be deceased Christians, then the most reasonable understanding is that these are people who are being baptized in the name of these deceased Christians.

Saint Paul has already referred us to this group of departed saints at the beginning of chapter 15, directly before he uses this example in verse 29. The apostle lists a great number of witnesses to the Resurrection of Christ, including the apostles and at one point five hundred people at once. Of these, many were still alive, but as St. Paul says, some had fallen asleep (v. 6). The use of "these dead" would most naturally refer back to those previously mentioned in verse 6.[8]

---

8   This use of the Greek article, meaning "previous reference," is the most common use of the article in the common Greek of the biblical period.

Saint Paul is speaking of people who, when they were being baptized, were being baptized in the name of one of these departed saints.

Putting this together with St. Paul's general understanding of baptism, we can see how someone taking the name of a departed saint at their baptism would create a relationship between the person being baptized and that saint. This relationship can best be described by the Roman understanding of patronage. A Roman patron was established in a social position within Roman culture and would then act in his position to assist someone who was beginning his own public life or career. In return, the patron's client was expected to act in such a way that it would bring further honor to his patron and to work diligently to achieve the kind of status that his patron had. The status that departed saints were seen to have within apostolic Christianity stood in relation to the well-developed understanding of God's divine council. This understanding of the departed saints' role in the life of the Church naturally resulted in the formation of such relationships with a patron saint at the time of entry into the Christian community at baptism.

Saint Paul, then, in 1 Corinthians 15:29 can be seen to be referring to the practice, already beginning in the mid-50s AD, of those who were being baptized doing so in the name of a patron saint. This practice had not yet but later would become universal in the Christian Church. The apostle's reference to it here in this context is to demonstrate the reality of the resurrection. If the dead are not raised, then no such relationship with a patron saint could exist, as that person would be dead and gone. The baptismal practice would make no sense whatsoever.

Saint Paul's reasoning here is roughly parallel to Christ's argument against the Pharisees in Mark 12:26–27 and Luke 20:37–38. God is the God of Abraham, Isaac, and Jacob, and He is not the God of the dead, but of the living. The apostles and witnesses of Christ's Resurrection who had already fallen asleep in the Lord at the time of the writing of 1 Corinthians had joined Abraham, Isaac, and Jacob in the resurrection. They could intercede for those in the Church in this world and especially for those who lived a life of faith in their name, bringing honor to their memory.

Saint Luke records Christ describing the destiny of humanity, that those who are sons of the resurrection will be "equal to the angels and sons of God." God is perfectly capable of existing without His creation. Even after creating, He is perfectly able to govern His creation without any assistance. God needs nothing. Yet out of love, He has created all things and has shared in the governance of His creation with His angelic creatures. Despite humanity's repeated falling away into sin, through the salvation found in Jesus Christ, human beings are brought into God's divine council and given, by grace, a share in His rule over creation.

PART THREE

Creation and Salvation

✠ ✠ ✠

CHAPTER 6

Creation and Chaos

TODAY, WE TEND TO ENVISION "being" in opposition to "nothingness." When we say something exists, we mean that it has some sort of material or concrete real-ness—it is a thing. Likewise, when we say something does not exist, we mean that it either is imaginary or somehow lacks real presence in space and time. Rooted in philosophical materialism, this paradigm makes it difficult to discuss the existence of God—who transcends temporal reality—as "a being." As a result, atheism has become the default worldview within our society. At the same time, our ability as Christians to challenge or even see outside the assumptions of atheism is limited because we, too, operate from the same premise, namely that only what is material or takes up space truly exists.

Yet this being-versus-nothingness understanding of reality has not always held sway. For centuries, particularly in Western thought, an understanding initiated by Plato (further elaborated by the Middle and Neo-Platonists) was the dominant lens for parsing the nature of existence. For Plato, the opposite of being was not a nonbeing or nonexistence but rather the state of becoming. In other words, some things simply are, and will always be, while other things are in motion or undergoing a process of change—continually becoming.

In the Platonic understanding, the things that "are" are superior to the things that are becoming because the latter are not yet the thing they are becoming. They can be recognized or understood only to the degree that they are like the thing they are turning into. This makes stasis, for Platonism, one of the highest virtues.

When this concept was integrated into Christianity, it produced an understanding of being not as an either/or phenomenon, but rather as a chain or spectrum. The simple, immutable God stood at the top, and the raw materials of creation lay at the bottom. All things, then, partake in being along a continuum. Aristotle, a student of Plato, made variation on this understanding that reveals the ancient view that had preceded it. Rather than being and becoming, he taught of potentiality and actuality. On one end of the chain was potential or "prime matter," which can be formed into anything but is not yet anything, just as a lump of clay can be shaped to form any recognizable figure, but until it is sculpted is not yet any of them. On the other end was pure actuality, a being who is unable to change, which is how Thomas Aquinas understood the Christian God as the "prime mover." Once again, all created things and their Creator are connected by being itself and are therefore related to one another analogously.

Even before Plato and Aristotle, however, in the most ancient understanding (reflected in the Hebrew Scriptures by virtue of the time and place in which they were composed), being was opposed not to nonexistence or fiction, nor the state of becoming. Rather, being was opposed to chaos. To exist is to dwell within a web of relationships that create meaning and purpose. It is to be ordered and structured. When a tower collapses into rubble, the constituent material of the tower is still there in the form of the rubble. The tower, however, no longer exists. Likewise, when an animal dies, its body dissolves into the earth, returning to its component elements, but the animal no longer exists. While people and their descendants may continue to exist after the collapse or destruction of a nation, the nation itself no longer exists following such an event.

That God brought all things from nothingness into being is the clear teaching of the Scriptures and the Orthodox Church. There are places within the Scriptures, however, in which Creation is described in other ways. In Genesis 1, the Creation of the world is described as being from nothing, but that nothing is primordial chaos rather than a timeless, spaceless void, if such a thing can even be conceived by human persons. In the beginning, the earth was formless and empty—but it was *something* in a material sense (Gen. 1:2). This state of formlessness is further described as a darkness above and the watery abyss below.

Over the ensuing sequence of days, God gave structure to the primal elements. Over the first three days, this took the form of organizing the formless elements to create regions. The creation of time from timelessness is not described, but on the first day, structure was given to time beginning with the day itself, evening and morning. On the second day, the spaces of the heavens and the seas were created. On the third day, the space of the dry ground was created. These spaces are in neither ascending nor descending order. In ancient experience, the heavens are the dwelling place of divine beings and manifest a perfect order. The land is the realm to which humans attempt to establish order. The seas, where no human can exist, continue to represent chaos and death, the two of which are closely linked.

On days four through six, God proceeded to fill each of these spaces in turn to solve the second problem, of emptiness. The heavens were filled with the sun, moon, and stars. The skies were filled with birds, and the seas with fish and creeping things innumerable. The land was filled with animal life and, finally, humanity. Contained within the story of the creation of humanity, however, is the idea that God's creative work is not complete. Humanity is created and

RELIGION OF THE APOSTLES

commanded to fill the earth and subdue it (1:28). Human persons were created to continue this work of giving order to the creation and filling it with life.

This ordering of the world forms the scriptural understanding of justice and expresses itself in the Torah in the form of commandments, through the keeping of which human life will bring that structure to the world as a whole. Sin as a force is opposed to this order and seeks to destroy it, reducing human life to chaos and death. It is only through these structures, however, that life can have meaning and purpose. Judgment, in Hebrew and Aramaic the same word as "justice," is the establishment or reestablishment of this order on earth. Justification is the setting of things or persons back into the proper order of things and the correct set of relationships with their Creator and the rest of the creation. It represents a new creative act.

Therefore, what it means to "live" or even to "exist" is to participate in these correctly ordered relationships with other human persons, the rest of the creation, and preeminently with God, the Holy Trinity. "This, then, is eternal life, that they might know you, the one true God, and the one whom You have sent, Jesus Christ" (John 17:3). Because these relationships define life and existence, without them there can be no concept of purpose or meaning but only brute material subsistence. Conceptually, order and meaning are inseparable. Therefore, the breaking of these relationships through sin, the disintegration of good order, or exile, constitutes death and nonexistence. The wilderness, that part of the world that resists being set in order, remains in this state of chaos and so is associated with nonbeing and death. In the Torah, it is ambiguous whether being "cut off from among the people" represents death or exile since, in context, these two states were the same thing. The sea continues to represent the same principles, which is why it ceases to exist in the new heavens and the new earth (Rev. 21:1). Likewise, the darkness of night, the time of sin and violence, ceases to exist (see John 3:19; Rev. 21:25).

152

Paradise, God's Dwelling

THE GARDEN OF EDEN, THE place where God dwells with His
divine council, is known in Greek translation as "Paradise." The
Greek term for "Paradise" (*paradeisos*), borrowed from Persian, refers
to a particular type of walled garden. Likely the most high-profile
example of a paradise garden in the world today is the Taj Mahal,
built according to Persian custom. (An aerial photo of the Taj Mahal
even reveals four waterways that mimic the biblical description.)
Eden's walls both protected it from the chaos of the world outside
and allowed for Adam and Eve to be expelled and kept outside of it.
Modern literalism has sought to pinpoint where the Garden of Eden
would have been located geographically, under the assumption that
at some point, usually the Flood of Noah, it was destroyed. While a
"this-worldly" interpretation of Eden is attractive to many, it fails to
explain the way Eden is referred to in the rest of the Old Testament,
and the way that Paradise is described as still existing in the New Testament. Eden does indeed exist, and understanding the way that Paradise, as a place, is depicted in the Scriptures clears up a great many
popular modern debates.

When Eden is introduced in the text of Genesis 2, contrary to
some modern claims, the seemingly geographic cues are not intended
as real-world coordinates. It is, first, stated to be "in the East" (Gen.
2:8), yet east of what is not stated. Attempts to physically locate the
Garden, therefore, typically focus on the four rivers that were said to
flow from the Garden (vv. 10–14), which are described in geographic
detail. The problem here is that sufficient geographic detail is given
to positively identify all four, as was recognized by interpreters even
several centuries before Christ. The four rivers that flow from Eden
are the Tigris, the Euphrates, the Nile, and the Danube. Even a brief
perusal of a map, ancient or modern, will reveal that there is no location in this world where the sources of those four rivers branch from

each other. The source these rivers do share, however, is that they were collectively the point of origin of the most ancient civilizations known to the biblical authors. The flooding of these rivers in the spring deposited fertile soil that could be used to grow crops, producing the first stable human civilizations along these rivers. Genesis here depicts these rivers, the source of life for these human communities, as flowing out from the Presence of God.

The location of Paradise "in the East" is an example of what is termed "cosmic geography." The cardinal directions, in ancient literature, have symbolic connotations. For example, evil dwells, in the Hebrew Scriptures, "in the North." While specific areas such as Mount Hermon and Bashan were to the north of most of Israel, this term can also refer to the cosmic dwelling place of evil. The Hebrew word *tzaphon*, used for the direction "north," is also used to mean a place that is "dark" or "gloomy." One of Baal's titles, Baal Zaphon, is a reference to his dwelling in the North on a particular mountain. His dwelling is "in the North." The North is the home of evil throughout the prophetic corpus of the Hebrew Bible (Is. 14:13, 41; 41:25; Jer. 1:13–15; 4:6; 6:22; 10:22; 13:20; 46/26:10, 20; Ezek. 8:3, 5, 14; 32:30; Zeph. 2:13). For this reason, the Resurrection Gospel reading of the Orthodox Orthros/Matins service, and in traditional Western liturgics the Gospel in general, is read toward the North—we are proclaiming the victory of Christ to His enemies. Likewise, Eden, the dwelling place of God Most High, is "in the East," and so prayers and worship are traditionally offered facing East.

In the ancient Near East, gods were considered to live in gardens and on mountains. Gardens were a dwelling place for gods because of the generally arid wilderness conditions under which most people lived. The famed hanging gardens of Babylon are an example of an ancient garden temple. Mountains were thought suitable dwelling places because they reached up toward the heavens and were inaccessible to humans. Eden is characterized as a mountain at several points in the Hebrew Scriptures, even after being clearly described as a garden in Genesis 2:8, 10 (see Ezek. 28:13–16). The mountain terrain of the Garden is also implied by the fact that the four rivers flow *down* from the Garden.

Adam was created from the dust of the earth and was then taken and placed in the Garden (Gen. 2:15). Here again, we see that Paradise is a location separated from the surrounding world; Adam was removed from the chaos of the world, and he was brought to live with God on His holy mountain. Eden was not the entire world, but the place within the creation where God had chosen to dwell. The Creation was not complete in the sense of fully completing its purpose, nor was humanity. Adam was created for a mission that would aid in bringing the creation to its intended perfection and bring himself to full maturity in the process.

Humanity was created, in Genesis 1, at the climax of Creation. At the beginning of God's creative activity, He is addressing two problems regarding the heavens and the earth. The earth is, in Hebrew, *tohu wubohu* (Gen. 1:2). It is formless or chaotic, and it is empty. Over the first three Creation days, the chaotic world is put into order (Gen. 1:3–10). Over the second set of three days, the creation is filled with life (Gen. 1:14–25). When humanity is created, however, they are commanded to "fill the earth and subdue it" (Gen. 1:28). This command directly parallels the initial problems: humanity is to fill the earth and bring order to it. Human persons are therefore God's coworkers to assist in bringing His works to completion (1 Cor. 3:9). Humanity was not created to, at that time, simply passively dwell with God forever in His Presence. Rather, humanity was created to, as God's image, spread Eden out into the world and make the whole world a Paradise in which God dwelt. Once this work was completed, then humankind would dwell with God and His heavenly hosts forever.

After their rebellion, however, Adam and Eve became mortal and were clothed with mortal flesh (Gen. 3:21). Adam and Eve had bodies already, but they were different from the bodies possessed in this world, just as those of this world differ from the bodies with which humanity will be clothed in the resurrection. They were then, as the Liturgy of St. Basil the Great describes it, "cast out into this present world." They were no longer able to stand in the presence of God or on His holy mountain (Ps. 24/23:3). They, therefore, did not take Eden with them when they came into this world and were unable to remedy the emptiness and chaos that they found. God's work in Creation remains incomplete, as Christ points out (John 5:17), until Christ Himself brings it to completion (John 19:30). After this, Christ rests on the seventh day and rises to begin making all things new (Rev. 21:5). In the end, the world becomes Paradise, filled with the knowledge of the glory of Yahweh as the waters cover the sea (Hab. 2:14), and God's Presence fills it.

Until Christ brings all things to completion, Paradise still exists as the place where God dwells atop His holy mountain, such that Christ Himself can promise the wise thief that He will be with Him there (Luke 23:43). Likewise, St. Paul could visit Paradise in a visionary experience (2 Cor. 12:2–4). Sinful humanity, however, is unable to ascend His holy mountain, despite rebellious attempts to do just this and bring God down as at the Tower of Babel (Gen. 11:4; compare John 3:13 and Rom. 10:6–8). Until man can once again come to dwell in the presence of God, Yahweh, the God of Israel, condescends to bring His dwelling place to humanity.

This is exemplified at Mount Sinai, which twice becomes the mountain of God, where He meets with Moses face to face (Ex. 3:1–6; 19:2–6). The people of Israel cannot even touch the mountain without dying (Ex. 19:10–13). The seventy elders of Israel, Aaron, and Aaron's sons, after purifying themselves, are able to ascend partway up the mountain and see Yahweh, the God of Israel (Ex. 24:9–11). Only Moses, however, can ascend to the peak (v. 12). In order to dwell with His people, therefore, Yahweh gave detailed instructions to Moses to pattern the tabernacle on God's dwelling place, which he had beheld on the mountain (Heb. 8:5). God, therefore, descended His mountain to come and dwell with humanity. This foreshadowed the Incarnation of Christ, when "the Word became flesh and tabernacled among us" (John 1:14).

Later, although He is under no compulsion to do so, Yahweh consented to dwell within the temple, and Mount Zion became the mountain of God for as long as He dwelt there (1 Kin. / 3Kg 9:3–9). The decorations of the temple were designed deliberately to evoke the Garden of Eden as a realization of the place where God dwells (7:15–50). This includes the imagery of flowers and fruit trees as well as imagery of the cherubim and other members of God's divine council who dwell there with Him. In Ezekiel's vision of the new and eternal temple, he sees streams of water flowing forth from it (Ezek. 47:1–12). Joel similarly uses the river imagery to connect the temple and Eden (Joel 3:18). Paradise is the place where Yahweh dwells, and so the place where Yahweh dwells becomes Paradise, and streams of living water flow from Him (Jer. 2:13; 7:13). It is for this reason that the Theotokos herself is poetically described as a "mystical Paradise," because Yahweh, the God of Israel, came to dwell within her womb.

Ultimately, the imagery of Paradise, the permanent dwelling of God, is applied to the Person of Jesus Christ Himself. This is the purpose of the language in the Gospels that identifies Christ with the temple (see John 2:19–21). Christ also identifies Himself as the source of the Water of Life (John 4:10–26). In the Troparion of His Nativity, Christ is called "the East from on high." In the new heavens and the new earth, the whole world drinks of the Water of Life that flows forth from the Presence of God (Rev. 21:6). There is no temple, not because the whole world is now a temple but because Yahweh the almighty God and the Lamb is their temple (Rev. 21:22).

For Christians, however, this promise becomes a present reality. The one who drinks of the Water of Life that flows from Christ

Himself, as Christ said at the Feast of Tabernacles, has a spring of water come to flow from within him (John 7:37–38). He is speaking of the coming of the Holy Spirit (John 7:39). When a Christian comes to be indwelt by the Holy Spirit, God Himself is dwelling within him, making that person a temple (1 Cor. 6:19). As St. Silouan put it: "The Lord has given the Holy Spirit on the earth, and in whomsoever He dwells, that one feels paradise within himself."[1]

Man, the Image of God

THAT HUMANS ARE CREATED IN the image of God is explicit from the first pages of the Scriptures (Gen. 1:27). Yet what exactly this means has become the subject of seemingly endless speculations, particularly when this reality is extracted from its specific context and purpose in the Genesis narrative. In contemporary theology, such discourses most often manifest in identifying "the image of God" in man with some characteristic or characteristics of the human person. Rationality, language, or freedom, for example, become the hallmarks of God's image within humanity.

This approach is problematic, to say the least. On one hand, as we advance in our knowledge and understanding of other creatures God has made, we see more and more that human consciousness is not necessarily unique but rather lies on a continuum with the consciousness other living things possess. Certain human qualities can also be found in animals, albeit to a lesser degree. On the other hand, some people lack certain uniquely human characteristics, generally near the beginning or end of life. The theological premise for the innate value of every human person is the notion that human persons are image-bearers. The nature of the divine image, therefore, cannot

---

1   St. Silouan the Athonite, *Writings*, IX.15

become the means of dehumanizing those incapable of reason, language, or substantive choice.

In order to understand the nature of God's image, it is better to turn directly to the scriptural texts in which this terminology is used in order to understand how it is being used in its original context. The narrative of Creation is the story of God creating a sacred space in which to dwell with His creation, humanity. God does not need a physical space in which to live, but humans, as finite creations, do. In describing such a space, the text of Genesis 1 and 2 follows the pattern of the construction of an ancient temple. In the religious imagination of the nations surrounding Israel, their gods lived in one of two places, either in a garden or on a mountain.

This is not to say that these pagans were correct, or that the God of Israel is like their gods. Rather, it is to say that when God spoke to ancient people, to describe to them this creation of sacred space, He spoke to them using language and imagery that they would understand. And so, the space that God creates in Genesis is a sacred garden. This garden imagery would later be further developed in the decorations of Solomon's temple. The tabernacle, on the other hand, followed the pattern of God's dwelling atop Mount Sinai, into which Moses entered (Acts 7:44; Heb. 9:11, 23).

The final step in the creation of an ancient Near Eastern temple was the installation of the god's image or idol. After its installation, a ceremony was performed in order to open its mouth and nose so that the spirit of the god could enter into it. This requires a word about idolatry, and how it functioned in the ancient world. Ancient people worshipped and sought to interact with, through acts of worship, spiritual powers. In order for the people to interact with these spirits, the spirits needed to take up residence in a body. The most common mode of this interaction was through the construction of a body for the god by its worshippers, an idol. After the construction of the body, a ritual was undertaken that would "open the nostrils" of the image so that the spirit could enter into it and take up residence. Once the divine spirit was inhabiting the image, the primary task of the priests was to care for the idol by keeping it clean, dressing it, bringing it food and drink, maintaining its home in the temple, and so on.

It is this that engendered the extended critiques of idolatry throughout Scripture (see Is. 44). It is not merely that humans are worshipping rocks and chunks of wood rather than the God who created them. There is inherent foolishness at work here. If a so-called god is unable to clean itself, dress, maintain its own home, or even pick itself up off the floor if tipped over, how could one possibly believe that such a being could bring rain or great yields of crops? If it cannot govern even the most basic functions of life, how could it govern a nation or the world? And yet all these rituals are aimed at one goal, to use the temple and the image to control the god and get it to do what one wants. The image of the god is the place where it encounters the human world.

What we see in Genesis is precisely the reverse of this pagan practice. Upon the completion of His own temple, His own sacred space, God then creates His own image. After creating a human person as His image, God Himself breathes into him the breath of life, opening his nostrils and causing him to live and function as God's image. The gift given to human persons is to be the means by which God acts in His creation. This is a privilege, as God does not need humanity in order to act in creation, any more than He needed a creation in which to act. The expulsion from Paradise then represents the failure of humanity to serve as the image of God. Rather than participating in the works of God, man undertakes his own work, another foreign motion of his will. At this point, as the Fathers distinguish between image and likeness, humanity lost the likeness to God, though human persons continue to be God's image, such that the reverence that is shown for a human person passes on to his Creator as does the lack thereof (Gen. 9:6; Matt. 25:31–46).

The true and full imaging of God in human nature, unfulfilled by humanity in sinfulness, finds its fulfillment in the Person of Jesus Christ. In Christ, God perfectly reveals Himself in and through human nature. Christ is, in fact, the express image of the Father (Col. 1:15; Heb. 1:3). This mystery is developed in Scripture in the context of a meditation on the formation of Christ's body, parallel to the creation of Adam. Hebrews 10:5–7 cites Psalm 40/39, applying its words to Christ. Specifically, Hebrews quotes the Greek rendering of verse 5, "a body You have made for Me." This is contrasted with the desire for sacrifices and offerings.

Here we see the inversion of the pagan view that God desires humans to fulfill some need on His part, which He will reward with blessings. Rather, God desires that human persons share in His life by participating in His working in the world, that they become righteous by participating in His righteousness, good by participating in His goodness, holy by participating in His holiness, and so on. He desires that they function as His image. Christ, as God Himself, gives perfect expression to the character of God, doing only the works of the Father (see John 5:17; 9:4; 10:37). The Hebrew of Psalm 40/39 uses the idiom of God having opened His ears, an idiom also used in Isaiah 50:5 to describe God's suffering servant, who, unlike Adam, does not rebel.

Through His death and Resurrection, Christ has restored human nature in its function as the image of God. This restoration brings about the descent of the Holy Spirit, which fills human persons in whom the image of God has been restored through baptism into Christ. It is in this way, the Holy Spirit coming to indwell the Christian, that human persons are empowered to serve as God's image in His creation. It is through the indwelling of the Holy Spirit that human persons come to participate in the working of God in the world, to do the works that He has prepared in advance for them to do (Eph. 2:10). These are God's own works, and so God can look on them and declare them to be good. In its turn, serving as God's image by participation brings about growth into God's likeness (Phil. 2:12–13). It is transformative of human persons, both restoring and healing them from the effects of sin, and ever more conforming them to the likeness of Jesus Christ.

Creation, New and Old

THE FEAST OF CHRIST'S ASCENSION represents one of the most important liturgical moments of the Christian year. Unfortunately, it is generally underappreciated. Because of where it falls in the cycle of feasts, it is sometimes seen as a sort of epilogue to Pascha. In our modern life, it falls in the summer, which has become a time for vacations, time off from work and school and even sometimes church. It falls in midweek, which in the modern working world makes participation in it more difficult for many people. For ancient people, however, the Feast of the Ascension of Christ would have been intuitively the most important. The Ascension represents the culmination of the gospel that was proclaimed throughout the world by the apostles.

Key to understanding the importance of Christ's Ascension is the understanding that this does not represent merely Christ flying into the sky or going away. Before the Ascension, Christ promises the exact opposite (Matt. 28:20). While St. John's Gospel uses the language of departing and going away, it is in the context of the coming of the Holy Spirit, which will bring the apostles to know Christ and the Father even more intimately (see John 16:7 and following). Rather, Christ's Ascension is the feast of His enthronement in the heavens. As we will see, the basis of worship, of ritual, of proclamation, of sacred architecture, of iconography, and of sacrificial piety in the ancient world was the enthronement of God. This was true in ancient Israel's worship in the temple, and it was equally true in early Christianity.

Ancient Near Eastern myth followed a similar paradigm regardless of culture, with strands of these ideas found in Egyptian and early Greek myth as well. The central story or epic cycle involved a divine rebellion, against a previous most high god, that represented the forces of chaos and death in the world. In this struggle, often as an accidental by-product rather than a deliberate act, the world and humanity are created. Following a victory in this struggle, the winner, still conceived as the son of a divine father, was enthroned in a newly created palace temple generally within a garden and/or atop a mountain. This structure can be seen in the case of Baal, Marduk, Zeus, and many others.

Individual temples are instantiations of that primary dwelling of the god. Within the worship of those pagan temples, the architecture and iconography were designed to retell this story. The story was told and sung directly. The story was reenacted and participated in by worshippers through ritual. The sacrificial meals were a victory feast, a celebration at the enthronement of the god as king of that city or empire.

Genesis 1—2 tells a parallel story regarding Yahweh, the God of Israel, but with important corrections regarding His identity and the Creation of the world. The first and most obvious is that although Genesis 3 describes a rebellion, it is not Yahweh rebelling against a previous god, but rather a failed attempt by a subordinate to rebel against Yahweh. All the other elements, including those representing chaos (i.e., the waters) obey the commands of the God of Israel immediately and perfectly. Even in the case of the rebellion of Genesis 3, the devil is simply thrown down to the realm of the dead by a divine command with no struggle or battle necessary.

While the imagery of Yahweh battling the monstrous forces of chaos is poetically referenced in the Old Testament (Psalm 74/73 and Isaiah 27 are but two examples), it is notably absent from Genesis 1—3. Genesis 1 describes Yahweh constructing the entire creation as

His temple palace in which He will reign as king. The "resting" of the seventh day is Yahweh's taking His throne to rule over the entirety of His created order. The final stage of the construction of an ancient temple was the placing of the image of the god within it. This is corrected in the description of the formation of human persons and their placement within the temple elaborated in Genesis 2 to serve as Yahweh's image.

The tabernacle and the temple, then, were constructed as images of Paradise in particular, and the entire creation of which it is a microcosm. The structures, the iconography, and the worship of the tabernacle and temple were built around telling this story of the enthronement of Yahweh over all creation. The central element of the inner temple was the two massive cherubim who represented the throne of Yahweh.[2] The story of Yahweh's Creation of all things in heaven and on earth and rule over them was retold liturgically in various ways. The story was told through the worshippers' surroundings, through psalms and hymns, through the reading of the narrative, and through ritual re-creation and participation. This proclamation was against the reality that human and angelic rebellions against Yahweh, though futile, were still ongoing within the God of Israel's creation (Ps. 2). This proclamation ended with the prophetic promise that Yahweh would return to His creation in a new act to put an end to these rebellions and reestablish justice and peace.

Daniel 7 prophetically describes the solution that will come to these rebellions. Daniel saw in his visions terrifying embodiments of these spiritual and human rebellions against Yahweh and His rule. In describing their final end, Daniel 7 directly utilizes the imagery of the enthronement of Baal by his father El while again correcting it. In Daniel's vision, Yahweh remains enthroned over all creation as the

---

2   These gigantic cherubim, after the destruction of the Second Temple by the Romans in AD 70, were taken and publicly displayed in the Jewish quarter of Antioch as a display of Roman power.

Most High God. Another figure is portrayed who is also Yahweh but appears as a human. This second hypostasis of Yahweh, the divine Son, is victorious over the rebellious powers and is enthroned with dominion over all the creation given by His Father. Another cycle of victory and enthronement will take place through the Person of God the Son.

The apostles repurposed the Greek word translated as "gospel," *evangelion*, to make this understanding clear. In its extrabiblical use, this word occurs almost entirely in the plural, *evangelia*. This term referred to the proclamation of the victories of a Roman general or emperor prior to his arrival at a city. The "gospel of God" or the "gospel of Jesus Christ," then, is the recounting and proclamation of the story of Christ's victory over the powers of sin, death, and Hades, culminating in His enthronement over the entirety of the creation. Saint Matthew's Gospel ends with Christ being invested with all authority in heaven and on earth (Matt. 28:18). The longer ending added to St. Mark's Gospel ends with the proclamation of the gospel to all the creation (Mark 16:15) and His subsequent enthronement (v. 19). Christ sits at the right hand of the Father because He is not a rebellious son who overthrows His Father to seize power like the pagan gods. Rather, He is an obedient son who receives dominion from the Father as glorification for His victory (Phil. 2:5–11). Saint Luke's Gospel concludes with Christ's ascent into heaven (Luke 24:50–53). The Acts of the Apostles begins in the same place, adding the detail that Christ is taken to heaven on a cloud, directly connecting this event to the enthronement in Daniel 7 (Acts 1:9).

The apostolic proclamation of the gospel of Jesus Christ sees His Ascension and enthronement as the climax of His victory (Acts 2:33–36; 5:31; 1 Cor. 15:24–28; Eph. 1:20–23). Church temples are constructed and adorned with iconography to retell the story of this victory before that place where Christ sits enthroned with the altar as His footstool. The story of this victory is retold through hymns, the reading of Scripture, and direct proclamation. This victory is celebrated and participated in through ritual and the sacrifice of the Eucharist. Through the life of the Church, the proclamation of the gospel, culminating in Christ's Ascension and enthronement, is made to the entire world in preparation for that day on which the same Christ appears to judge the living and the dead, establishing justice for eternity in a renewed and transfigured creation.

CHAPTER 7

Atonement for the Whole World

B EFORE DELVING INTO PARTICULAR PASSAGES of the Scriptures regarding atonement in the Old Covenant and Christ's
atoning work in the New Covenant, a working definition of *atonement* is needed. How does this term function in the Bible? What did it
mean in the original languages of Scripture our English translations
derive from? In answering these questions, we must disambiguate
scriptural and early Christian concepts of atonement from how it has
been construed and misconstrued in Western theology and popular
Christian discussion. Many of today's more unexamined concepts of
atonement rest on shaky theological assumptions that arose centuries after the Scriptures had been composed. At best, these misread-
ings of the Bible are merely confusing. At worst they create a sort of
confirmation bias by which it is difficult to meaningfully evaluate the
Scriptures on their own terms. It is therefore necessary to clear the
ground before proceeding to how atonement was understood in the
religion of the first century AD.

The English word *atonement* was created for the purposes of biblical translation and has no earlier etymological history. Wycliffe used
the phrase "at one-ment" in his fourteenth-century translations of the
Vulgate into Middle English to convey humanity's being reconciled

167

or "at one" with God. In the sixteenth century, this was combined into the word "atonement." Because the word was coined, it offers little insight into the concept as it is employed in the Scriptures. Some modern English translations have moved to the translation "reconciliation" in many instances to parallel Wycliffe's original usage. In contemporary scholarly sources, "purification" has become widely popular, with "purgation" as another popular alternative.

The origin of the term is in the Hebrew word group *kfr*. Hebrew words have three-letter roots that can then be used to form related verbs and nouns with connected meanings. A form of this word creates the name for the holy day Yom Kippur, the Day of Atonement. The *kfr* root appears to be derived from a parallel Akkadian word that formed the verb "to wipe." In Hebrew, it can mean to wipe, smear, or cover. In the Hebrew Scriptures, this invokes a deliberate wordplay on, for example, the description of the Day of Atonement ritual (Leviticus 16). The act of smearing or wiping blood in the sanctuary wipes away sin. By covering the objects in the tabernacle with blood, sins are covered from the sight of God. Similarly, incense covers the appearance of God Himself within the sanctuary on that day so that the high priest does not see Him and die.

This action is central to all Israelite worship. The lid of the ark of the covenant is "the atonement cover," though often translated "mercy seat" in English. The later temple is referred to as the "house of atonement" (e.g., 1 Chr. 28:20). Despite the centrality of the term in ritual contexts, it is also used throughout the Hebrew Scriptures with regard to human relationships. It is used, for example, when Jacob is preparing to meet his brother Esau for the first time in many years and sends offerings ahead of himself in the hopes that they will "cover," or more literally "atone" Esau's face (Gen. 32:20). The *kfr* word group not only pertains to the restoration of relationships between persons and community in a general sense but also includes ritual elements aimed at removing or covering over the cause of estrangement.

In Greek translations of the Hebrew Scriptures, the word *hilasmos* and other related words are used for the *kfr* word group. This choice has some of the same limitations as the English term *atonement* in providing additional information about the term's meaning. There are no known instances of the word *hilasmos* in Greek literature outside of Jewish and Christian texts and their influence before the first century AD. For the first few centuries of its known usage, then, this term was only a Greek substitute for *kfr* words. Hilasmos was used in a pagan context for the first time in the first century, around the time the New Testament was composed, in Plutarch. In every case, Plutarch used the term to refer to sacrificial offerings intended to placate an angered or offended god or spirit of a deceased human. This represents a narrower usage than *kfr* words, though the translators of Scripture and later Jewish authors such as Philo freely used *hilasmos* to convey reconciliation in both divine–human and human–human relationships. In Jewish and Christian thought, unity with God and with fellow human persons are inseparable concepts.

Beyond the clarification of terminology, however, there are further preconceptions related to atonement, for the most part grounded in Western theology, that need to be cleared away. Much, if not all, of contemporary discussion regarding atonement in general, and Christ's atoning sacrifice in particular, takes place surrounding various competing theories of atonement. These theories represent attempts that are to one degree or another systematic to explain how atonement, and specifically Christ's sacrificial death on the Cross, works. Sometimes, rather than "theory," the term "model" is used.

Within Western theology, a shift occurred in the seventh and eighth centuries concerning how certain teachings and doctrines fit together and how particular mysteries of the Church function. This trajectory in theology, at least in the context of atonement, shifted away from *describing* what Christ had accomplished on the Cross and toward *explaining* how and why He accomplished it in the particular way He did. The most famous example of this turn is, of course, Anselm's *Cur Deus Homo* ("Why the God-Man?"). This book, written in the eleventh century, still bore the connective tissue of earlier theology inasmuch as it integrated Christ's death with the Incarnation. Yet it followed in the new trajectory in the ways it sought to explain the how and why of Christ's atonement. Anselm saw the purpose of Christ's death as satisfying the demands of God's justice over His injured honor. Only a divine Person could fully satisfy God's wrath, and so the Son became man. In our own day, scholar Simon Gathercole has championed penal substitutionary atonement, a model derivative of Anselm's, as superior to all other models because it is the only one that provides a "mechanism," or explanation, for how atonement works.

Views such as this are based on a series of presuppositions that collapse under even the lightest pressure of scrutiny. There is, for instance, no reason to assume that God's ways operate according to "mechanisms" intelligible to the human mind. There is likewise no reason to believe that the many metaphors used by the Scriptures and the Fathers to describe Christ's atoning sacrifice were intended to serve as exhaustive or exclusive explanations for what happened on the Cross, much less as "theories" to be debated and pitted against one another. But most important, perhaps, is this: there is no reason to insist that the problem of human sin required a particular response from God to remedy, as though He—the Sovereign God—were subject to some overarching system of rules or justice.

Rather, the Scriptures and the Fathers understand Christ's atoning death as the revelation of His divine glory. Atonement as it took place in the Old Covenant, as described in the Hebrew Scriptures, represents a partial and preliminary revelation of the glory of Christ, which comes to its fullness in His death on the Cross. The Scriptures and the Fathers meditate on what is revealed about Christ in these events and on what He has accomplished in these mighty acts for the sake of His creation, including ourselves.

The purpose of this chapter's discussion is to return to see the way in which this revelation of Christ is described in Scripture. It is not to promote one of these "theories" over against others. The only critique that will here be offered of various models for the atonement will be the implied critique of their absence from the testimony of Scripture and therefore from the ancient religion that the Scriptures represent. Such theories, merely because they have been advanced or even become popular, do not need to be disproven. Rather, those who would seek to advance them must prove their legitimacy. More importantly, they must demonstrate the validity of the assumptions that led to them in the first place, which are reflected neither by the Scriptures nor by the Fathers.

The Wrath of God

THE WRATH OF GOD IS an unpopular topic today. Much theological ink has been spilled in an effort to explain away the idea, despite its clear presence in the Scriptures and in the writings of the Fathers. An entire, fully developed complex of ideas in later Western theology, including not only God's wrath but also a particular concept of His justice and of penal substitution, is seen by many modern commentators as an inextricably linked whole. The traditional Protestant understanding, which evolved over centuries, holds that God is bound by His own justice to fully punish all sin. The Cross is then seen as the place where the Father's wrath is poured out as punishment on the Son. This understanding of atonement is caricatured in various ways and rejected wholesale by those who find the picture of God it presents repulsive. Too often, in addition to rejecting the doctrines that have accrued in Western thought, such commentators also cast aside the idea that God has any wrath whatsoever. To reject the teaching of

the Church that underlies these later ideas, along with the later erro-
neous edifice built on it, is to deform the Christian Faith. Many of St.
Paul's original hearers, in the face of teaching on sin, sought to justify themselves. Postmodern thought demands that the faithful justify God. If any understanding of God's wrath is abandoned, it makes
the concept of true repentance utterly unintelligible or at best a bland
form of self-improvement. Worse, it makes the Cross of Christ an
embarrassment once again, as it was to so many in the ancient world.

Though the "wrath" of God, at first glance, involves the feeling of
anger, it is not intended to express a passionate or emotional state on
God's part. This is an important distinction in breaking the popular caricature of the angry, vengeful God. What the "wrath" of God
actually seeks to convey is a particular experience of God by human
persons and those who witness that experience, not to portray God
as fickle or intemperate. An oft-repeated theme in the Hebrew Scriptures is that God is slow to anger (in Hebrew idiom, literally "long of
nose"),[1] highlighting the long period of patient mercy that precedes
encountering His wrath.

To better understand how and in what contexts human experiences of God are conveyed as His wrath, two interlinked concepts
need to be understood. The first of these is the concept of justice
or righteousness. Both the Hebrew *mishpat* and the Greek *dikaios*
describe the world as being in a rightly ordered state. Existence and
nonexistence and therefore Yahweh's act of Creation in Genesis 1 are
conceived in the Scriptures as bringing order to chaos. Humanity
was originally created to continue the work of Creation in cooperation with Yahweh by bringing the order and beauty of Paradise with
them to make the whole creation into Eden. Humanity, however, was
expelled from Paradise into this present world of chaos and violence

---

1   This idiomatic phrase for patience or longsuffering is reflected in depictions of
     the saints with long noses in traditional iconography.

172

under the power of sin and death. The great promise of the Hebrew Scriptures is that a day, most often called "the day Yahweh," will come when He will establish perfect justice in the whole creation (Is. 13:6, 9; Jer. 46/26:10; Ezek. 13:5; 30:3).

Although the Old Testament passages above present a rather horrifying account of the Last Day, they also contain important images that illustrate the nature of God's wrath. The first of these is fire, specifically one that tries and tests—purifies—all things (see Mal. 4:1–5). This fire has different effects, depending on the kinds of people it tries. For some, the fire of God's wrath is destructive, consuming them utterly. For others, it is purgative, allowing them to emerge from the Day of the Lord purified as gold from the dross, cleansed from the stain of their sins and transgressions. This latter group are those who are justified, made righteous, or made just. Rather than being consumed along with their sins and wickedness, they are purified from them as though through a refiner's fire. This burning fire is rightly described by Scripture and the Fathers as God's wrath.

Undergoing this fiery trial, regardless of which result it brings about for a person, is "judgment" in its biblical sense. In the New Covenant, this justification, being made righteous or just—being set in order as God's creature—begins in this life, in this world. In his prophetic ministry, St. John the Forerunner engaged this motif when he described the wrath to come as cleansing fire (see Matt. 3:7–12). He also, however, linked this fire to the Holy Spirit, and specifically to baptism with the Holy Spirit (3:11). When St. John stated that he baptizes with water, the language directly parallels his statement that Christ will baptize with the Holy Spirit. It literally describes being immersed or submerged in the Holy Spirit and—as St. John clarified here—fire. Repentance is therefore tied to, and the precondition for, the cleansing fire of the Spirit. It is not seen as self-improvement or growth but as testing and refining fire. It is bringing one's self under

173

judgment now to remove the fire of judgment on the Day of the Lord (1 Cor. 11:31).

The other major motif surrounding the day of Yahweh in the Hebrew prophets is what one could call distributive justice (see Obad. 1:15). Criminal justice is a form of retributive justice—criminals are simply punished for their crimes. Distributive justice is more akin to civil law—someone has been wronged, the scales of justice are out of balance, and action is taken to level them once again and make the injured party whole. It is aimed at restoring wholeness and relationship rather than punishment for the sake of punishment. The state of this present world, as it is still God's creation, still reflects His character. Humanity still holds the image of God within it. Therefore what needs to be cleansed and purified by the fire described above is not abject chaos and destruction but rather a broken order of creation. The distributive character of judgment on the Last Day aims to repair the order creation is still imbued with. It is a restoration of the balance and order God spoke into His creation in the beginning. This transformation will necessarily affect some positively and others negatively based on their thoughts, words, and deeds (Rom. 2:6; 2 Cor. 5:10).

Many scriptural categories express the two poles of the experience of God—reward and punishment, blessing and curse, vindication and wrath. Punishment, curse, and wrath are all ways of describing the experience of those who suffer loss in this restoration. This does not merely refer to superficial regret; it entails profound suffering. For the Egyptians, their massacre of the male children of God's firstborn, Israel, was rebalanced by the death of their own firstborn sons. For two hundred years of apostasy, the Northern Kingdom of Israel was scattered back into nonexistence. For 490 years of ignoring the Sabbath year, the Southern Kingdom of Judah faced seventy years of exile in a foreign land. One of the constant themes in Christ's own preaching is that this same sort of massive upheaval awaits humanity on the Day of Judgment (see Matt. 19:30; 20:16; Mark 10:31; Luke 13:30; 16:25).

This twofold understanding of God's wrath—purifying fire of judgment and distributive justice—helps explain the various punishments or consequences for sin in the Torah. The Torah never imposes suffering or torture to make amends for sin (although this was not uncommon in other ancient cultures).[2] Rather, sin in the Torah is resolved either by death or by exile—being cut off from the community—or by restitution. In either case, although the perpetrator may suffer loss, the objective is to restore the right relationship of justice. A thief, for example, was required to pay back five times what he stole (Ex. 22:1). This notion of restitution as a critical element of repentance (Luke 19:8–9) gave rise to the concept of penance in the Church. It also helped shape the Church's understanding of asceticism.

The wrath of God is the experience of judgment and righteousness; thus God's wrath is experienced in His Presence. In Hebrew idiom, what is generally translated in English as being in God's presence is actually to be "before His face," which is itself a reference to seeing Him. God is righteous. God is holy. He is surrounded by the fullness of His glory. To say that God is righteous or holy or glorious does not imply that these qualities exist apart from God. God is not subject to or judged by some other standard. Rather, just as God is love, He is also righteousness, holiness, glory, and so on. And so for Moses, to see His glory would be to see God Himself (Ex. 33:18–20). Likewise, St. Paul can say that Christ is the righteousness of God (1 Cor. 1:30–31). The experience of a sinful human person coming into the presence of God is dramatized in Isaiah's prophetic call (Is. 6:1–13). The prophet experiences his own undoing in encountering the righteousness,

---

2   The Code of Hammurabi, which preceded the Torah by several centuries, for example, frequently prescribes public beatings and various forms of physical mutilation as punishment for offenses.

holiness, and glory of God (v. 5). In order for him to speak the words of God, his lips must be purified by fire (vv. 6–7).

The Torah refers to God's bringing judgment on the gods of Egypt and vindicating His people as "visiting His people" (Gen. 50:24–25; Ex. 4:31). The day of Yahweh is, therefore, also referred to as the day on which He will visit His people (Ex. 32:34; Lev. 26:16; Is. 23:27; 29:6; Jer. 15:15; 27/34:22; 29/36:10; 32/39:5). In the prophetic timeline, the day of Yahweh would be preceded by the appearance of Elijah and would come first on Judea. Judgment would be exercised first on God's people, through which a remnant would be refined by fire. After this would come a period, the last days, during which the nations would stream to Jerusalem to worship Yahweh, concluding in Yahweh's judgment of the entire creation and the completion of His creative work.

As the New Testament authors saw it, this timeline had lurched forward in their day. Jesus Christ is Yahweh, and He had come to His people in Judea. His very presence in their midst brought about judgment. Most were cut off through their rejection of Christ; however, a remnant found repentance and justification in Christ. Following this, the Gentiles were added to this remnant, reconstituting the assembly of Israel, the Church. The apostles bore witness to these events and attest to them in the Scriptures. This means, as they attest, that we are now in the latter days, during which Christ rules in the midst of His enemies.

At the conclusion of this period, described by St. John figuratively as a thousand years in his Revelation, Christ will again visit His creatures to complete the ordering activity of Creation, already begun by Incarnation and Resurrection. Thus, He will judge the living and the dead. The word *parousia*, used in the New Testament for Christ's return and generally translated in English as "return," more literally means "presence." All creation will be brought before the throne of Christ. All creation will stand in His presence. All will see His face.

This will bring all the works of God to order and completion. Human persons will be either justified—purified by fire—or purged, losing even what little they may presently possess. For the first group, this experience will be reward and joy, but for the second, punishment and wrath.

This understanding of the presence of Christ is firmly embedded in the Church's understanding of the Eucharist. In the Eucharist, a human person receives Christ Himself into his own person. The presence of Christ, as has already been seen, can bring either purification or destruction, forgiveness or wrath. Saint Paul speaks of this when he describes the consequences of receiving the Eucharist in an unworthy manner (1 Cor. 11:27–34). The priest's prayers reference the purification of Isaiah described above (Is. 6:6–7). The prayer of St. Symeon the Translator[3] after receiving the Eucharist is a profound meditation on these themes. Repentance and the purification of our souls and bodies can be painful and difficult, but they prepare us to stand before the face of our Lord Jesus Christ and for the eternal righteousness, holiness, and glory of the world to come.

Propitiation and Expiation

DEBATES SURROUNDING ATONEMENT THEOLOGY OVER the last several decades have centered on two terms, *propitiation* and *expiation*. Propitiation refers to an offering intended to please or pacify the recipient. Expiation refers to an offering that purifies the offeror. Both of these terms describe the function of particular sacrificial rituals. There is not a conflict between the core meanings of these two terms. They have come, however, to be emblematic of the totality of theological positions regarding the atoning sacrifice of

---

3   St. Symeon's prayer is one of those found in the post-Communion prayers of
      the Orthodox Church.

Christ. Clearing away the accumulated theological baggage from these terms allows them to highlight two important elements of the sacrificial system described in the Hebrew Scriptures, which will, in turn, reveal elements of the Gospels' portrayal of Christ's atoning death. Rather than summarizing two incompatible views or options or theories regarding "how atonement works," these elements, along with others, convey ways of speaking and understanding sacrifice that together produce a rich, full-orbed understanding of what our Lord Jesus Christ has done on our behalf.

Both propitiation and expiation in the Scriptures view sin through an ontological lens. It is a thing that exists in the form of a taint, an impurity, similar to a deadly disease. Like a deadly infection, if left uncontrolled it not only will bring death but will spread throughout the camp in the wilderness, the nation, and the world. While this is true of sin generally, the presence of Yahweh Himself in the midst of His people in the tabernacle and later temple elevates this danger. The Day of Atonement ritual, for example, is instituted in Leviticus in response to the fate of Nadab and Abihu, the sons of Aaron who entered into the tabernacle unworthily in their drunken sinfulness and were consumed by the fire of God's holiness (Lev. 10:1–2; 16:1–2).

In fact, the entirety of the Torah's commandments seeks to deal with sin and related contamination so Yahweh can remain in the midst of His people. To be in the presence of God is judgment, a judgment for which Israel was not prepared. In His patience and longsuffering, God made provisions to allow Israel to dwell in His presence until the time of the coming of Christ. The failure of Israel and then Judah to follow them results in the departure of Yahweh from the temple and the removal of the people from Yahweh's land. The sectarian debates during the Second Temple period primarily surround what must be done vis-à-vis the Torah and the way of life of the people to correct the resulting situation. The Christian proclamation within this debate is that Yahweh has visited His people in the Person of Jesus Christ. Christ has fulfilled the commandments of the Torah (in filling them to overflowing) and accomplished what the people, of themselves, could not. While the Torah prescribed a sort of sin management system, Christ has dealt with sin once and for all, so that the commandments of the Torah now function, empowered by the Holy Spirit, to cure the disease of sin and transform human persons into sons of God.

Sacrificial ritual occupies a central place within the overall system the Torah prescribes, and it is in this context we see principles of propitiation and expiation. Expiation, as a term related to atonement, refers to the removal of sin. The danger to the community posed by sin and its resulting corruption is remedied by the removal of sin from those it has contaminated and ultimately its excision from the entire community. Because propitiation has become a loaded term of sorts, it has become popular to emphasize expiation as the entire function of sacrifice. The direct connection of expiation to sacrificial ritual, however, is tenuous at best. It is not uncommon, for example, for people, even scholars, to shorthand sacrificial practice by saying that before killing an animal, the priest would place the sins of the offerer, or the people as a whole, on that animal and then kill it. Unfortunately, this is something that occurs nowhere in the sacrificial system as outlined in the Torah, nor anywhere in the pagan sacrificial rituals of the ancient world, for that matter.

The one ritual in which such a thing occurs is within the ritual of the Day of Atonement (as first described in Leviticus 16). Within this ritual, two goats are set apart, and lots are cast (vv. 7–8). One of these goats is then taken, and the high priest pronounces the sins of the people over it (vv. 20–22). This goat is not the goat "for Yahweh." This goat is not sacrificed. In fact, this goat cannot be sacrificed because, bearing the sins of the people on it, it is now unclean and unfit to be presented as an offering. The goat is so unclean, in fact, that the one who leads it out into the wilderness is himself made unclean by contact with it (v. 26).

The goat is sent into the wilderness, the region still controlled by evil spiritual powers as embodied in Azazel, such that sin is returned to the evil spiritual powers who were responsible for its production. This represents the primary enactment of the principle of expiation in Israel's ritual life, though the principle is found throughout the Hebrew Scriptures (see Ps. 103/102:12). The New Testament authors see this element of atonement fulfilled in Christ as He bears the sins of the people and is driven outside of the city to die the death of an accursed criminal (as in Matt. 27:27–44; Rom. 8:3–4; Heb. 13:12–13).

A much more widespread concept that falls under the category of expiation is that of purification, purgation, and washing from sin, often associated with blood. This is not so much expiation enacted within sacrificial ritual as it is a result of the sprinkling or smearing of blood that wipes away sin. This idea is at the core of the terms translated "atonement" in Hebrew itself. As part of the sacrificial offering of the other goat, the goat "for Yahweh," its blood is drained and is used to purify the sanctuary, the altar, and the rest of the accoutrements of the tabernacle (Lev. 16:15–19).

The annual Day of Atonement ritual took place in addition to the regular cycle of sin and guilt offerings that take place throughout that year and had as one of its key purposes the cleansing of the sanctuary itself. While sin has been managed through these other offerings, it has left a resulting taint and corruption in the camp, which is especially dangerous in the place in which Yahweh Himself resides, and so this must be purified. Once again, handling this blood, which absorbs and removes sin, renders the high priest himself contaminated, and so he must purify himself before he goes on to offer the rest of the animal to Yahweh (vv. 23–24). This element of washing and purification from sin is found throughout the Hebrew Scriptures (see Ps. 51/50:2, 7) and forms much of the basis of the understanding of baptism beginning with that of St. John the Forerunner. It is applied to the operation of the blood of Christ by the New Testament authors (as in Eph. 1:7; Col. 1:20; Heb. 10:3–4; 19–22; 1 Pet. 1:18–19; 1 John 1:7; Rev. 1:5).

The term *propitiation* carries heavy theological baggage. Specifically, it has been used as a sort of shorthand for the systematic view of penal substitutionary atonement. The word *propitiation* is taken, by itself, to mean appeasing the wrath of God incurred by a person or people for their sins by punishing a substitute in their place. Attempting to import this concept into the sacrificial system established in the Torah is simply impossible. Much of the sacrificial system of the Law does not even involve the killing of an animal, even though the offerings it calls for are always food. There is a sacrificial meal involved in which the offerer and those bringing the offering eat and/or drink a portion of the meal while a significant portion, the best, is offered to Yahweh.

Animals that are going to be a part of these offerings and meals are, of course, killed as they would be before being a part of any meal, but the Torah pays no attention to the way they are to be slaughtered. Precise details are laid out regarding how they are to be butchered and how the various parts of the carcass and cuts of meat are to be parceled out, while their killing is not even ritualized. This likewise means that some sort of punishment or suffering on the part of the sacrificial animal was no part of the ritual. Even in the case of whole burnt offerings—which stipulated that the entire animal be burned and thereby given to Yahweh—it is not sacrificed alive but is killed first, unceremoniously.

Propitiation itself, however, has a much simpler meaning. Literally, of course, it means to render someone propitious, or favorably disposed. At its most basic level, it refers to an offering that is pleasing to God. Unlike pagan deities, Yahweh does not require care and sustenance in the form of food from human worshippers. There are, however, significant instances of Him sharing a meal in a literal sense (see Gen. 18:4–8; Ex. 24:9–11; and, of course, numerous meals shared by Christ in the Gospels). The more common language used in the Scriptures for God's appreciation for His portion of sacrificial meals is that these sacrifices are a pleasing aroma (as in Gen. 8:21; Lev. 1:9, 13; 2:2; 23:18). This same language is applied to the sacrifice of Christ in the New Testament (in Eph. 5:2 and the Father's statement that in Christ He is "well pleased").

In the Greek translation of Numbers 10:10, the language of memorial is used to describe the sin offering as its smoke rises to Yahweh. This language is applied to prayers and almsgiving elsewhere in the Scriptures (Ps. 141/140:2; Acts 10:4; Rev. 5:8). The party who is being propitiated through atonement may be wrathful toward the one who makes the offering (as, for example, Jacob assumes in Genesis 32:21 regarding Esau), but this is not necessitated by the language of propitiation as such.

Understanding the wrath of God as a function of His presence, of His justice and holiness, there is another element of propitiation that is directly relevant to wrath. This is the protective function that sacrificial blood and incense offerings serve in relation to Yahweh's presence. Part of the Day of Atonement ritual is specifically oriented toward allowing Aaron to enter the most holy place without dying, as had his sons (Lev. 16:11–14). An obscuring cloud of smoke, as well as the blood of a bull to wipe away the sins of himself and his priestly family, are required because, on that day, Yahweh Himself would appear in that place (v. 2). The blood of the sacrificial lamb, the meat from which was utilized as a meal at the Passover, served a similar protective role (Ex. 12:21–23). This is not protection from a loving God. Rather, it is a means provided by that loving God to allow sinful human persons to abide in the presence of His holiness. This same sort of protection language is utilized regarding the blood of Christ (see Rom. 3:24–25; 5:9; Eph. 2:13; Heb. 10:19–22; Rev. 12:11).

Propitiation and expiation, themselves being seen from a variety of perspectives, are inseparable elements of what atonement means in the Scriptures. They, along with other elements already and still to be discussed, form the cohesive understanding of Christ's own sacrifice on the Cross. These are not abstract principles, theological rationales or arguments. They are not constructed ideas used to explain mechanisms by which salvation takes place. Rather, they are highlighted moments of experiential reality. The core of Israelite, Judahite, and Judean religion was sacrificial ritual that brought about states of being and consciousness in its participants and the world itself. As ancient people, the first Christians understood the self-offering death of Christ in terms of this lived experience. The study of sacrificial ritual seeks to reestablish access to this experience of God through delineating the shape of that experience for our fathers in the Faith.

The Handwriting of Our Sins

ONE TEXT CITED OFTEN WITH regard to the Crucifixion of Christ in the Orthodox liturgical tradition is Colossians 2:14, "He canceled the handwriting in the decrees against us, which were opposed to us. And He has taken it from our midst, by nailing it to the Cross." This verse describes how, as the previous verse says, we who were dead in our transgressions were made alive by having those transgressions taken away. The language used here offers us yet another window through the Scriptures to understand the atoning sacrifice of Jesus Christ for our sakes on the Cross. Though it may not be apparent in English translation, this "handwriting of a decree" is bound up with language used throughout the Scriptures to describe human sin and its relationship to death.

The Greek word translated typically in this verse as "handwriting" is translated so based on a woodenly literal rendering of a Greek compound word made up of the word for "hand" and the word for "something written." Its most common usage, however, in the first century AD was to refer to a promissory note or, more casually, an IOU. Its attachment here to the word translated "decree," which refers to an official public document, moves the meaning toward the latter usage, a promissory note or a public document describing a debt owed. Saint Paul is therefore here describing the effects of our transgressions, our sins, as an accumulated debt that represents a claim against us. Christ, through His atoning sacrifice on the Cross, cancels this debt. The certificate of that debt is nailed to the Cross and torn asunder.

The imagery of transgression as debt that St. Paul evokes here is also commonplace in the Gospels. Depending on the Gospel, the Lord's Prayer asks for the forgiveness either of "debts" or of "trespasses." The Lord's Prayer as rendered by St. Matthew's Gospel refers to the forgiveness of our debts as we forgive our debtors (Matt. 6:9–13). Immediately thereafter, however, as an interpretation of the prayer, Christ says that if we forgive the trespasses of others, then our trespasses will likewise be forgiven (vv. 14–15). Saint Luke, however, phrases the Lord's Prayer as referring to the forgiveness of our sins as we forgive our debtors (Luke 11:4). The concepts of debt and transgression are so closely aligned in Second Temple-era thought that they can be used interchangeably. In describing the forgiveness of sins, Christ uses debt in several of His parables (see Matt. 18:23–35; Luke 7:36–47).

This understanding of sin as a debt, however, goes well beyond merely an analogy to aid in understanding forgiveness. Though not so in most of the cultures of our day, in the ancient world the concept of debt was closely tied to the institution of slavery. Slavery in the ancient world was not primarily an instrument of racial or ethnic oppression. Rather, it was primarily an economic institution. With no concept of bankruptcy in the modern sense, the means by which a debt that could not be paid would be settled was indentured servitude. A person would work off the debt by becoming a slave. As the head of a household, not only a man who had incurred a debt would be sold as a slave, but his entire family. Children born into the family would be considered to be subject to the debt incurred by the father and might live their whole life in slavery, attempting to pay it back or otherwise earn freedman status. Until that point, their lives and actions were not their own but were under the control of the person who held their certificate of debt and so had a claim to ownership of them.

In his Epistle to the Romans, St. Paul uses this language of debt and slavery to describe the relationship between sin and death (6:16–23). Saint Paul posits that the wages of sin is death. Death is the means by which the debt incurred through sin is paid, and so death, through the slavery of sin, projects itself back through the life of the debtor, expressing itself in the form of continued sin, which in turn increases debt and further enslaves in a vicious cycle (Rom. 7:7–24). Because this debt has been owed by every human person who has ever lived, each person dies for his own sin (Deut. 24:16; Jer. 31/38:30; Ezek. 18:20). Further, the devil is connected to this imagery as the holder of the debt. After his rebellion in Paradise, the devil was cast down to the underworld and given, for a time, dominion over the dead. Through death and sin, he has been able to enslave the great mass of humankind, with this certificate of debt as his claim over everyone who sins.

A critical theme of St. John's Gospel is that Christ, as sinless, does not owe any debt to death. In fact, it would have been impossible for Jesus to be killed. Rather, He chooses to lay down His life and, having done so voluntarily, is able to take it up again (John 10:17–18). Because Christ is without sin, the devil has no claim over Him whatsoever (John 14:30–31). He cannot even lay claim to His body through decay (Jude 9; Acts 2:27). Because He had no sins of His own He was able to die for the sins of others (1 Cor. 15:3). Because His life is the ineffable, infinite life of God Himself, it is able to pay the debt owed to death for every human person, setting them free from bondage to sin, death, and the devil. The devil is thus rendered powerless and deprived of even his kingdom of dust and ashes:

> Since, then, the children have shared in blood and flesh, He Himself, in the same way, shared in the same things, in order that through this death He might destroy the one who has the power of death, that is, the devil, and might set free those who, through fear of death, were subject to a lifetime of slavery. (Heb. 2:14–15)

This language of emancipation and redemption, of being freed from slavery through Christ's sacrifice, is also entailed by the paschal language surrounding Christ and His death. Christ died not on the Day of Atonement but on the Passover. The celebration of Pascha was and remains for Jewish communities a celebration of freedom from slavery—slavery to a spiritual tyrant who wielded the power of death. Saint Peter can, therefore, speak of us having been purchased by the blood of Christ, the Paschal Lamb (Matt. 20:28; Mark 10:45; 1 Pet. 1:18–19). Saint Paul can say that Christ has been sacrificed for us as our Passover (1 Cor. 5:7). Saint John the Forerunner's primary witness to Jesus Christ is that He is the Lamb of God who takes away the sin of the world (John 1:29). It is the Lamb who was slain that St. John sees seated on the heavenly throne (Rev. 5:6).

Redemption in this sense, from the power of death and the devil, is universal. On the Last Day, all will be raised from the dead, not only the righteous (John 5:25–27; Acts 24:15; 1 Cor. 15:52; 1 Thess. 4:16). Death has been destroyed in Christ's victory over it. Saint Paul can say that Christ is the savior of all men, especially those who believe (1 Tim. 4:10). The power (*kratos*) of death that the devil wielded has been taken away from him so that now all authority in heaven and on earth has been given to Christ *Pantokrator* (all-powerful; Matt. 28:18; Eph. 1:21; Jude 25). Every human person now belongs to Christ, their Lord and Master (1 Cor. 6:19–20). He now rules over all creation, over those who accept and embrace him as Lord and Master of their lives and over those who continue in rebellion against him (1 Cor. 15:24–26). In the end, every knee will bow and every tongue will confess that Jesus Christ is Lord (Rom. 14:11; Phil. 2:10–11).

The heresy of universalism (or *apokatastasis*), the teaching that every person will necessarily eventually find salvation, which has arisen from time to time in the history of the Church, comes from a misunderstanding of this universal element of redemption. What is said about the resurrection of the dead and Christ's dominion is then taken to also be speaking of entrance into the Kingdom and eternal life. The Scriptures, however, are utterly clear that the resurrection of every human person who has ever lived is a precursor to Christ's judgment of the living and the dead. "Do not wonder at this, for the hour comes when all who are in the tombs will hear His voice and come out; those who have done good to the resurrection of life and those who have done evil to the resurrection of judgment" (John 5:28–29). Rather than removing judgment from all humanity as universalists suppose, Christ's victory over death makes him the sole judge of all humanity (John 5:22; Rom. 14:4). No one but Christ exercises judgment over human persons, including the devil and his demons. They no longer have any claim. Christ is the Lord and so the judge of all.

The gospel of Jesus Christ is the story of His great victory over the powers of sin and death and the devil, culminating with His enthronement at the right hand of the Father with dominion over all the earth. This is a proclamation that brings joy and freedom in being set free and receiving forgiveness of debts. But the gospel includes the warning that it is Jesus, too, who will judge the living and the dead. This warning inevitably raises the question, "What must I do to be saved?" The answer to this question has brought people through the centuries to live lives of repentance and faithfulness within the community of the Church.

The Tree of the Cross

THAT OUR LORD JESUS CHRIST not only died but died specifically by crucifixion is vital to our understanding of how the Scriptures function as a whole. As an instrument of torture and death perfected by the Romans, a cross is an odd choice to be the focal symbol of a religion. Not only does it represent a terrible death for which the word *excruciating* was coined to describe the pain involved, but it was also a means of public humiliation. Crucified individuals died naked, on public display, exposed to the elements, and left to die over the course of what sometimes took days. The Romans often then left the bodies where they were to decompose, throwing them into massive graves only if and when they needed to reuse the structure for another crucifixion. It was both a means of execution and a way to deter rebellion by projecting Roman power. Roman citizens who received the death penalty were not crucified. It was the means of executing slaves and peasants. To peoples governed by the Roman Empire, the image of a crucified victim represented degradation, forsakenness, and abandonment. To members of the Jewish communities under Roman domination, it represented even more.

Deuteronomy 21 gives special instructions regarding executions by means of hanging a victim on a tree (vv. 22–23). While it does not forbid this mode of execution, it does stipulate that the body must be removed from the tree and buried on the same day of the execution, not left there, even overnight. The reasoning for this in the text of Deuteronomy is that the person who is hung on a tree is cursed by God—leaving the cursed body hanging on the tree will defile the land itself. Again, it is not the mode of execution that defiles the land

and is thus forbidden. Rather, in this text, it is the curse of God on the victim of execution that defiles the land. This curse is drawn down onto the person by the method of execution and then must be alleviated through providing the victim with a proper burial.

The most prominent enactment of this curse by the Israelites takes place in Joshua 7 and 8 in the episode at Ai, which mirrors the flow of Deuteronomy 21. Israel had been commanded to devote the city of Ai to destruction, and they suffered a blistering defeat. It is discovered that this is because a certain Achan had, in violation of Yahweh's explicit command, stolen certain treasures for himself. The Israelites were in Canaan to execute the judgment of God against the Canaanites there, not to plunder and pillage in order to enrich themselves. Achan's disobedience had led to Israel's defeat, and so in a manner parallel to Deuteronomy 21:21, they purified themselves from the wickedness by stoning the involved parties to death. After this event, the city was destroyed and its people put to the sword. Following the victory, Joshua hung the king of Ai on a tree. But even in the case of this Canaanite king who has been punished by God with utter destruction, Joshua was careful to remove his body and bury it under a stone monument before nightfall (8:29).

The curse of God that comes upon human persons because of their sin affects not only the person involved or even that person and their community. In the contemporary Western world, we think of sin in juridical terms and so look at God's curse as punishment. We associate God's curse brought about by wickedness with a person's eternal destiny after death. Israelite religion, as well as that of the Second Temple period and early Christianity, however, had rather what might be called a "biological" view of sin. Sin is an infection. Things tainted by sin are treated in the same manner and according to the same purity regulations as those tainted by disease or mildew. Sin and the curse that it brings can be communicated from person to person and infects areas and objects and even the land. It not only must be forgiven as a transgression, but it also requires purification.

When Adam brought God's curse on himself in Genesis 3:17, not only was he cursed, but the ground was cursed because of him. When the curse is more fully elaborated at the conclusion of the Torah in Deuteronomy 28:15–68, human wickedness is described as affecting the sky and the soil (vv. 23–24). It is likewise directly associated with disease (vv. 21–22). It is this association that produces the close link between healing and the forgiveness of sins throughout the Gospels. Much of the conquest narratives of Numbers, Joshua, and Samuel/ Kingdoms must be understood as control of a deadly epidemic.

Saint Paul describes Christ's atoning work in terms of the curse in his Epistle to the Galatians. "Christ redeemed us from the curse of the Torah by becoming a curse for us. Because, as it has been written, 'Cursed is everyone who hangs on a tree'" (3:13). The apostle's language is repeated in the liturgical prayer said, among other places, at the Proskomedia service: "Thou hast redeemed us from the curse of the law by thy precious blood." Relatedly, in Romans 8:3, St. Paul speaks of God having condemned sin in Christ's flesh because He came in the likeness of sinful flesh. It has been common for centuries in the West to read these references on a surface level as referring to a form of substitution. These substitutionary ideas, however, miss the point of the way in which sacrifice in general, and atoning sacrifice in particular, functioned in Israelite and Second Temple religion.

What the Torah and the other Hebrew Scriptures describe in narrative was enacted, made real, and participated in by the community through ritual. At the core of ritual is enacting future possibilities. Positive future possibilities are enacted to bring them to pass. Negative future possibilities are enacted in order to ward them off. Within most ancient cultures, the lines between religious ritual and ritual magic are more or less blurred. In Israelite ritual, however, ritual was aimed not at bringing about a change in deity or making God perform certain actions on the community's behalf. Nor was ritual viewed as grounded primarily even in the repairing of the relationship between God and the community, though this was a secondary effect. Ritual was aimed at the transformation of human life as persons and as a community.

Positive future possibilities were not guaranteed by correct ritual performance, nor were negative futures warded off as by a fetish. When Israel took that view in its ritual life, Yahweh was quick to call for an end to sacrificial ritual (see Amos 5:21). Rather, ritual was a participatory means by which the people themselves came to repudiate negative future possibilities and embrace positive ones, and this expressed itself in moral action. We as modern people take for granted that there is a connection between religion and morality, but this close connection made Israelite and Jewish religion peculiar among the nations.

The curses of Deuteronomy, the curse of the law, had two prongs. The first and perhaps most obvious was death. The second was exile and abandonment to slavery to hostile foreign powers. Both of these are seen in the curse placed on Adam in Genesis 3 and writ large as applied to Israel as a nation. These two fates ultimately befell Israel and Judah respectively. Within the ritual of the Day of Atonement (Lev. 16), both of these possible fates are enacted, using two goats chosen by lot. One goat has the sins of the people laid on it; this goat, as mentioned previously, is not sacrificed. It cannot be. It is now infected with sin and is thus unfitting to offer to God. As the people drive this goat out of the camp or city and into the wilderness by spitting, striking it with reeds, and taunting it, they are condemning and rejecting their own sins in the flesh of the goat. They are rejecting the exile that will result from their sin by expressing hatred for that sin. The other goat suffers death, being slain, and its blood is used to decontaminate the physical sanctuary and, through it, the camp or nation as a whole. The people are brought to transformative

191

repentance through their participation in the ritual warding off of the curses of death and exile.

The New Testament writings express that Christ's death on the Cross fulfills ritual atonement in various ways. Matthew 27:24–61 shows this through narrative. Saint Paul touches on it in the arguments of his epistles with examples already given. Hebrews expresses this through direct analogy (Heb. 13:12–16). All, however, see this ritual as having been fulfilled in Christ's actual suffering of these two fates. Ritual is then not done away with but is transformed and brought to a new fullness in Christ. The New Testament narrative of Christ's atoning work is enacted, made real, and participated in by members of the Church as community through ritual. This participation produces repentance, which brings about forgiveness, cleansing, and the healing of sin.

For Israel and Judea, ritual represented a curse postponed and a deadly infection managed. Christ through His acceptance of the curse has removed His people from it. He has removed the threat of death and ended the exile by restoring humanity to Paradise in coming, as God, to dwell in our midst. At the sign of the Cross, human persons come in repentance to repudiate and hate our sin and to be cleansed from it. This is made real for human persons in the ritual life of the Church and expresses itself in a moral transformation of human lives as persons and in community.

Not Only for Our Sins, but for the Whole World

FIRST JOHN 2:2 STATES THAT Christ has offered Himself as an atoning sacrifice "not only for our sins but also for the whole world." For most of Christian history, this verse has been used as a football in various theological disputes. First, it was used as a proof text against the Donatists, who saw their churches in North Africa as the totality of the Church of Christ. Second, its meaning was debated in regard to universalism, whose proponents saw it as endorsing their teaching. Third, beginning in the period of the Protestant Reformation, it became a key text in the debate surrounding the Calvinist doctrine of limited or particular atonement. While what St. John has to say to the Johannine community in 1 John may apply in various ways to these later debates, it is quite clear that none of these applications reflect the original context. Saint John was not writing against hypothetical first-century Donatists or Calvinists. Nor was he writing in support of some universalist notion. Rather, St. John is applying a consistent understanding of atonement centered around the Day of Atonement ritual itself to the sacrificial self-offering of Jesus Christ.

Paradise is the place where God dwells. After the creation of humanity, they were brought into Paradise to dwell with God and with the already created spiritual beings. Humanity was meant to grow to maturity and then depart from Paradise, bringing Paradise, the presence of God Himself, with them in order to transform the whole creation into Eden. Instead, by partaking of the knowledge of good and evil, humanity became subject to corruption and ultimately death. The first humans were expelled from Paradise not because of their sin and uncleanness alone but because for them to live eternally in that state would have made them like the demons, unable to repent (Gen. 3:22–24). Rather than bringing Paradise with them, they brought their corruption with them and lived in difficulty within this present world.

The first transgression, in the Garden, took place at the instigation of the devil. This pattern, of wicked spiritual powers influencing humanity to perform evil deeds, continued and intensified. This began with Cain, the archetypal wicked man (Gen. 4:6–7). In Second Temple thought, Cain is the first and preeminent sinner and wicked man. While his father was told that the ground was cursed because of him, Cain himself was cursed "from the ground" (v. 11). While Adam would bring forth food from the earth by the sweat of his brow (3:17–19), the ground would not at all yield its fruit to Cain (4:12). Unable to live by the work of his hands, Cain founded a city so that he and his lineage could create commerce, culture, and warfare.

What was true of Cain plays out in his genealogy (Gen. 4:17–24). The corruption of the world continues and culminates in the figure of Lamech, whose song to his two wives is emblematic of his sexual immorality and violent murder, exceeding his forefather Cain exponentially by his own boast. This moral corruption was paralleled by spiritual corruption (Gen. 6:1–7). In the interpretations found within Second Temple texts, this relationship, as with Adam and Cain, is causal. Rebellious spiritual powers are at work in and through human rebellion to corrupt and destroy the created order. It is the purification of the world from this evil and corruption that necessitated the Flood, as prophesied at Noah's birth (Gen. 5:28–29). Saint John directly references these traditions surrounding Cain and his lineage in regards to the corruption of the world in 1 John 3:12–13. For St. John, the whole world lies under the power of the evil one (5:19) through this corruption. But Christ came to destroy the works of the devil brought about in the world by human persons (3:8).

The name attached to the leader of the supernatural powers involved in this corruption in league with Cain and his descendants in Second Temple literature is typically Azazel. So, for example, 1 Enoch 10:8 says, "The whole earth has been corrupted through the works taught by Azazel; ascribe to him all sin." The use of this name serves to connect these traditions about the corruption of the world to the Day of Atonement ritual itself. The first of the two goats utilized in the Day of Atonement ritual is the goat "for Azazel." It is entirely possible that this was, at the earliest stage of the text of Leviticus 16, not a proper name but simply referred to "the goat who takes away." This is the goat into which the sins of the people were ritually placed by the high priest and that was then sent into the wilderness to die. In later Second Temple traditions, this was understood to mean that the goat was taking the sins of the people back to whence they came, to the evil spiritual powers who had inspired them.

The annual Day of Atonement ritual took place alongside the regular cycle of sin and guilt offerings. This means that it served an additional ritual function above and beyond what those sacrifices accomplished. The Day of Atonement ritual, indeed all the commandments of the Torah, are aimed toward preserving the holiness, purity, and cleanness of the Israelite camp and the later nation. Sin was seen to leave a metaphysical taint, a stain of impurity, on those who committed it and on the world around them. It brings spiritual corruption in the world. For God to continue to dwell within the tabernacle at the center of the camp and later the temple in the midst of the nation, not only must sin be atoned for through sacrifice, but this stain and corruption must be purified.

This is enacted within the Day of Atonement ritual. The sins of the people are placed on the goat and sent away, and the blood of the second goat is used to cleanse the sanctuary, the place where Yahweh Himself dwells, because this is the place in which that corruption and taint are the most dangerous. When the Torah was kept, it preserved first the camp in the wilderness and then the nation of Judah as holy and pure islands in the midst of a world that had been subjected to evil spiritual powers through sin and death. The people of the nations, ruled over by demons whom they worshiped, were unclean. Animals from outside the camp were unclean. Even physical objects were unclean and had to be cleansed and dedicated before they could be used in the sanctuary and then annually cleansed at the Day of Atonement.

The same literature that connects the corruption of the world in the earlier chapters of Genesis to Azazel and to the cleansing ritual of the Day of Atonement also envisions an ultimate fulfillment of that ritual. Texts such as the Apocalypse of Abraham, which has been preserved in Slavonic by the Orthodox Church, describe an ultimate eschatological Day of Atonement. This day is connected with the coming of the Messiah, in which not only the sins of the people will be cleansed, but the entire world will be set free from the corruption of sin and death. This is fulfillment in the original sense, that the pattern of the Old Covenant is filled to overflowing by what is accomplished in the New Covenant. This event will represent a fulfillment of the entire Torah in that what the Torah merely managed and controlled on a small scale, this latter messianic fulfillment will deal with once and for all.

That Christ's atoning, sacrificial death represents this fulfillment is ubiquitous among the New Testament authors. The Synoptic Gospels, and St. Matthew's Gospel in particular, present Christ as fulfilling the role of both goats through His suffering and death. Saint Luke in his two-volume work, his Gospel and Acts of the Apostles, follows the same trajectory at the pivot point from one volume to the next. The end of St. Luke's Gospel culminates in Christ's self-revelation on the road to Emmaus, followed by the continued praise and worship offered by the original Christian community in the temple.[4] Saint Luke describes the rededication of the people as a temple. This rededication is followed at the beginning of the Acts of the Apostles by the coming of the Holy Spirit, the Presence of Yahweh Himself, to fill not a new building, but His people. The sacrifice of Christ not only had purified and cleansed them to allow the Spirit to dwell within them but had also expanded the boundaries of the camp to encompass the entire world, such that Gentiles and even wild animals were no longer unclean (Acts 10:9–23).

Though this final purification of the world is accomplished in principle in Christ's death and Resurrection, it finds its application in the world of time and space over the course of the period preceding

---

4   This parallels the events of the Maccabean revolt, in which the climactic battle at Emmaus was followed by the rededication of the temple after it had been desecrated and abandoned under Antiochus Epiphanes.

Christ's return. That all food is clean finds its expression in the lives of the faithful when that food is received with prayer and thanksgiving (1 Tim. 4:4). For St. John, Christ came to destroy the works of the evil one (1 John 3:8). This finds its fruition within the community of the Church. "We know that we are from God and that the whole world lies in the power of the evil one" (5:19). Just as those who are, like Cain, from the devil bring sin and corruption and death into the world, so also those who are from God bear fruit of purification and life. Just as they actualize the works of the evil one in time and space, so also the one in whom the Spirit dwells brings the works of God into the world of time and space. God calls these works "good" because they are His works.

Saint Paul tends to speak of this in Adamic terms. The body of the Christian, as the result of Christ's atoning death, is a temple of the Holy Spirit (1 Cor. 6:19–20). This means that, as was the intent with the first created man, the Christian has the Presence of God within him as he goes out into the world. The Orthodox Divine Liturgy culminates not in the reception of the Eucharist, but in the dismissal. The faithful, having received Christ into their bodies, are sent out into the world bearing Him with them. The entire creation is now the possession of our Lord Jesus Christ, who wields all authority within it. We, as His assembly the Church, bring that rule and its effects to realization within the world as we receive God's creation, bless it, and hallow it. This includes the baptismal reception of the people of the world but extends also to every level of the created order, animate and inanimate. This is the work of the Church in the world until the Last Day, when there will be no temple because the whole creation will be the dwelling place of the Lord God Almighty and of the Lamb (Rev. 21:22).

PART FOUR

God's People and His Law

✠ ✠ ✠

CHAPTER 8

God's People Israel

T HOUGH "ISRAEL" IS THE NAME used for the people of God in both Old and New Testaments, as a nation Israel occupied a fairly limited historical span. Depending on one's dating of the Exodus, Israel—as a united people group freed from Egypt—existed for between three hundred and five hundred years, and only for the final century of that interval did the entity constitute an actual kingdom with a (human) king. After this, at the end of Solomon's reign, the twelve tribes fractured, and the northern ten tribes continued to exist under the name "Israel" for roughly two hundred years before its complete destruction at the hands of the Assyrian Empire. Even during those two centuries, the Northern Kingdom was better known as "Ephraimite" or "the House of Omri" to most of its neighbors, rather than as Israel. Nevertheless, the prophets' promises of restoration all concern the restoration not only of Judah (the Southern Kingdom) but also of Israel. Likewise, when the New Testament refers to the salvation of God's people, it is not only latter-day Judea[1] or the Judeans who are addressed but rather all Israel (see Matt.

---

1   After the return from exile, Judea (the Kingdom of Judah, or the Southern Kingdom, prior to captivity) was created as a Persian province, became briefly independent, and then ended up a Roman province.

2:6, 20–21; 8:10; 9:33; 10:6, 23; 15:24, 31; 19:28; 27:42; Acts 5:31; Rom. 11:26; Heb. 8:8–10).

At the Tower of Babel, God dispersed the nations and disinherited them, assigning their governance to angelic beings who later became corrupt and whom those nations came to worship as gods (Deut. 32:8, 17). God did not then choose one of the existing nations to purify and make His own, electing Israel from among the abandoned nations. Israel is nowhere to be found in the list of the seventy nations of the world in Genesis 10. Rather, God created a new nation for Himself, creating a people who, before His creative action, were not (Deut. 32:6, 10). When God revealed His name to Moses— "Yahweh"—it is in this context. Though it is impossible to determine with absolute certainty, the name *Yahweh* appears to mean "He who causes to be." The God of Israel, therefore, is the One who creates, the One who causes things to be that previously were not.

While Yahweh began this process with Abraham, Abraham's significance extends beyond his status as the ancestor of Israel. God promised to Abraham that many nations will come from him, and many do—Edom, Moab, Ammon, the Ishmaelites, and others from his family descent in addition to Israel. The further promise made to him was that all the nations of the world would bless themselves in him (Gen. 22:18).

The History of Israel in the Old Covenant

ACCORDING TO THE HEBREW SCRIPTURES, Israel came into being as a people and a nation at the Exodus (see Hos. 11:1; Ex. 4:22; Ezek. 16:4–7), specifically during the cycle of events from the Passover to the reception of the Torah at Sinai—from Pascha to Pentecost. While the Torah would later prohibit intermarriage between the people of Israel and their neighbors—whether Semitic or otherwise—the patriarchs (ancestors of Israel prior to Moses) did not consistently apply this rule. Yes, Abraham and Sarah guide Isaac to take a wife from "their own people." This meant that Isaac was to marry someone from Mesopotamia, Abraham's ancestral home, rather than someone native to the land of Canaan in which he sojourned (Gen. 24:2–4). Similarly, Joseph does not incur criticism when he takes an Egyptian woman for his wife, the daughter of a pagan priest (Gen. 41:45, 50; 46:20). During the four centuries spent by the family and descendants of Jacob in the Nile delta region of Egypt, living among other Semitic migrant peoples (called "Asiatics" by the Egyptians) and native Egyptians, there is every indication that they intermarried (Ex. 11:2). Some significant portion of this family became a part of Egyptian culture and religion (Ezek. 23:19).

When Moses was sent back into Egypt to redeem God's people from slavery, he began with the faithful remnant of the household of Jacob, whose name had been changed to Israel. As Yahweh struck Egypt and its gods with plagues, the region where these faithful Israelites dwelt was spared their effects (Ex. 8:22–23; 9:4–6, 25–26; 10:22–23). This also meant that the non-Israelite neighbors and faithless Israelites dwelling in the same region were also spared. When the time came, however, for the birth of Israel to begin with the final plague on the firstborn, those redeemed—purchased—by Yahweh out of slavery were not defined by the geographical region in which they dwelt or by their ethnic descent. Rather, they were defined by their faithfulness to their God, and that faithfulness was expressed in ritual.

The Passover event, including that its ritual celebration was to continue in perpetuity, was described in detail before the first Passover occurred (Ex. 12:3–20). The initial shape of the nation and the people of Israel, therefore, is defined by those marked out by the blood of the Passover lamb. This marker is not only initial but ongoing, as the celebration of the Passover allows future generations to participate in this event and thereby become members of Yahweh's redeemed people. Important to note is that when this people left Egypt, it included an ethnically mixed group of Egyptians and other Semitic migrants (Ex. 12:38). This mixed group of people is not mentioned later in the Torah as a separate group because these families are integrated into the nation and the people of Israel and became some of its founding members.

A prominent example of one of these people who was not biologically related to the person Israel (Jacob) and yet became a founding Israelite is Caleb. Of all the generation that came out of Egypt, only two men, Joshua and Caleb, entered into and took possession of the Promised Land (Num. 13:26—14:24). All the rest, including Moses himself, died in the wilderness as a result of various episodes of faithlessness. Caleb became one of the spies sent to search out the land of Canaan because he was a chief of the tribe of Judah (Num. 13:6). Caleb was, however, the son of Jephunneh, who is repeatedly identified as being a Kenizzite (Num. 32:12; Josh. 14:6, 14). The Kenizzites were a Canaanite people who already lived in Canaan at the time that Abraham had arrived there (Gen. 15:19). Caleb and his family were among the many Semitic migrants to Egypt during this period, and yet through his faithfulness to Yahweh and his participation in the events from Passover to Pentecost, he became a part of the tribe of Judah, even one of its chief men, and an inheritor of the promises to Abraham (Josh. 14:13–14; 21:43–45).[2]

After the people's deliverance through the sea, they arrived at Sinai, which became the mountain of assembly, the mountain of God

---

2   Evocatively, most of the named Levites of the first generation have Egyptian names. In the case of Moses, adopted into Pharaoh's household, this makes logical sense. But Aaron and his grandson Phinehas also bear them without explanation. Miriam, the sister of Moses, bears an Egyptian name that contains a theophoric for an Egyptian god. *Mry-mn* is the Egyptian name meaning "beloved of Amun."

on which His divine council convened. Moses, Aaron and his sons, and the seventy elders from the tribes of Israel were invited partway up the mountain to see Yahweh, though only Moses himself went and remained in the presence of the God of Israel for forty days (Ex. 24:1–2, 9–12). Here Yahweh issued a covenant (*berith* in Hebrew) to the newborn nation of Israel. This covenant follows the form of contemporary suzerainty treaties, which were issued by a conquering king to his new vassals to identify himself, describe what he had done for them, and define their responsibilities to maintain peaceful and prosperous relations with their king. Gathered at the base of the mountain, Israel agreed heartily with the covenant given them (Ex. 24:7). Connecting this founding moment of the nation to the marking out of the people at the Passover, this covenant was ritually sealed when Moses sprinkled the people with sacrificial blood, the blood of the covenant (Ex. 24:8). This event also became an annual feast to allow for the ritual participation of future generations as the Feast of Pentecost.

Yahweh, the God of Israel, kept His promises to the people by settling them in the land in their allotments. They lived for some centuries as a coalition of tribes before becoming a monarchy under Saul, David, and Solomon. In reality, this period saw not so much a united kingdom as the southern tribes of Judah and Benjamin able to project their rule over an increasing area of the northern tribal lands and peoples. This arrangement collapsed following the death of Solomon, with Solomon's son Rehoboam retaining kingship over only the southern territories of Judah and Benjamin. Jeroboam the son of Nebat, one of Solomon's officials, rebelled and formed a new northern monarchy, which took for itself the name Israel. Jeroboam himself set up a new religious system centering around idolatrous shrines at Bethel and Dan in the north. Later generations would seek to syncretize this idolatrous form of Yahweh worship with the Baal worship of neighboring lands to the north. Omri, the founder of a later northern dynasty, would purchase a hill and build the city of Samaria to serve as a northern capital within the territory of Ephraim, the largest and most prominent tribe of the north.

At no point in its relatively brief history was this Northern Kingdom faithful to their God or righteous in their ways. This resulted in the complete destruction of the ten northern tribes barely two hundred years after the founding of their independent kingdom (2 Kin. / 4Kg 18:9–12). The Assyrian Empire, as a standard policy, in order to prevent a future rebellion of conquered peoples, deported those peoples from their native lands to other parts of the Empire and brought peoples from those other regions to the newly conquered lands. The foreigners brought in to the region around Samaria intermarried with the remaining Israelites to produce the Samaritan peoples. The people of Israel deported to Assyria, after several generations of intermarriage and assimilation, disappear into the larger Gentile population and cease to exist as a separate people.

The Southern Kingdom of Judah survived the Assyrians, and although it went into Babylonian exile, a remnant was allowed to return after seventy years, establishing the province of Judea. Yahweh's promises to restore Israel in the latter days through His prophets were made specifically to Israel as a whole, not to Judea or the Judeans (the name translated "Jews" in most English translations of the Bible). These two terms—Israel and Judea—are not synonymous in the context of the promise of restoration, which clearly and specifically apply to the Northern Kingdom (Israel).

Jeremiah prophesied at the time of the destruction of Jerusalem, 150 years after the beginning of the Assyrian deportations and at a time when the Kingdom of Israel and its tribes had long since ceased to exist, speaking the promise: "I will build you again, and you will be rebuilt, virgin of Israel. You will plant vineyards again on the hills of Samaria. Because there will be a day when watchmen on the hills of Ephraim cry out, 'Arise, and let us go up to Zion, to Yahweh our God'" (Jer. 31/38:3–6).

In Jeremiah's vision, not only will the northern tribes be restored, they will worship their God in truth in Jerusalem, which had not yet occurred in their history. "'In those days and at that time,' declares Yahweh, 'the sons of Israel will come. They and the sons of Judah as well will go, weeping as they go, and it will be Yahweh their God whom they seek. . . . They will ask the way to Zion, setting their faces in that direction'" (Jer. 50/27:4–5).

Ezekiel, prophesying in captivity in Babylon, was told by Yahweh:

> Son of man, take a stick and write on it, "For Judah, and the people of Israel associated with him." And take another stick and write on it, "For Joseph, the stick of Ephraim, and all the house of Israel associated with him." Join them one to another into one stick, that they may become one in your hand. And when your people say to you, "Will you not tell us what you mean by these?" say to them, "Thus says Yahweh God: See, I am about to take the stick of Joseph that is in the hand of Ephraim and the tribes of Israel associated with him. And I will join with it the stick of Judah, and make them one stick, that they may be one in My hand." (Ezek. 37:15–19)

In the vision of the Hebrew prophets, Israel would be reconstituted when the messianic king came. "I will save them from all the transgressions in which they have sinned and will purify them, and they will be my people, and I will be their God. My servant David shall be king over them, and they will all have one shepherd. They will walk in My rules and be careful to obey My statutes" (37:23–24). This would necessitate not only redeeming the remnant of Judea but also reestablishing all Israel, including the northern tribes who had been dispersed among the Gentiles and ceased to exist. To do this would require a new act of creation by the hand of the God of Israel—or, as Ezekiel 37:1–14 would have it, a resurrection.

The Restoration of Israel

DESPITE THE DISSOLUTION OF THE Northern Kingdom of Israel, the prophets promised that God would one day restore and redeem not only the remnant of Judea but the entirety of the twelve tribes. This had been made seemingly impossible by the fact that the ten northern tribes had been "lost," not to history so much as to cultural assimilation. Over generations of intermarriage, the people of the northern tribes became indistinguishable as a particular people group. Their identity as a people had been dissolved among the nations, dispersed among the Gentiles.

This meant that the northern tribes could be restored only from among the Gentiles. Hints of this are seen already in the Old Testament. Following Israel's return from exile, those who assisted the nascent Judea in rebuilding were reckoned as members of one of the northern tribes. The Hasmonean Kingdom, after the Maccabean revolt, formed a treaty with the Spartans in which they are said to be descendants of Abraham (1Mc 12:21). To restore these missing tribes would mean that people such as Caleb and the mixed multitude who came out of Egypt alongside Israel would again have to be merged into a renewed nation.

It had been prophesied that the means of Israel's rebirth would be the reestablishment of the ten tribes from among the Gentiles. Israel is described throughout the Old Testament as Yahweh's portion, His inheritance (Ex. 34:9; Deut. 4:20; 32:9; Ps. 68/67:9; 78/77:71; 79/78:1; 106/105:5; Is. 19:25; Jer. 10:16; 16:18; 51/28:19; Mic. 7:14, 18). Nonetheless, after the Word of God has judged the gods of the nations, Yahweh will inherit from all of them (Ps. 82/81:8). These Gentiles are not naturalized citizens or converts to the religion of

Judaism; rather they, like Caleb, are integrated into one of the tribes of Israel, considered children of Abraham, and become heirs of the same promises.

> On the holy mountain stands the city He founded. Yahweh loves the gates of Zion more than all the dwellings of Jacob. Glorious things are said of you, O city of God. Among those who know Me I mention Rahav and Babylon. See Philistia and Tyre with Cush. They say, "This one was born there." Then of Zion, it will be said, "This one and that one were born in her." Yahweh records as He registers the peoples, "This one was born there." (Ps. 87/86:1–6)

The birth of this new people would, in turn, require a new Pascha and a new Pentecost in which the reestablished, regenerated Israel would be marked out by blood through the shared experience of deliverance. To this end, the New Testament writings portray the death and Resurrection of Christ as the new Passover and new Exodus. He is the "Lamb of God" (John 1:29, 36; Rev. 5:6; 7:17; 14:10; 15:3; 19:6, 9; 21:23; 22:1, 3). Christ was slain at the Passover (Matt. 26:2; Mark 14:1; Luke 22:1). Saint John's Gospel presents Christ dying at the same time the lambs were slaughtered for Passover (John 19:14). Likewise, St. Paul identifies Christ directly as the Passover Lamb who has been sacrificed for us (1 Cor. 5:7). Christ's blood redeems His people as at the Passover Yahweh redeemed the firstborn of Israel from the destroyer (Acts 20:28; 1 Pet. 1:9; Rev. 1:5). And as at Sinai at the first Pentecost, the sprinkling of Christ's blood marks out the people who receive His New Covenant (1 Pet. 1:19).

As was the case with the series of events between the original Pascha and Pentecost, which demarcated and created Israel as God's people, so also the new Pascha and Pentecost are participated in by subsequent generations, all of whom become grafted into God's people and inheritance through ritual. Saint Paul, for example, parallels the events of the Exodus with Christian mysteries. At the sea, the people were "baptized into Moses," and in the wilderness, they "ate spiritual food" and "drank spiritual drink" (1 Cor. 10:1–4). They were baptized not only in the water but in the cloud of the Presence of the Holy Spirit (v. 2). Baptism brings the Christian into participation in the death and Resurrection of Christ, while chrismation brings participation in the new Pentecost. Just as the Passover meal was instituted and proclaimed as a participation in the events of the first Pascha before those events took place, Christ instituted the Eucharist before His death and Resurrection. He describes His blood in the Eucharist as the "blood of the covenant" (Matt. 26:28; see also 1 Cor. 11:25; Heb. 12:24) in fulfillment of the blood sprinkled by Moses at Pentecost (Ex. 24:8).

Christ Our Passover

IT WAS NOT A COINCIDENCE that Christ's death and Resurrection took place at the time of the Passover. He could have chosen for it to take place on any date of the festal calendar or another date entirely. The writers of the New Testament not only record that Christ died at Passover; they emphasize it. The Scriptures see Passover as one important lens through which to view and understand Christ's death and Resurrection. In 1 Corinthians 5:7, St. Paul bluntly states that Christ our Passover has been sacrificed for us. Though St. Paul's identification is particularly clear and straightforward, references to Christ as the Passover Lamb, and His death and Resurrection as a new Passover, are ubiquitous in the Scriptures.

In Orthodox liturgical practice in English, we tend not to translate the word Pascha—it is simply the Greek word for Passover wherever it occurs liturgically. Therefore, we call our festal celebration of Christ's death and Resurrection "Passover" on a regular basis. The Old Testament establishes patterns of God's working with humanity and in His creation, including for our redemption. These patterns are then taken up and fulfilled, that is, filled to overflowing, by Christ. Though Christ's death and Resurrection, in contemporary theological discussion in the West, are most commonly discussed with reference to atonement, it is the Passover that is the primary pattern the Scriptures and Christian liturgical tradition use to interpret these events in Christ's life as filled with meaning and salvific power.

The overarching theme of the Passover is deliverance from slavery. It is quite obvious in the case of the first Passover that the Israelites were slaves in Egypt and that the Passover was the key event in their release from that bondage. It may be assumed then that they were slaves, broadly, to the Egyptian people, but this envisions the slavery under which they suffered as parallel to the slavery practiced by the Greeks and Romans or later chattel slavery in the Western world. This assumption would then lead to an understanding that the plagues, culminating in the Passover, represent God's wrath and judgment against the Egyptian people. This is not, however, the way in which the text of Exodus presents Israel's deliverance. Yahweh, the God of Israel, is quite clear that He is executing judgment not against human persons, but against the gods of Egypt (Ex. 12:12). Pharaoh considered himself to be one of these gods in bodily form (specifically Horus). The biblical text does not dispute this, seeing Pharaoh as indeed being the embodiment of the spiritual powers of evil in Egypt. It is for this reason that the Paschal canon refers to Pharaoh as "the persecuting giant."

The Israelites (and the Egyptians for that matter) were enslaved to powers and principalities in the heavenly places who desired evil through Pharaoh as their agent. It was Pharaoh who utilized the Israelites as slave labor in building cities and monuments to his own greatness. The power by which these dark powers, acting through Pharaoh, carried out this enslavement was the power of death. Only Yahweh can create and give life. At the opening of the Book of Exodus, creational language is used regarding the people of Israel. Their "becoming numerous" utilizes the same verb used for the lives that teemed in the waters and the sky during the Genesis account of Creation (Ex. 1:7). God's commandment to newly created humanity, reiterated after the expulsion from Paradise and again after the Flood of Noah, was to be fruitful, multiply, and fill the earth. The Israelites were fulfilling this commandment faithfully but were opposed by rebellious spiritual powers who stood behind Pharaoh. Pharaoh's response was to use death to prolong and reinforce their enslavement. First, he ordered all the male Israelites to be killed (Ex. 1:16). When this plan failed to work because the Egyptian midwives refused to participate, he gave a blanket order for male Israelite children to be drowned in the Nile (1:22).

The Passover event, vis-à-vis the final plague, the death of the firstborn, responded to this along several trajectories. The first is simple justice. Pharaoh murdered the male children of the Israelites with the Egyptians as willing accomplices; Pharaoh and the Egyptians experienced the death of their firstborn sons as balancing the scales. All the plagues, including the tenth, exhibited the powerlessness of Pharaoh and the other gods of Egypt. Every one of the plagues brought death. For a few of them, Egyptian magicians were able to partially mimic the plague, which only caused more death. But in no case had any of the gods of Egypt been able, as they claimed, to prevent the death being visited on Egypt or bring life to counteract it. Pharaoh and the other gods do not have the power of life and death. Yahweh, the God of Israel, brings judgment and wrath on the gods of Egypt and out of it brings new life, the newborn nation of Israel.

While this describes what God was doing in the Passover event, there is also the question of the ritual, both at the original event and in its subsequent annual practice. It must be noted immediately that there is very clearly no element of substitution in the Passover ritual. There is no indication that the lamb is being killed instead of a firstborn human losing his life. This is clear for several reasons when the text is read carefully. No attention is paid by the ritual text to the killing of the lamb. This means that its death is incidental to the ritual, not part of it. Rather, the focus is on how the lamb is to be cooked and eaten (Ex. 12:3–11).

This is in keeping with the norm for sacrificial ritual. The lambs are not apportioned according to the lives that are going to be spared. It is not "one lamb per firstborn male in a household" such that some households would need to offer several lambs and others would not have to offer any. Rather, the lambs are apportioned one per household (Ex. 12:3). Important to note, however, is that a very small household that could not eat an entire lamb in one night could share that lamb with another small household (12:4). Therefore, the apportionment is according to what a given household is able to eat, not based on the quantitative reckoning of firstborn children's lives that must be spared.

Finally, any sort of substitution would assume that God in His judgment and wrath required the death of the firstborn not only of Pharaoh and the Egyptians but also of the Israelites. There is no indication that this was some sort of requirement; rather, it was an action taken by Yahweh, the God of Israel, to publicly defeat His enemies, the gods of Egypt. Through their defeat, He delivered a people and made them His own. Furthermore, there is no intimation that this plague was aimed at Israelites and Egyptians indiscriminately. A major element of this plague is the establishment of justice for the Hebrew children murdered by Pharaoh and his people. Yahweh taking the lives of more Hebrew children makes no sense in this context. The previous plagues fell on the land of Egypt but left the Israelites untouched (Ex. 8:27; 9:4, 26; 10:23). Why would one assume that this one would fall indiscriminately? This not only is not implied by the text but runs counter to what the text actually states.

Rather, Yahweh, the God of Israel, Himself revealed what the ritual in its practice would do. To the contrary of the previous assumption, He stated that the Passover ritual would make a distinction between Israel and Egypt (Ex. 11:4–7). The previous plagues fell on all the land of Egypt, but not on the land of Goshen, where the Israelites dwelt. But the distinction that Yahweh made was not based on the region in which people dwelt or on ethnicity, but between His faithful people and those who wished to remain in slavery to the Egyptian gods. The Passover enacted this distinction through sacrificial ritual and through the marking with the blood of the lamb on the household's door. Israel was constituted, and the people living in Egypt became Israelites, through worship and obedience to Yahweh's command regardless of ethnicity. The faithless, regardless of ethnicity, became Egyptians that day. The faithful, regardless of ethnicity, became part of God's people Israel on that day and in subsequent generations through participation in the Passover.

Christ's death and Resurrection fulfill—and fill to overflowing—the first Passover. In the Passover, the people of Israel were set free from enslavement to spiritual powers of wickedness and from death in a provisional way on a small scale. Through Christ's death and Resurrection, the new Passover, those spiritual powers are defeated and thrown down once and for all, and the power of death is made powerless. Just as being an Israelite meant participating in the first Passover through ritual and obedience, being a Christian means participating in the death and Resurrection of Christ through sacramental worship and a life of obedience. As the Paschal canon proclaims, "Today a sacred Passover is revealed to us, a new and holy Passover, a mystical Passover, a Passover worthy of veneration, a Passover that is Christ the Redeemer."

The Assembly of Israel

THE GREEK TERM TYPICALLY TRANSLATED as "Church" in the English New Testament (*ekklesia*, which can also mean "assembly") is used throughout the Greek Old Testament to refer to the gathering together of the people of Israel. Its meaning is the same as in the New Testament—the Church is the assembly of Israel, God's people, which has been renewed and restored. The tribes formerly lost have been reconstituted from among the nations into which they were dispersed. The notion that the Church has "replaced" Israel or is somehow a "new Israel" is nonsensical once one understands the language the Scriptures speak. The Church *is* Israel. Specifically, the Church is the assembly of Israel, God's people, set apart to offer worship, praise, and sacrifice to Him. It is not that God's people have ceased to be an ethnic group or nation, but rather that they were never an ethnic entity, and only ever so briefly a national one.

Saint Paul takes this a step further and argues that this reconstituted Israel was God's plan from the very beginning and throughout His people's history. The God who "gives life to the dead and calls into being the things that do not exist" made Abraham the father of His people Israel and in so doing established him as the father of many nations (Rom. 4:13, 16–17). Abraham is the father of all those who believe (Rom. 4:11–12). Just as Moses came to redeem a remnant of the descendants of Jacob from Egypt who became the core of the new people of Israel, so also Christ came first to redeem that remnant within Judea (Matt. 15:24; John 4:22; Rom. 1:16). This remnant was gathered for Him first through the ministry of St. John the Forerunner. This remnant was preserved by Yahweh, the God of Israel, throughout the apostasy of the northern tribes and kingdom as exemplified in the ministry of the Prophet Elijah (Rom. 11:2–5). That judgment would reduce Judea to this remnant was always a part of the prophecy of Israel's restoration (Rom. 9:27–29).

The fate of the northern tribes represented a theological problem for Second Temple religion and later Rabbinic Judaism that St. Paul sees resolved in the fulfillment of the promises to Abraham in Jesus Christ. The larger part of the nation of Israel, ten tribes, had an

all-too-brief existence marked by continuous apostasy, which culminated in dissolution, leaving only the smaller Judah to exist inde-
pendently for another 140 years. Did this mean that God's promises
to Israel had failed or that He had dealt unjustly with them?

In response to these questions, St. Paul reminds us of Pharaoh,
whom God raised up despite his wickedness precisely so He could
display His power to the entire world (Rom. 9:17). To this might be
added the example of Judas, called by Jesus and given all the teaching, power, and authority of the rest of the twelve, though he was a
devil (John 6:70). God created Pharaoh and gave him a position of
authority and privilege despite His knowledge that Pharaoh would
abuse that power and come under judgment. Christ called Judas to be
one of the twelve despite His knowledge that Judas would later betray
Him. The judgment that came on these men, and on the Northern
Kingdom of Israel, was a result of their faithlessness. The blessings
they received before that judgment were the product of the mercy
and love of God for even His most disobedient creations.

Jeremiah had prophesied from the potter's house that Yahweh,
the God of Israel, shapes nations like clay, and if one of them turned
to evil, He would take it, crush it, and form it anew (Jer. 18:1–12).
Echoing this language, St. Paul proclaims that God was just in His
treatment of the Northern Kingdom, whom He patiently bore with
despite their wickedness, delaying the judgment that would result
from that evil. During this period of time, He not only delayed judgment but bestowed His blessings on them for three hundred years
before their destruction (Rom. 9:20–22). The purpose, however, of
this patient endurance of Israel's wickedness was to prepare to start
anew and create vessels of mercy prepared for glory, the renewed
Israel of God (vv. 23–24).

Later in his Epistle to the Romans, St. Paul uses another metaphor: the olive tree. Here, God allowed the unbelieving branches
of Israel to grow so that once they were pruned, they would create a

216

place for other, believing branches to be grafted in (Rom. 11:17–24). These wicked branches, the greater part of the originally constituted Israel, came to exist and were blessed despite their apostasy to create room within God's people. They were dispersed to the Gentiles as punishment so that when the Gentiles returned and came to fill their space, they would be restored. In the end, all Israel would be saved (Rom. 11:25–27). This is the fulfillment of the prophecy of Hosea, after Yahweh had declared Israel to be "not My people," that Israel would be restored when a people that did not yet exist would be called His people, while at the same time those who had been rejected would be declared to be His people once again (Hos. 1:10; 2:23; Rom. 9:25–26).

While Pascha and Pentecost have created the renewed, restored, resurrected Israel, this people in its fullness is still being gathered through the mission of the Church in the world. Saint Paul calls this body that will ultimately fill Israel "the fullness of the Gentiles" (Rom. 11:25). Saint Paul receives this phrase from the blessing of Joseph's sons, Manasseh and Ephraim, by his father Jacob. Ephraim, though younger, received the blessing of Jacob's right hand. As the largest and central tribe in whose territory lay the capital of Samaria, Ephraim was often used as a reference to the Northern Kingdom. The particular wording of this blessing, however, prophesies not only Ephraim's importance within Israel but that his offspring will become "the fullness of the Gentiles" (Gen. 48:19).

Christ Himself, likewise, referred to the time between the constitution of the people of Israel and their arrival in the Promised Land and the kingdom as "the time of the Gentiles" (Luke 21:24). It is for this purpose that Christ sent His apostles, the twelve and the seventy, after beholding Him risen on the mountain, to make disciples from all nations (Matt. 28:19). The latter days, then, this final period between Christ's Ascension in glory and His glorious appearing, can be described not only as the regathering of the nations in response to

Babel but also as the regathering of Israel from the nations. These are, in fact, the same event.

The New Covenant at Pentecost

ISRAEL AS A PEOPLE BEGAN as a mixed ethnic group from a core of the descendants of Jacob. Being an Israelite meant being marked out by the blood of the Passover lamb. Israel was delivered from Egypt through the sea, culminating in the reception of God's covenant at Sinai with the sprinkling of blood. Subsequent generations were integrated ritually into Israel through the celebration of the Passover and Pentecost within the yearly ritual cycle. After most of Israel had been dispersed to the nations, it was resurrected with Christ at the second Pascha by the reintegration of the nations around a core of the remnant of Judah. The culmination of this renewed Israel and its assembly as the Church of Christ happened at a second Pentecost.

The Feast of Pentecost, before the Pentecost of Acts 2, was the annual celebration of the original giving of the Torah, God's covenant with Israel, fifty days after the Passover. Pentecost was, in the Second Temple period, a feast of covenant renewal in which the faithful would repent of their sins of the previous year and recommit to the covenant made with their fathers. Among diverse other realities manifested by the coming of the Holy Spirit is the fulfillment of Pentecost in the granting to the restored Israel of the New Covenant.

That there would be a New Covenant was one of the central promises of the prophets regarding the regathering of Israel as the people of God. There are two primary prophetic passages that describe the New Covenant's coming and nature. The first is Jeremiah 31 (38 in the Greek text). The second is Ezekiel 36. In both cases, the chastisement and discipline suffered by Judah are described, while at the same time the promises of redemption and regathering are also extended to the tribes of Israel who have been dissolved into the nations (Jer.

218

31/38:5–6, 9, 18–20, 27; Ezek. 36:1, 8, 19–22). The promise is of a regathering from all the nations and resettlement in the land (Jer. 31/38:4–5, 8–9, 12–14, 16–17, 21–22, 27–28; Ezek. 36:8–15). Finally, the promise is of a new, transformative covenant. Just as the reception of the Old Covenant was the climax of the birth of Israel, so also it is the culmination of Israel's rebirth. It is therefore appropriate that at the second Pentecost there was a gathering of the remnant of Judea from the nations of the world (Acts 2:9–11).

As the people were being deported into exile under the Neo-Babylonian Empire, Jeremiah prophesied that the time was coming when Yahweh, the God of Israel, would issue a New Covenant to the house of Judah and the by-then already vanished house of Israel (Jer. 31/38:31). This would implicitly indicate that as the first covenant had been issued after Yahweh's victory over the gods of Egypt and the redemption of His people (v. 32), this new and greater covenant would be proceeded by a new and greater victory. This victory is the gospel. The core description of this New Covenant is that:

> Yahweh declares, "I will put My law within them, and I will write it on their hearts. And I will be their God, and they will be My people. No more will each teach his neighbor and each his brother saying, 'Know Yahweh,' because they will all know me, from the least of them to the greatest . . . for I will forgive their wickedness and no longer will I remember their sin." (vv. 33–34)

Here, already, is the first point at which the New Covenant is superior to the Old Covenant. The Torah was the product of Yahweh's desire to dwell among His people. What prevented this was Israel's sin and impurity. Because of this, humanity had been expelled from God's dwelling place in the beginning (see Gen. 3), and afterward humanity had become increasingly corrupt. This corruption reached a pinnacle that required God to purify creation from humanity, which was poisoning it with the pollution of sin, through the Flood (Gen. 6—9). Though God declared peace thereafter with humanity, the problem of sin and pollution had not gone away. The Incarnation, death, and Resurrection of Christ were already the divine plan for dealing with the problem of sin and corruption as well as death and the hostile spiritual powers. In the meantime, however, until that plan and victory came to fruition, a system was required to manage sin and the resultant pollution within Israel's camp in the desert and in the land so that Yahweh could continue to dwell in their midst in the tabernacle and temple.

The Torah represents this system in identifying sin and corruption and providing a means to manage it and the resultant stain on human persons and on the land itself. Israel and then Judah's failure to follow this system, allowing instead abomination and pollution to build to a point of crisis, resulted in the departure of Yahweh from their midst, destruction, and exile. The New Covenant offers forgiveness, the removal of our sins as far as the east is from the west (Ps. 103/102:12), and complete purification from its pollution (1 John 1:9). This represents the fulfillment (in the true sense, being filled to overflowing) in Christ of the sin management system of the Torah. For this reason, in meditating on this passage in Jeremiah, Hebrews sees the Old Covenant as now obsolete by virtue of being surpassed (Heb. 8:6–13).

During the exile, through the Prophet Ezekiel, the promise of the New Covenant was described as the Torah being written on the hearts of all people, through which they would all come to know Yahweh. This would be completed when He gathered together all Israel from "the nations . . . all the countries" in which they had been scattered (Ezek. 36:24; see also 11:16). Note that the exiles from Judah are all in one place, Babylon, such that Ezekiel can travel to them (11:24). The ten tribes of the Northern Kingdom had literally vanished through intermarriage and assimilation with residents of Mesopotamia. Yet Yahweh says that He will be regathering His people—all Israel—from the distant nations they had scattered to, to reassemble them as a new people and give them this New Covenant.

Again the themes of purification and cleansing are invoked to illustrate how God will cleanse and save this newly gathered people. They will have clean water poured over them, and they will be clean (Ezek. 36:25); they will be cleansed from their wickedness (36:33). Unlike the Old Covenant—which mandated the tabernacle to be cleansed of the people's sin once a year so Yahweh could continue to dwell there—the blood of Christ cleanses not a sanctuary but human persons (1 John 1:7) so that God may reside within them. The Holy Spirit came upon the apostles at the second Pentecost because of this cleansing and as the fulfillment of the promise of the New Covenant. "I will put My Spirit within you and make you walk in My command-ments and be careful to obey My rules. . . . You will be My people, and I will be your God" (Ezek. 36:27–28).

This means that the knowledge of God—that is, knowing God rather than just knowing about Him—is offered to every person who has received the Holy Spirit. Yahweh is not someone who must be taught about, who dwells in a (perhaps remote) temple, but rather One who dwells within each of His people. When the people assem-ble for worship, in the power of the Spirit, Christ is in their midst. The apostolic generation was purified and set apart through St. John's baptism and the ministry of Christ to receive the Holy Spirit at the second Pentecost and the giving of the New Covenant. Subsequent generations have come to participate in the New Covenant through the ritual of baptism, cleansing from sin, followed by the receipt of the Holy Spirit. This covenant is renewed continuously in the Eucharist, when communicants receive Christ's blood of the New Covenant.

Notice that even as Jeremiah and Ezekiel looked beyond the Old Covenant, they neither abolished nor rescinded the Torah but rather perceived through its lens something greater that is yet to come. The

221

Torah, for them, would be filled to fullness and then to overflowing. Both prophets promised that in the New Covenant, the Torah would be written on the heart by the Spirit and that this Spirit would keep the Torah within each member of Yahweh's people Israel. While the Torah could point to sin and prescribe means of managing it, it could not eradicate or overcome sin. These latter things, St. Paul states, could be accomplished only by Christ, who dismantled sin so that the Spirit could come to dwell within us and fulfill the righteous requirements of the Torah (Rom. 8:3–4). The Spirit being present within us naturally brings not only repentance through the knowledge of God and His commandments, but also good fruit that blossoms forth into eternal life (John 4:36). "The fruit of the spirit is love, joy, peace, patience, kindness, goodness, faithfulness, gentleness, and self-control. Against these things, there is no law" (Gal. 5:22–23).

In later prophetic literature, the blood of the first Pascha and the blood of the covenant at Sinai were referred to as the blood of Israel's birth (see Ezek. 16:4–7). Subsequent celebrations of the Feast of Pentecost were, therefore, a sort of "birthday" for God's people Israel. As the giving of the covenant was remembered, it was a day to take stock of one's obedience to God, and a day of repentance and recommitment. While it has become something of a commonplace to refer to the second Pentecost of Acts 2 as "the birthday of the Church," some have objected because the Church had already existed. It is true that the *ekklesia*, or assembly, of Israel existed from that day of the first Pentecost when the people assembled to be sprinkled by Moses with the blood of the covenant (Ex. 24:8). However, on that particular anniversary of that assembly, Israel was reborn as what we call today the Orthodox Church. Appropriately, therefore, the kneeling prayers of Pentecost represent a time to again take stock, to offer prayers of repentance, and to intercede for the living and the departed. Pentecost is a birthday, the anniversary of the covenant that created God's people Israel.

Israel, God's Inheritance

As St. Paul composed his Epistle to the Romans, the Jewish people, which had been the primary recipient of God's promises as a birthright, now found itself estranged, in large part, from those promises in favor of the recently redeemed Gentiles who already were coming to represent the greater part of the Church. Saint Paul elaborates on the fact that this pattern has happened before in the Scriptures, the disastrous effects of allowing this transition to evolve into enmity, and most important, the blessings that are promised when the Jewish people are reconciled to Christ and to their Gentile brothers within His body the Church. These particulars, however, raise the question of the general case. What does it mean that in the Old Covenant, Israel was elect, was God's chosen? Is this related to salvation? What does this say about all the other people of the world throughout history before the coming of Christ? And what does it say concerning the Church as restored Israel?

When St. Paul speaks of election in general and the election of Israel in particular, he speaks in the language of inheritance and birthright. His use of the story of Jacob and Esau in Romans 9 is only one such example. His description of salvation in Christ uses this language in Romans 8 (vv. 14–17, 29). He uses this language to describe the richness of the heritage that belongs to the Jewish people, Israel according to the flesh (9:4–5). This connection and this language are not inventions of St. Paul. This is the language that is used throughout the Old Testament to describe the promises that God made originally to Abraham (Gen. 12:7). This is the way in which those promises were understood going forward, at the time of the conquest.

The Hebrew *nachalah*, usually translated in English with the word "inheritance," is used 223 times in the Old Testament. Of these occurrences, forty-eight are found in the Book of Joshua to describe the land of Canaan as it had been promised to Abraham. Inheritance also constitutes a major theme in the Book of Numbers, as particular tribes and families are allotted portions of land as their inheritance to be handed down to future generations. Israel's chosen, or elect, status is therefore defined as their receipt of an inheritance from Yahweh, the God of Israel. There are many nations in the world, but Israel is the nation created by Yahweh to be the recipient of this inheritance. In Romans 8, St. Paul describes election as a linked group of processes (vv. 29–30) that ultimately create sons and heirs of God (vv. 16–17). The faithful are called, justified, and glorified. Later in Romans, these same terms are ascribed to the nation of Israel as further definitions of its status: election and calling in 11:28–29; adoption in 9:4; and foreknowledge in 11:2.

Inheritance in the ancient world, as seen, for example, in the case of Jacob and Esau, was mediated through the firstborn son. In the case of the patriarchs, we see that the firstborn son of Abraham and Sarah, Isaac, was the son who received the promises. In the next generation this would have been Esau but through a reversal came to be Jacob. This did not, however, mean that all the other children were disinherited or cast out of the family. Families were large in the ancient world not primarily through a large number of children but because they included the entire extended family.

Neither Lot nor Ishmael was Abraham's heir, but they were both members of the family and received an inheritance for themselves and their descendants within the land that was promised initially to Abraham. Likewise, Esau, though he forfeited his birthright through unbelief, was not removed from the family but received an inheritance for himself and his posterity likewise. Jacob, however, was the recipient of the fullness of the promises. Israel is referred to repeatedly in the Old Testament as God's firstborn, a people whom He created Himself (Ex. 4:22–23; Hos. 11:1).

Israel's status as elect or chosen, then, does not mean that the promises were exclusively for Israel, but that it is through Israel as the heir that the promises and blessings of God were mediated to the entire human family. When the promises were made to Abraham, they were made as gifts given by God to Abraham's seed, but, through these gifts, all families of the earth would call him blessed (Gen. 12:3). The promise to Abraham was not that from him God would make a great nation to whom alone His grace would be given, but rather that a multitude of nations would be born from him (Gen. 17:4–6). Among these nations that were Abraham's offspring, Israel would have the status of firstborn. Israel was not blessed for its own benefit only, but it was to be a light to the nations (Is. 49:6).

Though the temple of Yahweh, the God of Israel, was only one and existed in one place, where God dwelt in the midst of Israel, at the temple's dedication Solomon expressed its purpose as ultimately being a place where those of all the nations of the world would come to worship Israel's God (1 Kin./ 3Kg 8:41–43). Isaiah prophesied that when the Messiah has come, this will be realized as foreigners come to worship the God of Israel and the temple becomes a place of prayer for all the nations of the world (Is. 56:3–7). Israel was chosen and called to be the vehicle through which God would work in the entire world, not called to be removed from it. God loves the entire world, and He chose in the Old Covenant to express that love in and through the nation of Israel. It could therefore rightly be said that "salvation is of the Jews" (John 4:22).

Saint Paul describes a situation in Romans in which, whereas once it was Israel, the firstborn and heir, through which the promises of God were mediated to the world, now it is the Church, which was already coming to be predominated by Gentiles. He parallels this with Jacob and Esau. Though Esau was technically the firstborn, it was Jacob who was the father of Israel. It is now through the Church that the God of Israel works in His creation, as St. Cyprian of Carthage said in his famous dictum, "Outside the Church, there is no salvation."[3] This is not, in St. Paul's understanding, a situation in which Israel has been cut off completely and the Church has now replaced it. Nor is it a shift in firstborn status from Israel to the Church directly. Rather, St. Paul sees this change as having taken place in Christ. The heritage of Israel from the patriarchs to His birth culminates in Him (Rom. 9:5).

Christ, the only-begotten Son of God, is the singular seed of Abraham in whom the inheritance finally comes to rest (Gal. 3:16–18). Faithfulness for the patriarchs had consisted of living in faith that the promises of God would be kept. Faithfulness for St. Paul is thus faithfulness to Jesus the Messiah, in whom those promises have been fulfilled. Christ, therefore, is the One who truly has the elect and chosen status, hence St. Paul's constant phrasing that all the grace and blessings of God are ours "in Christ." It is Christ who fulfills the calling of being the light to the Gentiles (Luke 2:32–33). Membership in the family of Abraham and thereby a share in his inheritance is, for St. Paul, possessed by this faithfulness (Gal. 3:7). Those who do not maintain faith in the fulfillment of the promises in Jesus Christ, though they may be ethnically descended from Abraham according to the flesh, have cut themselves off from that family (Rom. 9:6). Abraham's family is also the family of God, and so the adoption of believers within the Church is adoption into a family centered around Christ as firstborn (Rom. 8:29). Human persons become fellow sons and fellow heirs with Christ (8:14–17).

Further, for St. Paul, Christ is the Firstborn of all creation (Col. 1:15). This is not to say that Christ came into existence at some point in time before the creation did. "Firstborn" is a status, not a matter of historical chronology. All the words of the Triune God, from the Creation of the world to its salvation, and beyond that to the eventual transfiguration of all things, takes place through and for Christ (1:16–20). The

---

3   *Letter* LXXII.

inheritance fulfilled in Christ is not a piece of land or a bodiless enjoy-
ment in an ethereal realm, but the entire earth, the entire creation itself
(Rom. 8:19–23; Heb. 11:16). The chosen, or elect, status of the Church,
therefore, derives from the elect status of Christ Himself. Saint Paul
moves quickly from the imagery of Christ as the firstborn and inheritor who distributes the inheritance to His brethren to the imagery of
Christ as head of the body (Col. 1:15–18). All the benefits of being chosen by God belong to the faithful in Christ, including adoption (Eph.
1:3–10). What this election in Christ means is that in Him the faithful receive an inheritance (Eph. 1:11–14). This inheritance comes with
being a part of the household of God (Eph. 2:19).

Chosen to Bear Fruit

ALTHOUGH IT MAY SEEM COUNTERINTUITIVE, the most
important biblical text for understanding the Christian gospel as
St. Paul proclaims it is the Book of Deuteronomy. This text sums up
the Torah in its presentation of Moses' final sermon to the people of
Israel before His death and their entrance into the land promised to
their forefathers. Israel had been redeemed from slavery in Egypt and
brought through the wilderness. As God's people, they had received
His covenant and now were preparing to receive an inheritance. The
title Deuteronomy literally means "second law." This doesn't mean
that it is only a reiteration of commandments that have come before
in the Torah. As a preacher, Moses was applying what had come
before to the new situation in which the people of Israel were about to
find themselves. He was telling them what the teaching of the Torah
meant for how they would now live their lives. He specifically wanted
to emphasize the responsibilities and requirements that come with
being the chosen of God and the recipients of His covenant.

Israel was chosen by God to receive an inheritance, and in the
Book of Joshua, following on Deuteronomy, Israel took possession

of it. Israel was chosen for this purely by God's grace. He chose to work through Abraham and his descendants. He chose to treat Isaac as the firstborn for purposes of inheritance, and Jacob even though he was the younger brother. He chose Israel out of all the nations of the world for His own possession, to work in the world through them. Israel did not earn this status. God did not give them the law in Egypt and then, when they had kept it perfectly, bring them out of Egypt and give them the land. As Deuteronomy 9:4–6 says:

> Do not say in your heart, after Yahweh your God has thrown them from your presence, "It is because of my righteousness that Yahweh has brought me in to possess this land"; rather it is because of the evil of these nations that Yahweh is driving them out from your presence. Not because of your righteousness or the straightness of your heart are you going in to inherit their land, but because of the evil of these nations Yahweh your God is driving them out from your presence, and that he may confirm the word that Yahweh swore to your fathers, to Abraham, to Isaac, and to Jacob.

This is the same language of righteousness and lack of a reason for boasting used by St. Paul in Galatians, Romans, and Ephesians.

This concept also lies at the core of the dispute between Christ and the Pharisees. The Pharisees believed that God would act and the Messiah would come when Judea once again became completely obedient to the law. They would earn the restoration of their inheritance. This made tax collectors and sinners bitter enemies of the people, who needed to be done away with, as they prevented the Messiah's arrival and the restoration. Christ, in contrast, tells them that He came to seek and save the lost. He had come not to reward the righteous according to the law and condemn the wicked, but to reconcile the wicked through repentance and the forgiveness of sins. This is the core of the Parable of the Prodigal Son, who has squandered his inheritance but finds forgiveness when he repents and returns. This is also what lies behind the older brother and his bitterness. Christ condemns the Pharisees for not truly understanding the Torah, which was so precious to them. Their beliefs were never a part of its teaching.

But this inheritance for which Israel was chosen is not the end of salvation; it is the beginning of salvation. God had chosen Israel so that the world would be saved through it. Israel itself would find salvation by fulfilling this calling for which they were specially chosen. The central portion of Deuteronomy, summarizing and explaining the law, was the description of how Israel would fulfill its calling. It described how they would live their lives as individuals and as a community in order to serve as a light to the nations that would draw all the nations of the world to come and worship Yahweh, the God of Israel. Saint Paul sees his own life in this context. He was known by God and chosen from his mother's womb (Gal. 1:15), called to proclaim the gospel of Jesus Christ to all the nations of the world.

This is also how he sees salvation functioning in the lives of those who receive his epistles. Saint Paul begins his Epistle to the Romans by proclaiming the salvation that has come to Christians by the grace of God, which they did not earn, for Christ died while all were still sinners. This is received by faithfulness to the promises received from God, which are true. But this is the beginning, not the end of salvation. The Holy Spirit, received at baptism, is the down payment on the Church's inheritance (Eph. 1:14), and He comes with a call on the lives of the faithful. Saint Paul continues, in each of his epistles, to describe how those within the New Covenant are to live, as individuals and in community, to accomplish the calling for which the faithful have been chosen by God.

Fulfilling this call is what makes the status as called and chosen by God actual, real, and efficacious. Just as being a physical descendant of Abraham was not enough in the Old Testament, so also having chosen and called status is not enough in the New Testament.

His divine power has granted to us all things related to life and
piety through the knowledge of Him who called us to His own
glory and virtue, by which He has granted to us His precious and
very great promises. . . . Make all effort to add to your faith with virtue. . . . Be even more diligent to confirm your calling and election.
(2 Pet. 1:3–10)

Saint Paul states that for the elect to find salvation, something else
must occur in their lives, and his purpose in writing his epistles was
to aid in this coming to pass (2 Tim. 2:10).

The product of a life lived as a Christian and lived in the community of the Church is compared biblically to fruit. Christ says, "You
did not choose Me, but I chose you and appointed you in order that
you might go and you might bear fruit and that your fruit might
remain, in order that whatever you might ask the Father in My name
He would give to you" (John 15:16). This same imagery is found
throughout the New Testament as the description of a true Christian
life and the purpose of the Church as a whole (Matt. 3:8, 10; 7:17–19;
13:23; Mark 4:20, Luke 3:8–10; Luke 6:43; 8:15; 13:9; John 12:24;
15:2, 4–5, 8, 16; Rom. 7:4–5; Col. 1:6, 10).

Fruit as a metaphor for faithfulness was not a New Testament
novelty. It is first found in Deuteronomy 29:18, which describes any
man, woman, clan, or tribe who turns away from Yahweh to follow
the gods of the other nations as a root bearing poisonous and bitter
fruit. Throughout the rest of the Old Testament, it functions prophetically to describe the remnant of Israel that will emerge in the last
days, which will, unlike Israel of old, bring forth fruit for God (2 Kin.
/ 4 Kg 19:30; Ps. 92/91:14; Prov. 12:12; Is. 11:1; 37:31; 45:8; Jer. 17:8;
Ezek. 17:8, 23; 47:12; Hos. 9:16; Joel 2:22; Mal. 3:11).

The close of Deuteronomy's sermon describes the judgment that
will come upon Israel. In Deuteronomy 28—30, death and life, blessings and curses are set before Israel, which will come upon them

based on whether or not they fulfill their calling. If they follow the ways of the Lord and bring about salvation in the world by actualizing it in their personal and communal lives, they will receive every good thing from God, and their inheritance will increase and abide forever. If they turn away from Yahweh their God, who has done these things for them, then they will receive curses and will be driven from their inheritance. All God has given them by His grace will be taken away if they abandon faithfulness.

In the same way, the conclusion of the gospel as presented in the New Testament in general and by St. Paul in particular is that Christ will return to judge the living and the dead according to their works. This, too, is compared in Scripture to a harvest of the fruits of the field. Every branch that does not bear fruit will be cut off and thrown into the fire (Matt. 7:19; John 15:2, 6). When the Son of Man comes in glory with His angels, He sends them forth to harvest the wheat and burn the chaff in the fire (Matt. 3:12; 16:27).

Christ as the Firstborn is the heir and recipient of all the promises of God and receives them as an inheritance upon His own death so that He can distribute them to the Church, which constitutes His body (Heb. 9:15–28). As adopted sons of God and fellow heirs, the faithful receive a share of this inheritance in Christ (Rom. 8:17). They receive the Holy Spirit as a down payment on the inheritance that is to come, in baptism. In granting His Spirit, God chooses us and places a calling on the lives of the faithful to bear fruit. The faithful strive to live in Christ and in His Church to bring forth these fruits, for the time of harvest is coming when all will give an account for what they have done in their lives with the deposit of the inheritance they have received (Matt. 25:14–30; Luke 19:12–27).

CHAPTER 9

The Law of God

I N MATTHEW 5:17, CHRIST STATES that He has not come to abolish the Torah or the Prophets, but to fulfill them. What is meant by "fulfilled," here, has important ramifications for how Christian communities understand themselves in proximity not only to the Law but also to the saving acts of Christ. If, by Christ's words, we understand that the Law has been taken care of or done away with, it effectively means it can be ignored. Yet, as Christ takes great strides to clarify in this same passage, not the tiniest letter or stroke of a pen will pass from the law until the end of this age. He adds that greatness in the Kingdom of heaven will be based on doing and teaching the commandments of the Torah, even down to the very least of them. However we understand "fulfill," then, it must involve doing and teaching all the commandments of the Law for the remainder of this present age in our world. Throughout history, Christian communities have found different ways of negotiating the meaning of these words, and more generally the function of the Law in the New Covenant.

In our own day, one of the more common ways to integrate the Law with Christianity—particularly in Protestant theology—is to divide the commandments into three categories, with some carrying more weight for Christians than others. This view, first set forth by

John Calvin, perceives the Law as consisting of civil, ceremonial, and moral commandments. Civil laws deal with the administration of the government and criminal justice systems of the nation of Israel in the Old Testament. Ceremonial laws deal with the sacrificial system and other parts of Israelite worship, as well as the rules concerning cleanness and uncleanness. Moral laws deal with moral conduct. For adherents to this threefold distinction, Christ has fulfilled the whole law, and consequently Christians are no longer bound by the civil and ceremonial commandments. The moral commandments, however, continue to apply to Christians as they always have to all human beings.

In this threefold conception of the Law, Christ's proclamation of "fulfill[ing]" the Torah is interpreted to mean different things in regard to each of the three categories of the Law (even though Christ is using the term in only one context). Christ is seen to have fulfilled most of the ceremonial law, which centers on the sacrificial system. His sacrifice having taken the place of the many animal sacrifices, these commandments no longer apply. The rest of the ceremonial law, such as the dietary laws, Christ fulfilled by keeping those commandments in His own life, and therefore they are said to no longer apply. Christ fulfilled the moral commandments in precisely the same way—by keeping them in His own life—yet they are said to still apply to Christians as a kind of universal moral system for all humans. Finally, Christ is said to have fulfilled the civil commandments by never being subject to their penalties, being without sin, and this too, in some unclear way, renders them all no longer applicable.

As tempting as it may be to parcel out portions of the Law that seem antiquated or irrelevant in Christ, however, this approach is problematic on several fronts. First and foremost, in Matthew 5, Christ is clear that every one of the commandments should be maintained "until the end of this age." It seems unlikely that by this last phrase Christ had meant until the Church begins, since by the time these words were recorded, the Church was already in existence. Indeed St. Matthew is directing his Gospel to the Church. Additionally, while civil, ceremonial, and moral may seem like logical or helpful categories, these distinctions are not found in the Scriptures, neither in the Torah itself nor in the New Testament. The Torah and its commandments are a coherent whole—there are no actual divisions in the text that make some commandments important for Christians and others obsolete. What divisions or categories can be assigned are only heuristic or descriptive.[1]

Just as the Law in its entirety is not compartmentalized into categories, the Ten Commandments—a kind of microcosm of the Law—is not subdivided, not even between the first four (which initially seem focused on the proper worship of God) and the final six (which seem more concerned with the proper functioning of human relationships). Idolatry is treated everywhere in Scripture as a moral offense, not a ceremonial one. The statements of moral offense in the Law are almost always accompanied by civil penalties that result from the violation of these commandments or ceremonial prescriptions for expunging the offense, or both. A typical commandment format might be, "If a man commits manslaughter, he shall be put to death unless he offers a ram and a young lamb as

---

1   Saint Paul applies even a seemingly obscure law directly to the life of the Christian communities that he initiated in his missionary journeys. In response to a reticence to provide for the livelihood of their community's leader, the apostle writes to Corinth and cites Deuteronomy 25:4, "You will not muzzle an ox while it treads out the grain" (1 Cor. 9:8–10). He affirms that this commandment was "for our sake." For St. Paul, this obscure law governing the proper treatment of animals not only was still in force but had spiritual significance—he uses it as an argument that the community at Corinth had an obligation to support their leaders in the work of the Church. If God requires care and compassion for animals who serve us, how much more does He require for the humans who serve our spiritual needs? The application of this particular commandment is reiterated in 1 Timothy 5:18 as a general principle.

a sin offering." This is a simple example to show how a single commandment could fall into all three of the categorizations Calvin and others have proposed. Christ never taught only one-third of these commandments were to be done and taught. But even if He had, it would be difficult to identify the strictly moral laws in the Torah with certainty, given that so many of them overlap in the complex web of human life on earth.

The alternative to picking and choosing which commandments Christians are to follow is to simply take what Christ said in St. Matthew's Gospel seriously. This does not entail following the Torahic commandments as they were followed in ancient Israel during the Second Temple period, or even by Orthodox Judaism today; neither does it mean to cast them aside as practically and spiritually irrelevant. Instead, it means to understand and follow them in a richer, deeper way—through Christ. In Christ, the Church is called to implement all the commandments in their lives in this more full sense. They have been filled full, to overflowing, by Christ.

The Scriptures' Understanding of the Torah

THE THREEFOLD COMPARTMENTALIZATION OF THE Law—commonplace in Protestant theologies—falls apart on close inspection because it applies a theological distinction to Scripture that is actually foreign not only to the Scriptures themselves but also to the mentality of Scripture. The three categories Calvin initially proposed were based, instead, on what had become an existing political-theological tradition and practice. In the sixteenth century, Christian civil governments in Europe no longer utilized the commandments of Scripture as the basis for civil law. Likewise, Christians no longer followed the dietary laws, and Christian worship looked very different from that commanded in the Old Testament. Worship was, within Protestantism, moving even further from the Old Testament model. Despite these discontinuities, however, the Christian moral compass still relied heavily on the Old Testament at least in broad strokes. The threefold division of the Law explains why a large number of commandments were and could be ignored. It originated as an invented theological distinction to justify a practice rather than an approach coming from the Scriptures to elaborate what belief and practice ought to be.

On the contrary, in keeping with Christ's statement in Matthew 5, every commandment of the Torah is done, taught, and continues to live in the life of the Orthodox Church. All the commandments—both as a united whole and in their particulars—continue to be relevant and applicable. They apply in a deeper, fuller sense because of what Christ accomplished in the gospel. Fulfillment is here seen as a lens through which the commandments are read rather than a veil, as now, knowing Christ, one can understand the real meaning, force, and life-giving power of the commandments.

To give an example of this sort of fulfillment other than as pertaining to a commandment, one need only look to the promise to Abraham that God would give to him and his posterity the land of Canaan. This promise was made in Genesis 15:18–21 to Abraham and later confirmed to his descendants. In Exodus and following history, God kept His promise by delivering Abraham's descendants from slavery in Egypt, bringing them to the land, and giving it to them. By the end of the Book of Joshua, it can be said:

> Thus Yahweh gave to Israel all the land that He swore to give to their fathers. And they took possession of it, and they settled there. And Yahweh gave them rest on every side, just as He had sworn to their fathers. Not one of all their enemies had withstood them, for Yahweh had given all their enemies into their hands. Not one word of all the good promises that Yahweh had made to the house of Israel had failed; all came to pass. (Josh. 21:43–45)

Although these promises were literally fulfilled and completed in the Old Testament (Israel entered and took possession of the Promised Land, for example), the writers of the New Testament still believed them to be living and active promises in the lives of Christians. The Epistle to the Hebrews states that the real promise to Abraham was of a heavenly city and promised land (Heb. 11:10, 16). Saint Paul frequently describes the Christian life in terms of the wilderness wanderings of Israel en route to the Promised Land, where there will be rest. Such references were not intended merely as allegories of or metaphors for Old Testament promises. Rather, the true reality and content of the original promises were now known and fulfilled through the revelation of Jesus Christ.

The Sabbath: A Pattern of Fulfillment

THE SABBATH IS ONE OF the most basic commandments of the Torah, one that Genesis describes as written into the creation itself (Gen. 2:2–3). While the Torah draws out particular applications of what the Sabbath means and how it ought to be observed, its existence as a structure of reality precedes not only the covenant given at Sinai but even the call of Abram from Ur. Nonetheless, the correct understanding and observance of the Sabbath became a chief issue between Christ and the Pharisees (Matt. 12:1–12; Mark 2:23–28; 3:1–4; Luke 6:1–9; 13:10–16; 14:1–5; John 5:1–18; 7:22–23; 9:14–16). In seeking to find fault with Jesus Christ, the Pharisees repeatedly accused Him of violating the Sabbath by performing works of healing and other signs.

Likely because of its centrality, the Sabbath represents a portion of the Torahic commandments Christ interacted with directly in the Gospels on more than one occasion. This in turn provides a framework for understanding not only the commandments from Christ's perspective but also what He means when He asserts He has fulfilled particular commandments. In Christ's interactions with the Pharisees concerning the Sabbath, He did not merely seek to argue that he had not violated the commandments. Rather, He expressed an entirely different understanding of these commandments and of the commandments in general. This, in turn, explains the way in which the application of these commandments has been transformed, through Christ, in His Church.

The various days of Creation in Genesis 1 and the acts of God associated with them seek to solve two problems that plagued creation almost from the beginning: formless chaos and emptiness (Gen. 1:2; see chapter 6 for a more detailed discussion). At the beginning of God's creative activity, the earth is formless and empty. In three days, He sets the earth in order by dividing the light from darkness, sky from sea, and sea from dry land. In three days, He fills the heavens with lights, the skies and seas with life, and finally the dry land with life. God is then enthroned in the temple that He has constructed and reigns from His rest. The observance of the Sabbath at the end of the week was then, for Israel, participation in the rest and reign of her God Yahweh and an anticipation of the rest that awaited her people at the end.

Already within Genesis 1, however, there is an indication that the work of setting the creation in order and filling it with life was not complete. Newly created humanity was commanded to "fill the earth and subdue it" (Gen. 1:28). These two commands parallel the two problems expressed in Genesis 1:2. While the first Adam failed in this mission through his rebellion, the second Adam—Christ—fulfills them. Christ points to this understanding when questioned by the Pharisees (John 5:17), namely that Yahweh's work of Creation was not yet finished even in the day of His earthly ministry. The Father was working even until that very day, and there was, for Christ, no rest until that labor was complete.

It is this completion to which Christ points later in St. John's Gospel as He gives up His life on the Cross, saying, "It is finished" (John

19:30). The Greek verb here used by St. John is the same verb used in Genesis 2:1 at the completion of the work of Creation, leading to God's rest. Christ, therefore, rests in the Tomb on the seventh day of the week, fulfilling the Sabbath. In three days He completes the work of Creation, rising again on the first day of the week. The Sabbath was, thereby, fulfilled.

The first day of the week, then, becomes the Lord's Day. It is the day of Resurrection. Rather than participating in the reign of Yahweh as participation in future rest, the people of God now participate in the Resurrection of Christ in anticipation of their own resurrection and eternal life in the world to come. Everything that was true of the Sabbath is true of the Lord's Day, only more so. All the commandments regarding the Sabbath find their fullness in the Lord's Day and in the worship of the Father in Spirit and in Truth. Creation is complete, and a new creation has begun with the coming of an eighth day. The Sabbath is not abolished but fulfilled.

The Council of Jerusalem

ACTS 15 PRESENTS THE PROCEEDINGS of what has become known as the Council of Jerusalem. This apostolic gathering became the paradigm for future Church councils and is considered to be central to our understanding of how the apostles viewed the continued relevance, or irrelevance, of the commandments of the Torah to the life of the Church. A group of Pharisees who had embraced Jesus as the Messiah was putting forth the argument that the Gentiles, who were by that time entering into the nascent Christian communities en masse, should be subject not just to the Old Covenant law but to their Pharisaic interpretation thereof.

The apostles who gathered—prominently Ss. Paul, Peter, and James—issued a letter against this position in which only four broad commandments were to be applied to the new Gentile faithful. This event and the passage that describes it have become a rhetorical tool for arguments of all kinds that wish to marginalize Old Testament texts. More recently, it has been deployed by those attempting to overturn the Church's historic teaching regarding human sexuality. Prominent figures state that the Council of Jerusalem decided that the law doesn't apply anymore for Christians.

First, context is necessary. The apostles were in agreement that the influx of Gentiles coming to worship the God of Israel was the result of an act of God in the Holy Spirit. They affirm as much in their statements in this chapter and that this act was prophesied in the Old Testament Scriptures. Saint James quotes here from Amos, but the inclusion of the Gentiles is prophesied throughout the Old Testament prophetic books, beginning with the prophecy regarding Noah's sons Shem and Japheth in Genesis. It is, for example, a major theme in Isaiah, as in 56:3–7, 58:6–12, 60:1–3, and 66:18–23. In addition to all that they had already seen fulfilled in Christ, the apostles were now seeing these prophecies fulfilled in their time as well.

To understand the apostles' understanding of the law, in this case it is perhaps best to begin with the four commandments issued by this council as applying to the entire Christian community, whether Jew or Gentile. Often when Acts 15 and the Council of Jerusalem are referenced rhetorically, these commandments are ignored, considered quaint, or otherwise not seriously considered. After all, it is said, two of them, concerning blood and meat with blood in it, are ignored by contemporary Christians. It is often said that St. Paul publicly disregarded the commandment against food offered to idols, though a careful reading of all of St. Paul's statements on the issue reveals otherwise. This leaves for them only the fourth of the commands, sexual immorality, which modern readers then see as suitably vague and malleable. These four commandments, however, are not arbitrary, cultural, or selected without a particular reason.

Leviticus 17—26 is often referred to as the "Holiness Code." It represents a series of commandments, directed to the forming nation of Israel, that if kept will allow the people of Israel to continue to dwell in their new land rather than being vomited out of it like the Canaanites before them. These sections of commandments are, for the most part, prefaced with Yahweh telling Moses to "Speak to the sons of Israel, saying . . ." These are commandments for the people of Israel, the keeping of which will separate and distinguish them from every other nation on earth. The Israelites are never commanded to enforce these commandments on the other nations of the world.[2] Rather, by keeping them, they are to serve as a light to the other nations, which will draw them to also worship Israel's God. And so, the dietary laws of Leviticus 11 are never applied to those who are not Israelites, nor are the laws concerning childbirth in Leviticus 12.

There are, however, a few passages within the Holiness Code that reflect something different. The eating of blood is discussed within the context of sacrificial regulations and therefore within a context of pagan worship in Leviticus 17. When the eating of blood, or meat with blood in it, is discussed in verses 10–14, the commandment is given to the house of Israel *and* to the foreigners who dwell among them. Anyone from either group who violates the commandment will be cut off. There is no prohibition in Leviticus 11 of foreigners eating unclean animals, but there is here a strict command against those foreigners eating blood.

Likewise, Leviticus 18 gives a variety of commandments regarding human sexuality, which are again applied to all the Israelite nation and to foreigners who dwell among them. Further, the reason given for this expansion of the commandment is that sexual immorality defiles the land itself, and therefore the land will vomit them

---

2   This represents a major difference between Israelite and Islamic understandings of law.

out if this sin is tolerated within it (vv. 26–28). Again, in chapter 20, regarding idolatry in general and Molech in particular, the commandment is given to the sons of Israel and the foreigners who dwell with them (vv. 2–5). Within Leviticus, these four commandments are singled out as applying not only to Israelites but also to anyone who is going to dwell among them.

A close reading of Leviticus reveals that the apostles were doing the exact opposite of saying that the Torah doesn't apply to Christians. Rather, they were proclaiming that a very literal reading of the Torah will be the basis for the structure of the life of the Church community just as it was the basis for the formation of the nation of Israel. The Gentiles who come to worship Christ do not become Jewish by virtue of coming to dwell in Israel. They remain Greeks or Romans or Egyptians or Syrians. But in order to be a member of the community of God's people and not draw the wrath of God down on the community, they must refrain from all idolatry and sexual immorality. Further, the apostles' interpretation here means that what is meant by sexual immorality in this apostolic proclamation is not vague or subject to interpretation. Leviticus 18 describes in detail what constitutes sexual immorality for the Christian community. Saint James does not feel the need to elaborate further because, as he says after listing these commands, the Torah has been proclaimed in every city of the world through the synagogues, and so the Gentiles who receive his letter will know and understand what this entails (Acts 15:21).

The core of this understanding, that idolatry and sexual immorality, in particular, cannot be tolerated within the Christian community, can be seen in the practice of Christian communities throughout the history of the Orthodox Church. It lies behind the emphasis on virginity and the withdrawal from pagan public life in the early persecuted Church. It lies behind St. Constantine's dismantling of the public sacrificial system as one of his first acts after his conversion. It lies behind the de-paganization of the Empire begun under Theodosius. It lies behind the prohibitions of sexual immorality in St. Justinian's *Nomocanon*, which explicitly uses the language of the land vomiting out the people if it is defiled by these sins.

Far from proclaiming that the Law no longer applies to Christians, the Council of Jerusalem in Acts 15 directly, strictly, and literally applies the Torah to the life of the Christian Church. The Law is not here rejected, but established. The dispute it resolved was not between a pro-Torah and an anti-Torah party but instead concerned how the Torah should be interpreted, understood, and applied in light of the revelation of Jesus Christ.

Unclean Foods

CHRISTIAN COMMUNITIES VERY QUICKLY BECAME composed of a majority of Gentiles and ceased following the dietary laws of the Old Testament. The reasons most modern Christians give for no longer following these commandments are that they are from a category of commandments that no longer apply, or that Acts 15 states that Christians do not have to follow them. Both of these ideas have been shown not to be true. Why is it, then, that Christians do not follow the kosher laws regarding food in the Old Testament? Not only do they not strictly keep these dietary laws, but many of the foods that Orthodox Christians are allowed to eat during fast periods were considered unclean under the commandments of the Torah.

It must first be said that there is no good evidence that the apostles, including St. Paul, stopped following these dietary laws during their earthly lives. There is some, albeit slight, evidence that they did continue to follow them. It is absolutely clear that they did not impose these food regulations on the Christian communities they established throughout the world. The New Testament documents show that the apostles had come to a different understanding of cleanness and uncleanness, and this included food.

Acts 10 is the primary passage that deals with the unclean status of animals used for food. Just before he was invited to the home of Cornelius, a Roman centurion and God-fearer, St. Peter received a vision in which he is commanded to kill and eat a variety of unclean species. He protests that these are unclean animals. The response from heaven is that he must "not call unclean what [God] has made clean." The thrust of this passage is to communicate to St. Peter that the Gentiles are no longer unclean and that he can go into Cornelius's home. Further, the apostles, in general, can travel and preach the gospel to the nations without concern of becoming unclean through contact with their people. For this imagery to effectively communicate the message, however, the underlying principle—that God has now made these animals and the Gentiles clean—must be true. What is changed here is not the status of the commandments, but the formerly unclean status of the Gentiles and animals.

To understand how the Gentiles and these animals were made clean, it is best to begin with how they became unclean in the first place. Certainly, the animals were not unclean when God created them. Jews and Gentiles were descended from the same humans whom God had created and so were likewise not created unclean. At the time of the fall into sin, in Genesis 3, Adam was told, "Cursed is the ground because of you" (v. 17). Human sin tainted the physical world around them. The prophecy in Genesis 5 makes it clear that God was using the Flood of Noah to save the created world from the sin of human beings.

Within the Law itself, it is important to note that on the Day of Atonement, there are two separate elements as described in Leviticus 16. Atonement is first made (by a sin offering) for Aaron's sins and for the sins of the people, then the blood is taken to make atonement for the sanctuary itself, to purify the physical sanctuary, and by extension the Israelite camp, from the uncleanness of the people (Lev. 16:19). This uncleanness must be removed for God to remain present in the sanctuary and in the camp with His people. If the uncleanness remains, He must either depart or send the people away; otherwise they will be consumed by the fire of His holiness.

The understanding that the atonement is not only for sin but for the uncleanness of the material world that results from human sin (as described in chapter 7) is part of St. Luke's understanding of the great transformation that takes place in the final chapters of his Gospel and the first chapters of Acts. Christ's atoning sacrifice not only triumphs over the web of the world's sin; it also purifies the physical world from the uncleanness that has resulted from it. While atoning for the sanctuary allowed God to dwell there, Christ's atonement allows the Holy Spirit to come to dwell in the entire world, and in all the world's people, as He is about to come and dwell within Cornelius. This cleansing of the material world is final and does not have to be repeated because Christ's atonement is final and not repeated (Heb. 10:1–18).

The notion of sacred space that was so integral to the temple worship of the Old Covenant is not discarded in the New. By atoning for the whole world, Christ effectively cleansed the material creation from the taint left behind by human sin and sanctified the world as sacred space. As a result, there is (still) no neutral or meaningless ground in all creation, nor do material objects and places simply occupy "secular" space. Just as the material world came under the curse through the taint of human sin, so also Christ exercises His reign over His creation through the assembly of the Church.

It is for this reason that the Church cleanses, rededicates, and consecrates physical spaces. Saint Cyril of Alexandria translated the relics of martyred Ss. Cyrus and John the Healers to the former pagan Egyptian temple of Isis to cleanse it from the demonic influence that had pervaded it. Homes and nearly everything in them are blessed for the faithful. Objects brought into the Church for sacred use and even water itself are blessed not to bestow on them some sort of magical power but to cleanse them and reclaim them for the Kingdom. While Christ's victory is already won, the creation is reclaimed piece by piece and not without setback due to human sin and error. The fact that uncleanness is no longer attached to the physical creation does not mean the commandments of the Law regarding uncleanness no longer apply. Christ Himself points out that it is not what a person eats that makes him unclean, but rather the evil and sinfulness that comes out of him (Matt. 15:11).[3] A person can still defile herself through sin and wickedness, so all are still commanded to stand apart from the world's corruption and touch no unclean thing (2 Cor. 6:17). This does not mean to separate oneself from the material world through laws against tasting and touching (Col. 2:21), but rather to separate oneself from sin and wickedness and be united to a life of holiness. In fact, this new state of affairs intensifies rather than diminishes the demand for moral cleanness among Christians—the body itself, not merely a temple or sanctuary, has become the sanctuary of God since the Holy Spirit now dwells within the faithful (1 Cor. 6:19–20). Just as the Israelites faced destruction if they were to remain unclean in God's presence, so also unrepentant sinfulness presents a danger to those in the presence of Christ's holiness, leading to St. Paul's warning about receiving the Eucharist (1 Cor. 11:27–30).

Christians, therefore, are called on to "keep kosher" in a deeper and truer sense than outward compliance with the Torah's commandments. As in Acts 10, the freedom to eat all kinds of food and thereby enjoy the restored goodness of God's creation in Christ is an

---

3   It is important that here Christ is not setting aside the dietary laws as invalid. There is no commandment in the Torah requiring the washing of hands before eating or classifying someone who does not as unclean. This was a commandment added by the Pharisees. Christ points out that in the Torah, it is those things that come out of a person, blood and other bodily fluids, which render that person ritually unclean. He then applies that understanding to all those dark things that lie within the human heart and overflow from the mouth as likewise rendering a person unclean.

image of the even greater restoration of humanity in Christ, so that there is now in Christ no Jew or Greek, slave or free, male or female. There is no one who is unclean in and of themselves. But as people for whom Christ has made atonement, who have thereby been consecrated as holy to God, it is more critical than ever that none defile themselves with sin and uncleanness, lest they render themselves subject to judgment.

The Penalties of the Torah

ONE ELEMENT OF THE TORAH the vast majority of Christians see as obsolete or annulled following the death and Resurrection of Christ is the system of death penalties prescribed for a variety of offenses. While there are still many Christians who see the death penalty as appropriate in cases of murder or other specific crimes, few would argue for its application in cases of, for example, disrespect to parents or the fraud of a woman found not to be a virgin on her wedding night. The fact that Christians do not embrace a literal application of the penalties of these commandments from the Torah is then used as an argument to attempt to relativize the seriousness of other sins that require the death penalty in a literal reading. Others would argue that the prescribed death penalty serves to indicate that these are "mortal sins" or "sins unto death." Asserting that sin is serious is a far cry from asserting that it is worthy of death.

To understand how the apostles, and the Church who has followed in their footsteps, have continued to apply this portion of the Torah, one first has to understand how the Torah views life and death as they relate to the community under the law. This understanding begins in the opening chapters of the Book of Genesis. In our modern era, so much of our discussion has concerned the historicity of the various narratives in this book that we are prone to lose sight of its place in the Torah. In its canonical form, Genesis is not an independent entity but rather serves as the historical and theological prologue to the Torah as a whole. The major themes of the law are, therefore, to be found initially in Genesis. Genesis must shape the understanding of the events and teachings related in the texts of Exodus, Leviticus, Numbers, and Deuteronomy.

Life, in Eden, was to eat from the Tree of Life and thereby to live forever in the place where God is. In the day that humanity's first parents chose to eat from the tree of the knowledge of good and evil, they died in being cut off from the Tree of Life and expelled from that place where God's presence is. Throughout the Torah, this is the understanding of what life and death mean, including biological life and death. The living God dwells in the land of the living and the slain in the grave are cut off from His life-giving hand. Here the ideas of death and exile are brought together and united.

Later in the Torah, the common phrase is that certain sins require that a person be "cut off from among the people" (see Num. 15:30–31). It is ambiguous whether this refers to expulsion from the community or a literal death penalty, not because of a lack of historical knowledge, but because both ideas are so closely united in the vision of the text. After the Exodus, God came to dwell in the tabernacle at the center of the Israelite camp. Later, He was present in the temple at the center of the nation. To be expelled or cut off from the place where God is, from His presence, is death. The situation continues, and is the subject of meditation, in the postexilic psalms and prophets.

It is worth noting, too, that the status of being cut off from among the people and from the presence of God was not irremediable. Following the pattern established in Genesis by Abraham's sacrifice of the ram in lieu of Isaac, the Law required sin offerings to be offered as atonement for the transgressor. Discussion of the Torah and its penalties often neglects the concrete means of repentance and restoration it provides. The Torah is not merely a means of governance for Israel; it represents the expression of what is required of Israel now that God dwells among them, which by necessity entails the means of restoring right relationship between God and man when it has been disrupted. Numbers 15 explicitly ties the cutting off of a person from the community to their lack of repentance in addition to the nature of their sin. When sin enters the community through a person, this can be remedied either by the repentance of the person or by the removal of that person from the community.

Saint Paul applied this part of the Torah quite directly in 1 Corinthians 5. A man in Corinth was guilty of sexual immorality with his stepmother, which under the law required him to be cut off from among the people, but the Church in Corinth had done nothing about it. Saint Paul pointed out that this situation could not be allowed to remain—the man had to be removed from the community. But even here, he left room for hope that this penalty would work toward the man's repentance and salvation.

Excommunication from the Church community, the remedy for unrepentant sin throughout the New Testament, is the direct equivalent of exile from the Old Covenant community (see Matt. 18:17; 2 Thess. 3:6; 1 Tim. 1:20). In addition to being expelled from the place where Christ dwells, one is excluded from eating from the Tree of Life, as fulfilled in the Eucharist, the ongoing source of life in the Kingdom (John 6:53–57). Far from being a "watering down" of the juridical penalties of the Law, excommunication from the Church community, as taught by the apostles and practiced by the Church through the centuries, is a direct application of the principles, and the penalties, of the Torah understood in their deepest sense. The life given by Christ, eternal life, is "real" life. Biological life is an image or a shadow of that reality. Basic to Christianity is the understanding that biological life in this world is not all that there is.

Worship According to God's Commandments

WORSHIP OUGHT TO BE THE offering made to God that He wishes to receive from us. When Cain and Abel presented their sacrifices to God, one of them was accepted by God, and the other was rejected. Consistent with this, the Torah provides detailed instructions for how to structure both the place and the patterns of worship. These laws even take precedence over many of the moral commandments in the Law. In fact, the command to celebrate the Passover precedes the actual Passover in Exodus 12. It is clear from the text that commandments regarding worship are serious matters—Aaron's sons Nadab and Abihu die after offering incense at the wrong time and in the wrong manner.

Despite the clarity of these commandments and their strict application throughout the Old Testament, the default assumption among Christians today is either that most of the commandments in the Law that deal with worship have been invalidated or that their spiritual significance has diminished. Protestant approaches to worship tend particularly in this direction, lending credence only to explicit commands found in the New Testament regarding religion. The basis for this hearkens back to the artificial division of the Law into three categories mentioned earlier, with the commandments regarding worship being considered part of the "ceremonial law" that Christ's fulfillment of the sacrificial system abolished. In Roman Catholicism, this shift was more subtle, with human imagination and therefore input in the form of religion becoming gradually more and more allowed and even emphasized since the schism with Orthodoxy, culminating in Vatican II's relativizing of the forms and spaces of worship.

Over against this, the Orthodox Church has consistently continued to apply the commandments of the Law to the life of the Church in this area as it has since the first century. Just as in other cases, these

251

commandments are applied through the fulfillment that has come in the Lord Jesus Christ. A key scriptural text for understanding this transformation of worship is John 4:19–24, a passage often used by proponents of the opposing view. The Samaritan woman asks Christ a question regarding the proper place of worship, the Jerusalem temple or the Samaritan site on Mount Gerizim. Christ's ultimate answer, that in the future God's people will worship Him "in spirit and in truth," is then interpreted to refer to the idea that in the future, God may be worshipped anywhere, at any time, by any person. Often it is taken further to argue for the complete individualization of religion, as this text is seen as invalidating the Old Testament commandments regarding the places, times, and ordained persons involved in worship. This understanding of the text, however, ignores the details of the text. A close reading reveals something very different.

In His full answer to the question, Christ speaks specifically of worship of the Father, not merely of God in a general sense, as a Samaritan worshipper would have been used to. He immediately dismisses the issue of which of the two places is correct by stating that it will not be long before the Father is not worshipped in either place. The Samaritan temple had long since been destroyed by John Hyrcanus, and the Jerusalem temple was soon to fall to Titus in AD 70. Christ then reframes the question by pointing out that the Samaritans worship what they do not know, while the Jews worship whom they know because it was the Jews who have received God's revelation of Himself.

It is this situation, of the Jews knowing God and those outside not knowing, that Christ then says will be remedied in the future worship of the Father. The Fathers, in commenting on this passage, note two things. First, when the word "spirit" or "spiritual" is used in the New Testament, it almost always refers to the Holy Spirit. Spiritual does not mean "ethereal," "unreal," or "subjective." Second, and more directly related to St. John's Gospel, Christ identifies Himself as "the

Truth" (see John 14:6). In Christ, the true revelation of God's identity, the Holy Trinity, comes into the world, and not only to the Jews but to all nations, such that now all humanity, when worshipping the Father, worships Him in the Spirit and in Truth, in the Holy Trinity.

Christ does not abolish the commandments regarding worship but fulfills them in bringing the full knowledge of God, which transforms and deepens them in a new context. We see this borne out in the practice of the apostles, who did not reject the existing Second Temple worship, which still existed in their times. Quite to the contrary, not only St. James but also St. Paul were willing and eager to participate in the taking of a Nazirite vow, complete with sacrificial offerings at the temple (Acts 21:23–26). Saint Paul did not shun synagogues but rather went to them first in all his missionary journeys, participated in their worship, and preached Jesus there as the Christ, the fulfillment of the Scriptures, which were read and taught there.

Even more tellingly, despite their understanding of Christ's sacrifice in relation to the sacrificial system, the apostles did not abandon the other worship of the temple in Jerusalem while it still stood. In St. Luke's Gospel, the events surrounding Christ's Resurrection from the dead and Ascension into heaven culminate with His followers being continually in the temple. In the Acts of the Apostles, St. Paul indicates his desire to return to Jerusalem for the feast of Passover, and when he is unable to, he commits to being there for Pentecost. At the same time, however, St. Paul in 1 Corinthians speaks of keeping the Feast of Unleavened Bread, but with the transformation that now "Christ, our Passover, is sacrificed for us" (5:7–8). It is worth noting that this letter is addressed by St. Paul to a primarily Gentile community.

This mode of applying the Torah's commandments regarding worship, begun by the apostles, is what lies behind the patterns and structures of Christian worship. Just as the Passover was the "first of days" in the Torah, around which the Israelites structured their year, so also Pascha, now the celebration of the Resurrection of Christ, is the first of days for Christians around which the cycle of many of the Church's great feasts is structured. Just as in the Torah, that year is structured around a cycle of feasts commemorating the great events in the history of our salvation. Just as in the Torah, one day in seven is set apart to the Lord. Christ, having rested in the Tomb on the seventh day, has fulfilled the Sabbath, and so that day is now the day of His Resurrection, the first day of the week. The Tuesday and Thursday fasts have moved to Wednesday and Friday, connected to Christ's betrayal and Crucifixion.

The most basic structure of Christian worship remains the offering of incense at morning and evening with prayer and the lighting of lamps (Ex. 30:7–8). Christian worship spaces are adorned on the walls and the iconostasis with images of the hosts of heaven, just as the tabernacle was, though now these hosts include the saints in resurrected glory, owing to the Resurrection of Christ. There is a distinction between a holy and most holy place, though now, consecrated in the blood of Christ, all the faithful enter into the holy place as a Kingdom of priests.

At Mount Sinai, every form of idolatry was strictly prohibited (see Ex. 20:4–6; Deut. 4:15–18; 5:7–10). The tabernacle, however, being made according to the plan seen by Moses on the mountain when he stood in the divine council, was designed to mirror it. The ark of the covenant was closely associated with the throne of Yahweh (as in Ex. 25:17–22). It was, therefore, surrounded by images of the cherubim, the throne guardians who surround Yahweh's throne (Ex. 25:17–22; 26:10; 37:9; Num. 7:89). The inner courts of Solomon's temple were decorated likewise (1 Kin. / 3Kg 6:23–30; 2 Chr. 5:7–8). The former accoutrements of the tabernacle were directly commanded by Yahweh.

It is because of these commandments that iconography continued to exist in synagogues, as continues to be revealed by archaeological excavations in Galilee and elsewhere. This practice persisted in Christian churches. In the Christian context, however, the coming of Christ transformed iconography in one major way: angelic beings in the divine council were accompanied by the saints in glory, depicted in the heavens with Christ Himself as they rule and reign with him, serving as priestly intercessors in His presence.

Because in Western Christian circles worship is largely regarded as a matter of personal taste, Orthodox worship—indeed, traditional Christian worship—tends to be understood as just one of many preferences for how to worship. "Smells and bells," as it were. It is assumed to be some form of Greek, Russian, Middle Eastern, or other arcane cultural expression of Christian worship. This, however, is far from the truth. The patterns, and even details, of Orthodox worship are based on a consistent interpretation of God's commandments in the Torah, now grasped more fully and deeply in Christ. New Testament worship did not start over with a clean slate after abandoning the worship of the Old Testament. The apostles applied the commandments of the Torah regarding worship to the Christian communities they founded. This apostolic worship is continued in the liturgical life of the Orthodox Church. This is the worship that God has given to humanity to allow them to make a pleasing offering to the Father, united to the Son, in the communion of the Holy Spirit.

Baptism and Circumcision

CIRCUMCISION OCCUPIED A POSITION OF centrality in the Old Covenant equivalent to baptism in the New Covenant. It was the marker of membership in the people of God. Its ritual establishment and significance preceded the giving of the Old Covenant to Moses by centuries. It constituted the people of Israel not as a national entity but as a family, the family of God. Moses' failure to follow this most basic of Yahweh's commandments nearly led to his own death

(Ex. 4:24–26) and resulted in his loss of the priesthood to Aaron and his line. It was nearly inconceivable, then, to the greater body of the faithful in Judea that someone could come to be a member of the people of God and partake of Christ as the new Passover without first being circumcised (Ex. 12:48).

Saint Paul argues fiercely against the necessity of circumcision for those who were coming from the nations into the people of God. This argument not only is the major focus of his Epistle to the Galatians, but it also sets the stage for the council of Acts 15. While there seems to be a clear connection in function between baptism and circumcision, surely, then, has not the significance of circumcision, along with its necessity, been set aside in the New Covenant? A surface reading would seem to indicate it has. While the intuitive connection between baptism and circumcision is a correct instinct and is important to the understanding of the propriety of infant baptism, to merely say that baptism has replaced circumcision is to move too quickly and pass over the ways in which St. Paul, above all New Testament writers, continued to utilize the language and commandments regarding circumcision.

Circumcision as a sign was first given to Abraham (Gen. 17:1–14). In the wake of the rebellion at Babel, Yahweh had dispersed the nations, assigning them to the governance of angelic beings. He will use a nation that will serve collectively as priests for all the nations of the world until that nation brings forth Christ as the culmination of its ministry. Rather than choosing one of the seventy nations already in existence at the time, Yahweh created one anew, from one man of Ur named Abram. At the giving of His initial covenant with Abram, He changed his name to Abraham, promising to make him the father of many nations, to bless all the nations of the world through him and his descendant. The way in which someone was made a part of this people was through circumcision—circumcision not only or even primarily of one's self, but of all the males of one's household, including even slaves. In a deliberate wordplay, anyone not circumcised was cut off from this covenant and the people whom it created.

The covenant, as St. Paul would later strongly argue, was therefore not based on biological ethnic descent. Rather, it was based on faithfulness in keeping the commandment of circumcision and "walking before the Lord in righteousness" (Gen. 17:1). For St. Paul, this righteousness is a function of this faithfulness. The faithful one is the one reckoned to be righteous. Righteousness comes by faithfulness. It was therefore always those who were faithful, like Abraham, who were His children (Gal. 3:7). Abram of Ur was a Chaldean (Gen. 11:28, 31). The term "Chaldean" is anachronistic; it refers to the Neo-Babylonian Empire that existed roughly fourteen centuries after the time of Abram. Abram is called a Chaldean to connect him to Babylon, the place of the Tower of Babel and later capital of the Mesopotamian region from which Abram came. He is called out of Babylon, the capital of the worst of the world's sin, to become the foundation of a new nation. Circumcision is his first act of cutting himself off from the world, and its captivity to darkness, that he came from.

This cutting off takes place in relation to the genitals because it is not primarily an individual act of devotion or a pledge made by an individual. Rather, it is constitutive of community and therefore involves not only the male but his spouse and his progeny. The broader community of Israel was a family, the family of God. It began with the family of Abraham and was always composed of tribes and clans, family units. These units always included strong elements of adoption, of incorporation of outsiders into family and clan. Newcomers, both by birth and by adoption, shared in this cutting off as the ritual means of integration. Women and female children were integrated through their family bonds to the circumcised male who was the head of the household, as only males were circumcised. The circumcised male cut the family unit off from the world, setting apart and therefore definitionally making it holy. It was the responsibility of the women of the household to maintain the purity and holiness of the household in both a physical and a spiritual sense, while it was the responsibility of the males who ventured out into the world to not yield to its impurity and bring sin and impurity back into the home. The circumcision of the flesh was to embody the circumcision of the heart, which needed to be cut off from the world and its desires and temptations (Deut. 10:12–17; 30:6; Jer. 4:4; 9:26).

Saint Paul reveals that every element of circumcision finds its fulfillment in Christ. This does not mean that it is done away with. Rather, every element is filled to overflowing in such a way that Christ represents the truth and reality that stood behind the shadow of the ordinance of circumcision (Col. 2:17). To return to the circumcision of the flesh, then, is to forsake reality and fullness for image and shadow and remove one's self from Christ, if not outright deny that Jesus, the Christ, has come as that fullness. Basic to St. Paul's understanding of the Crucifixion of Christ is that it represents an inversion of the curse of the Torah (Gal. 3:13). In his suffering and death, Christ was cut off from among the people. Christ's receipt of the curse, however, did not cut him off from life. Rather, being God, his cutting off was the final cutting off of the world and its prince, the dark powers and the passions and wickedness that had infested the creation, from God. It is, therefore, the world as a system, as represented by its capital, Babylon, that is judged and dies (Rev. 17:1—18:8). The person then who is in Christ has been cut off from the world and the world from him (Gal. 6:14). That person is a new creation (2 Cor. 5:17). This transformed way of being was foreshadowed by the new name given to Abraham following his circumcision, and the ritual of circumcising his male descendants on the eighth day of life to signify the new creation (Gal. 6:15).

Participation in Christ's death and Resurrection and the reality of this cutting off and new creation takes place in the Mystery of Baptism. To be baptized is to be baptized into Christ and thereby to put on Christ (Gal. 3:27). To be baptized into Christ is to be integrated into the family of God (v. 26). It is to leave behind whatever life in the world and its system of relationships consisted of, to be grafted into a new people created by God (v. 28). Although this people is new to the one baptized, it is the same family, the same people, created by Yahweh through Abraham to exist eternally (v. 29). Before His death, His cutting off, Christ sanctified Himself (John 17:19). Those who are baptized into Christ are set apart and made holy by Him through participation in His family (Heb. 2:11). Saint Paul can, therefore, say that we have all been circumcised with Christ's circumcision in baptism (Col. 2:8–12).

Christ has established the spiritual and material holiness of His house and His household members. It is the responsibility of the Church to protect and maintain that holiness because she is His bride. It is in precisely this sense that the Church is spoken of in feminine terms. Saint Paul applies this theological understanding of the deep connections between circumcision and baptism found in Christ's fulfillment practically in ways that stem directly from the understanding of circumcision. In addressing faithful Christians married to non-Christians, he applies the principle that the circumcised father sanctifies, or renders holy, mother and children (1 Cor. 7:12–16). This happens, however, in both directions. A faithful wife renders husband and children holy in the same sense as a believing husband would. This is because the holiness that comes to these families is not the holiness of a human man who has set himself apart in the flesh or even in his heart. It is the holiness of Christ Himself, in whom the faithful, baptized Christian participates, whether male or female.

That this still holds true reveals that baptism, like circumcision before it, was never an individual act or pledge. Rather, it has always been, from the very beginning, a communal act of family, clan, tribe, and nation; the new nation that is called by Christ's name, the

Church. The Church integrates new members, both by birth and from outside, through the ritual means of baptism. This renders them coheirs of the promises with Christ (Rom. 8:17), members of the family of God, a people holy and set apart from the world, which is perishing (1 Pet. 3:20–21), and a new creation in Christ. Circumcision, in the Church, is not abolished but fulfilled.

The Sacrifice to End All Sacrifices

THE FACT THAT THE EARLIEST Christian communities never offered the animal sacrifices of the Old Testament has been used to marginalize the Torah's commandments regarding worship as a whole. While the idea that Christ's sacrifice rendered the entire sacrificial system of the Old Testament irrelevant is attractive in its simplicity, it distorts the scriptural understanding of sacrifice. Further, this idea has led the vast majority of Protestants to question whether there is such a thing as a New Covenant priesthood. This blanket Protestant denial of the ongoing sacrifice taking place in the Christian community, namely in the form of the Eucharist, is itself a response to accumulated Roman Catholic doctrine regarding the propitiatory sacrifice of the Mass. Many Protestant groups see the sacrificial system as essentially abolished, with no ongoing reality in the life of Christian communities. Rome, in contrast, has often erred by seeing the offering of the Eucharist as being identical to the historical event of Christ's death on the Cross. It thereby neglects the sense in which that historical event was a fulfillment of previous sacrifice.

The first reality that must be kept in mind is that the sacrificial system is not made up entirely, or even primarily, of sin offerings. The sacrificial system commanded in the Torah includes grain offerings, drink offerings, firstfruits of crops and livestock, offerings for firstborn male children, and still more occasional offerings. As already described, the sin offerings were not centered around an act of killing but were themselves meals like the many others. Portions of the meals were eaten by priests and offerers; the best portions were offered to God Himself, generally by burning.

For this reason, the result of the burning of these offerings is described throughout the Torah as an "aroma pleasing to Yahweh" (Gen. 8:21; Lev. 1:9; 2:2; 23:18). The same language is applied both to animal offerings and to grain offerings in the Old Testament, not to mention to the sacrifice of Christ in the New Testament (Eph. 5:2). Bearing this in mind, the conventional Protestant understanding of the Eucharist as a meal, not a sacrifice, is incoherent from the point of view of the apostles. Sacrifices from their perspective *were* communal meals, leading to the very early crisis regarding meat offered to idols (as dealt with primarily by St. Paul in 1 Corinthians).

The fate of the sacrificial commandments and their ongoing application in the life of the Church become clear when the language used in the Second Temple period regarding sacrifice is understood. In Greek translation, Numbers 10:10 refers to the sin offerings of the tabernacle as "remembrances," not because in giving these offerings the worshippers remember some past event or remember their own sins, but because through the dedication of a pleasing offering they bring themselves and their need for mercy to the remembrance of God.

This language is picked up by the New Testament authors, for example, in Acts 10. The centurion Cornelius received a vision urging him to send for St. Peter in order to receive the gospel and baptism at his hands. What occasioned this angelic visitation is that his prayers and his giving of alms had gone up before the Lord as a "remembrance." Prayer and almsgiving are here associated with sacrifice. More important, however, is that when Christ instituted the celebration of the Eucharist, His command to His disciples and apostles was to "do this as My remembrance" (Luke 22:19; 1 Cor. 11:24). This is not to say that the Eucharist has replaced the sacrificial system but that in Christ's voluntary self-offering, the sacrificial system has been fulfilled. The Eucharist is the reality foreshadowed by those sacrificial commandments. They, and the sacrifices they commanded, served to prepare God's people to understand the sacrifice of Christ.

In the Eucharist, humanity offers to God the fruit of its labors, bread and wine, in fulfillment of the offerings of firstfruits, of grain offerings and drink offerings. This is in specific imitation of the offering of Melchizedek (Gen. 14:18), after whose priesthood Christ's is patterned (Ps. 110/109:4; Heb. 7:13–17). With these gifts, the people offer themselves, their labors, their whole life, and their collective being as a community unto God. In return, Christ offers Himself. In fulfilling the atoning sacrifices, Christ has once and for all cleansed His people of sin and its effects on the created order by offering Himself, His labors, and His whole life as a pleasing sacrifice to the Father. Therefore, no further sacrifices are required to this end (Heb. 10:10–18). Rather, in the eating of Christ's body and the drinking of His blood, we come to participate ever more fully in that once-and-for-all sacrifice and to receive in ourselves as human persons the effects of that sacrifice, namely purification from sin and the life of God Himself.

The many commandments regarding the sacrificial system in the Law, therefore, are far from obsolete. These commandments represent the means, the many vantage points, from which to view the sacrifice of Christ on our behalf. They represent the means by which we understand the transformative effect of that sacrifice on ourselves as human persons and on the creation in which we dwell. They represent, too, the way this transformation works itself out in each of our lives through the Eucharist, the center of our worship and our lives. Christ's sacrifice is at once the sacrifice that makes animal sacrifices unnecessary and the sacrifice that gives our liturgical and unbloody sacrifice its meaning and reality.

The Shepherds of Israel

THERE IS A COMMON MISUNDERSTANDING of the origins of clerical orders within the Church. It is argued that the Christians of the apostolic era, including the apostles themselves, believed that Christ would certainly return within their own lifetime. It is only when that clearly did not occur, when the apostles—or at least most of them—had died, that the concept of the Church came into being, as well as varied understandings that evolved over time as to how the newly constituted Church ought to be governed. It is thought that these structures were deeply influenced by the prevailing culture at the time, most especially Roman culture, as the Church by this time was primarily Gentile.

This narrative has been put forward with such force that it has been used to argue for a later dating of any book of the New Testament that mentions the Church or her orders. In the case of the Pastoral Epistles, it is used to argue that they must be minimally sub-Pauline, reflecting later developments after the end of the apostle's life. This view, however, requires rejecting the entirety of the ethos of the New Testament authors as well as everything that can be historically known and determined regarding the earliest Christians.

The prophets of the Hebrew Bible testified that a time would come when judgment would come upon Israel after their return from exile. At this point, much of Israel would be cut off, but a remnant would be purified and preserved by the fire of judgment (see Mic. 2:1; Jer. 23:3; Joel 3:5; Obad. 17; Is. 6:13; 7:3; 10:22). This remnant would become the basis for a new Israel, into which the nations would stream (see Is. 60:10–14; 19:16–25; Zech. 14:16). It is St. Paul's understanding in the uncontroversially Pauline Epistle to the Romans that this had taken place in the coming of Christ (Rom. 11:1–24), an understanding also found in St. John's Gospel. The Church is a new people of God, a renewed Israel, made up of the faithful remnant of Israel of the Old Covenant into which Gentiles who have come to Christ have been grafted. Those returning from the nations replace the tribes scattered to the nations so that in the end all Israel will be saved.

All the terminology of the New Testament regarding the Church reflects this continuity. The word ekklesia, which we typically translate as "Church," is the same word used in the Greek text of the Old Testament and generally translated "assembly." Throughout the Torah in particular, "the assembly" represents the gathering of God's people. After they had come to the inheritance of the land, other national descriptors became more commonly used. The New Testament writers understand the Christian assembly, the new people of God, to be in this life journeying toward the promised inheritance, and so again, "assembly" becomes the best descriptor (see 1 Cor .10:1–5; 1 Pet. 2:9–12). The concept of the "Church" itself then can be clearly seen to be based not in the establishment of an institution because of the unanticipated delay of Christ's second coming, but rather in the continuity of the New and Old Covenant peoples of God.

The formation of the assembly and, important to note, its established leadership does not begin in a group of later epistles at the end of the first century. Rather, it is seen to begin in the life of Christ. The gathering and purification of the remnant of Israel began before Christ's public ministry in the ministry of St. John the Forerunner, who gathered a group of disciples at the Jordan River who became the followers of Jesus Christ. The constitutive event for the formation of the Old Covenant people had been baptism into Moses (1 Cor. 10:1–3), and they had been led through the Jordan by the Old Covenant's Joshua to defeat spiritual forces of evil and claim an inheritance (Josh. 3:9–17). This newly assembled people is no more a loose collection placed under the sole leadership of Christ than the Old Covenant community was under Moses.

Rather, Christ put structures of authority in place that paralleled those of the Old Covenant. The twelve, identified first as disciples and then as apostles, are directly connected to the twelve patriarchs, who were the progenitors, the fathers, of Israel (Matt. 19:28). In the same way, the apostles would become the fathers of the new assembly (1 Cor. 4:14–15). In addition, Christ appointed the seventy (or seventy-two in some manuscripts), giving them authority within His assembled followers (Luke 10:1–20). Preserved within the Church's memory is the awareness that many of the early leaders of the Church whom we see emerging within the Acts of the Apostles and the epistolary literature came from this second group.

This group of apostles parallels the elders (*presbyteroi*) appointed by Moses to assist him in governing the people, who were also seventy (or seventy-two in some manuscripts) in number (Num. 11:16–17). This institution had endured throughout the Old Covenant and had become the Sanhedrin of the first century. While they might not have had formalized and disambiguated titles, within the ministry of Christ there were new patriarchs, new elders (*presbyteroi*) of the people, and men and women who served Jesus and accompanied Him. These last paralleled the Levites who served in and around the tabernacle and temple and the women who served at the tabernacle's gate (Ex. 38:8).

Just as the apostles and the Christian assembly gathered around them continued to pray at the temple in Jerusalem and attend, even preaching in, the synagogues, so they maintained these authority structures within their community. As in the case of the twelve patriarchs, the particular role of "apostle" was not passed on to subsequent generations, nor could it be. As in the case of the twelve patriarchs, the apostles served the role of progenitors, and basic to that order was their ability to serve as a direct witness to the Person of Jesus Christ (Acts 1:21–22; Gal. 1:11–12).

However, in 1 Corinthians 4, St. Paul describes the apostolic ministry. As part of this description, he not only describes the role of an apostle as father and progenitor but also describes a particular relationship that he has with St. Timothy (v. 17). Saint Timothy is his son in the sense that a son is the image of his father. Saint Timothy's ministry is an extension of St. Paul's: in the case of 1 Corinthians, an extension in space; in the case of the ministry to which St. Paul later commits him, in time. This allows for the two to address an epistle to a community as coming from a single authority (2 Cor. 1:1; Col. 1:1–2). Saint Timothy is able to appoint elders (presbyteroi) of the people and those who will serve (exercise *diakonia*) within that assembly (1 Tim. 3). This relationship, which also existed between the other apostles and their own disciples, is the basis of apostolic succession. This has two elements, both a historical continuity of relationship expressed in the laying on of hands and, what is more crucial, this relationship of imaging. Saint Timothy is St. Paul's successor in that he proclaims St. Paul's gospel and mirrors all that St. Paul teaches and the way in which he lives his life (1 Cor. 4:17).

In the New Testament texts, in the earliest documents describing Church order (see the Didache), and in the Apostolic Fathers, there is an ambiguity in the way those in authority are described. For example, it is not uncommon to see the apostles referred to as presbyteroi. This is by analogy to their role as respected elders in the community. *Episkopos*, a word used to translate "herdsman" in the Greek text of the Old Testament, is sometimes used interchangeably of a given person with the word *presbyter* for the same reason. "Herdsman" or "shepherd" was commonly used as a generic for all of Israel's leaders in the Old Covenant.

It is clear, however, that certain offices were not invented within a nascent Church structure; rather, traditional roles within the assembled people of God were continued within the new Christian assembly. There were, in the earliest layer of the Church, indeed within the early ministry of Christ Himself, clearly apostles and their successors, elders of the people, men who served, and women who served as four distinct orders or roles within the community. These four clear and distinct orders would, by the middle of the second century, come to be consistently labeled as the episcopate, the presbyterate, the male diaconate, and the female diaconate. This understanding of the Church's structure not only is biblical, but it also stems from a proper understanding of the very earliest layer of the Old Testament.

The Epistle to the Hebrews tells us that Christ is the same yesterday, today, and forever (Heb. 13:8). The Person who appeared to Abraham, Jacob, and Moses is the same One who lived and ate with the apostles. The One who gave Moses the teaching of the Torah also explained it to His disciples and fulfilled it in His life and work. Therefore, there are not pieces of the Torah that are applicable to Christians and others that are now irrelevant. There are not portions of the Holy Scriptures that are now to be ignored. The exact opposite is true. Through Christ, in the life of the Church, guided by the Holy Spirit, the commandments of the Torah can finally be fully lived out. The life of Christians in the Orthodox Church continues the way of life of the apostles and the earliest Christian communities. Even more, it continues the way of life that God established for His people from the very beginning.

The Orthodox Faith of the Apostles

THE PRIMARY AIM OF THIS book is to demonstrate the absolute continuity of ancient Israelite religion, the religion of the Second Temple, first-century Christianity, and the religious life preserved and practiced in the Orthodox Church. The structures, patterns, and teachings now extant within the Church were already present in the Church of the first century because they had been present already in the religion in which the apostles were raised and which they practiced throughout their lives. They worshipped in the temple and in the synagogues. They prayed according to traditional hours of prayer. They offered incense and lit lamps at morning and evening. They strove in the power of the Spirit to keep the commandments of Christ, given by Him to Moses at Sinai. They worshipped the Holy Trinity, known through the Hebrew Scriptures but now known to them personally in the Person of Jesus Christ and the coming of the Holy Spirit. They saw the religious ritual that structured their lives as the means of spiritual warfare against the powers of evil. They saw at the end of their lives the hope of receiving a good judgment before the throne of Christ and being granted to participate in His rule over the creation in this age and the age to come.

This has, of course, always been present in the New Testament texts themselves, and these continuities have always existed. Until the middle point of the last century, however, much of the data that manifests these continuities had been obscured by history. Within that evidentiary vacuum, speculation produced an array of reconstructions of the New Testament Church and its practices. These reconstructions were, in general, based on the projection of present-day beliefs, perceptions, and controversies back onto the ancient past. Every generation has assumed that all previous generations (or at least those aspects of them we deem favorable or recognizable somehow) are in direct line of identity with the present. It is often taken for granted that people of the past, in general, and the apostles, in particular, are analogues of the scholar, researcher, preacher, or theologian who examines them. The ancients must, certainly, have experienced God, the world, and religious faith in the same way that we moderns do.

Beginning in the second half of the twentieth century, the discovery of ancient texts by archaeologists and the broader availability of texts preserved in far-flung monastic settlements has brought about a revolution in our understanding of apostolic Christianity. Archaeological discoveries have shed light on the nature and structure of first-century synagogues and the first Christian churches. In the light of these revelations, many of the previous reconstructions have crumbled. While the beliefs and practices based on these reconstructions may continue based on tradition and inertia, their fundamental basis has been shown to be false.

In no other area is this clearer than in relation to ancient Judaism, if such a thing can even be spoken of following these revelations. Through the history of the Church in the West, it has been commonplace to project the present shape of Rabbinic Judaism back into the past. The shape of religion in Judea in the Second Temple era, and of Judeans in the diaspora during that same period, has become increasingly clear. It has likewise become clear that there is between that religion and Rabbinic Judaism a major disjunction. This disjunction is a product of the history of the period.

In the period following the advent of Christianity and the destruction of the Jerusalem temple in AD 70, followed by the destruction of Jerusalem itself at the end of the Bar Kochva rebellion, Rabbinic Judaism was born. It was born, however, through a repudiation of Christianity and of Second Temple traditions that lent themselves to or resonated with Christianity. Nearly universal views such as, minimally, a Binitarian Godhead were repudiated as heresy. The vast range of literature produced during the Second Temple period vanished from Judaism in a generation as a result of a ban on writing not lifted until centuries later as the Talmudic tractates were composed. The entire reading of the Hebrew Scriptures was transformed, as was the ritual life of Judaism, in direct reaction and counterpoint to the parallel Christian structures. Rabbinic Judaism is a new religion that came into being in the fourth and fifth centuries AD.

Meanwhile, following the apostles, the spiritual understandings and practices, the worship, the authority structures within the assembly, and even the literary activity of the Second Temple period continued uninterrupted in the Christian Church. The texts of the Second Temple period, beyond the shrunken canon of the Hebrew Scriptures received by Rabbinic Judaism, were preserved through the centuries by Christian scribes in Christian monastic foundations of the East. The religion of ancient Israel as it continued into the Second Temple period continued unabated within Christian communities, while dissenting Judeans broke away and formed a new set of religious traditions. It is therefore not only possible but correct to speak of the Christianity of ancient Israel or Second Temple Christianity. That religion, practiced by the Orthodox Church, is the religion of the apostles.

Bibliography

The following bibliography presents not only works that served as source material for this book but also a list for further reading on various topics contained herein. Many of these sources do not write from an Orthodox Christian perspective, and therefore their inclusion here does not constitute a wholesale endorsement.

Annus, Amar. "On the Origin of Watchers: A Comparative Study of the Antediluvian Wisdom in Mesopotamian and Jewish Traditions." *Journal for the Study of the Pseudepigrapha* 19, no. 4 (June 2010): 277–320.

Bauckham, Richard. *Jesus and the Eyewitnesses.* Grand Rapids, MI: Eerdmans, 2006.

Beard, Mary, John North, and Simon Price, eds. *Religions of Rome.* 2 vols. Cambridge: Cambridge University Press, 2013.

Boyarin, Daniel. *Border Lines: The Partition of Judaeo-Christianity.* Philadelphia: University of Pennsylvania Press, 2004.

———. "The Gospel of the Memra: Jewish Binitarianism and the Prologue to John." *Harvard Theological Review* 94, no. 3 (July 2001): 243–84.

Burkert, Walter. *Greek Religion.* Malden, MA: Blackwell, 1985.

———. *Homo Necans.* Berkeley: University of California Press, 1983.

Charlesworth, James H. *The Old Testament Pseudepigrapha.* 2 vols. New York: Doubleday, 1983.

Eisenbaum, Pamela. *Paul Was Not a Christian.* New York: HarperCollins, 2009.

Gregory the Great. *Moralia in Job.* Translated by John Henry Parker and J. Rivington. Oxford: Oxford University Press, 1849.

Gruenwald, Ithamar. *Rituals and Ritual Theory in Ancient Israel.* Atlanta: Society of Biblical Literature Press, 2003.

Irenaeus of Lyons. *On the Apostolic Preaching.* Translated by John Behr. Crestwood: St Vladimir's Seminary Press, 1997.

Josephus. *Works*. 9 vols. Translated by H. St. J. Thackeray. Loeb Classical Library. Cambridge, MA: Harvard University Press, 1966.

Lopez-Ruiz, Carolina. *When the Gods Were Born: Greek Cosmogonies and the Near East*. Cambridge, MA: Harvard University Press, 2010.

Markschies, Christoph. *God's Body*. Translated by Alexander Johannes Edmonds. Waco, TX: Baylor University Press, 2019.

Naiden, F. S. *Ancient Supplication*. Oxford: Oxford University Press, 2006.

———. *Smoke Signals for the Gods*. Oxford: Oxford University Press, 2013.

Oden, Thomas C., ed. *Greek Commentaries on Revelation: Oecumenius and Andrew of Caesarea*. Translated by William C. Weinrich. Ancient Christian Texts. Downers Grove, IL: InterVarsity Press, 2011.

Parker, Simon B., ed. *Ugaritic Narrative Poetry*. Atlanta: Society of Biblical Literature Press, 1997.

Patrick, James E. "Living Rewards for Dead Apostles: 'Baptised for the Dead' in 1 Corinthians 15.29." *New Testament Studies* 52:71–85.

Philo of Alexandria. *Works*. 12 vols. Translated by F. H. Colson and G. H. Whitaker. Loeb Classical Library. Cambridge, MA: Harvard University Press, 1962.

Plato. *Works*. 12 vols. Translated by Chris Emlyn-Jones and William Preddy. Loeb Classical Library. Cambridge, MA: Harvard University Press, 2017.

Roberts, Alexander, and James Donaldson, eds. *Ante-Nicene Fathers*. Vol. 1. Peabody, MA: Hendrickson, 1999.

Segal, Alan F. *Two Powers in Heaven*. Waco, TX: Baylor University Press, 2012.

Smith, Mark S. *Where the Gods Are*. New Haven, CT: Yale University Press, 2016.

Sommer, Benjamin D. *The Bodies of God and the World of Ancient Israel*. Cambridge: Cambridge University Press, 2011.

Wiley, Henrietta L., and Christian A. Eberhart. *Sacrifice, Cult, and Atonement in Early Judaism and Christianity: Constituents and Critique*. Atlanta: Society of Biblical Literature Press, 2017.

Wright, Archie T. *The Origin of Evil Spirits: The Reception of Genesis 6:1–4 in Early Jewish Literature*. Tubingen: Mohr Siebeck, 2005.

Wright, N. T. *Paul and the Faithfulness of God*. Minneapolis: Fortress, 2013.

Scripture Index

Note: The Old Testament books are ordered according to the Western, Protestant reckoning. For chapters and verses which differ between the Hebrew and Greek versions, the Hebrew is listed first, followed by the Greek after a backslash. Extra-canonical books are gathered together at the end. Discussions about specific books as a whole can be found in the subject index.

Exodus (*continued*)
8:27, 213; 9:4, 213; 9:4-6, 203; 9:25-26, 203; 9:26, 213; 10:22-23, 203; 10:23, 213; 11:2, 203; 11:4-7, 213–14; 12:3, 213; 12:3-11, 213; 12:3-20, 203; 12:4, 213; 12:12, 211; 12:21-23, 182; 12:38, 204; 12:48, 256; 13:21, 54; 15:11, 126; 17:6, 18; 17:16, 68; 19:2-6, 156; 19:10-13, 156; 20:2, 17, 54; 20:4, 80; 20:4-6, 254; 20:24, 59; 22:1, 175; 23:20, 16, 46; 23:20-21, 58; 23:23, 17; 24:1-2, 205; 24:7, 205; 24:8, 205, 210, 222; 24:9-11, 156, 182; 24:9-12, 205; 24:12, 157; 25:17-22, 254; 26:10, 254; 30:7-8, 254; 31:18, 32; 32:34, 176; 33:7, 55; 33:7-9, 32–33; 33:11, 33; 33:18, 33; 33:18-20, 175; 33:20, 22, 33; 33:21-23, 33; 34:9, 208; 37:9, 254; 38:8, 265

Leviticus: 1:9, 182, 261; 1:13, 182; 2:2, 182, 261; 9:24, 55; 10:1-2, 178; 10:2, 55; 11, 242; 11:44-45, 126; 11:45, 17, 54; 12, 242; 16, 168, 191, 194, 245–46; 16:1-2, 178; 16:2, 32, 182; 16:7-8, 179; 16:11-14, 182; 16:15-19, 180; 16:19, 246; 16:20-22, 179; 16:23-24, 180; 16:26, 180; 17-26, 242; 18, 242–43; 18:2-5, 243; 18:20, 243; 18:26-28, 243; 19:2, 126; 19:19, 112; 20:7, 126; 20:26, 126; 21:6, 126; 22:9-11, 112; 23:18, 182, 261; 26:16, 176

Numbers: 7:89, 254; 10:10, 182, 261; 11:16-17, 265; 11:16-30, 55; 13:6, 204; 13:22, 94; 13:26—14:24, 204; 13:28, 94; 13:33, 94; 15:30-31, 249; 15:40, 126; 16:3, 126; 21:31-35, 93; 23:19, 26; 32:12, 204

Deuteronomy: 2:10-11, 94; 3:1-11, 93; 3:11, 93; 4, 83; 4:15-18, 254; 4:19, 80; 4:19-20, 81–82; 4:20, 208; 4:37, 54; 5:6, 17, 54; 5:7-10, 254; 5:8, 80; 9:4-6, 228; 10:12-17, 258; 12:5-21, 59; 14:23-24, 59; 16:1-11, 59; 17:3, 80; 17:17, 132; 21:22-23, 188–89; 24:16, 185; 25:4, 235n1; 26:1-2, 59; 28-30, 231; 28:15-68, 190; 28:21-22, 190; 28:23-24, 190; 29:18, 230; 30:6, 258; 32:6, 202; 32:8, 70–71, 76, 77, 82, 88, 131, 202; 32:9, 208; 32:10, 202; 32:16-17, 92; 32:17, 71, 82, 202; 33:2-3, 126; 34:5-6, 124

Joshua: 3:9-17, 264; 3:15-17, 139; 7-8, 189; 8:29, 189; 11:21-22, 95; 14:6, 204; 14:13-14, 204; 14:14, 204; 21:43-45, 204, 237

Judges: 2:1, 17, 46, 54; 2:1-5, 20; 2:4, 17; 6:11, 16; 6:14, 16; 6:20-21, 16; 6:23, 16; 6:34, 56

1 Samuel (1 Kingdoms): 3:1, 20; 3:7, 20; 3:10, 20; 3:15, 21; 3:21, 21; 10:10, 56; 16:13, 56; 16:14, 56; 16:14-16, 112; 17, 95; 18:10, 112; 19:9, 112; 28:13, 109

Isaiah (*continued*)
28; **19:16-25,** 263; **19:25,** 208;
23:4, 25; **23:27,** 176; **24:21,**
80; **26:14,** 94, 112; **26:17-18,**
25; **27,** 164; **29:6,** 176; **30:27,**
60; **34:4,** 80; **36:11,** 22; **37:31,**
230; **40:3,** 140; **40:3-31,** 140;
41:25, 154; **44,** 160; **45:8,** 230;
45:10, 25; **49:6,** 225; **50:5,** 161;
51:12, 27; **54:1,** 25; **56:3-7,** 225,
241; **58:6-12,** 241; **60:1-3,** 241;
60:10-14, 263; **63:10,** 58; **66:7-
8,** 25; **66:18-23,** 241
Jeremiah: **1:4,** 21; **1:5,** 4, 21; **1:7,**
21; **1:9,** 21; **1:13-15,** 154; **2:13,**
157; **4:4,** 258; **4:6,** 154; **6:22,**
154; **7:13,** 157; **9:26,** 258;
10:16, 208; **10:18,** 208; **10:22,**
154; **13:20,** 154; **15:15,** 176;
17:8, 230; **17:23,** 230; **18:1-12,**
216; **23:3,** 140, 263; **23:18-22,**
137; **27/34:22,** 176; **29/36:10,**
176; **31/38,** 218; **31/38: 31,**
219; **31/38: 32,** 219; **31/38:
33-34,** 219; **31/38:3-6,** 206;
31/38:5-6, 218; **31/38:9,** 218;
31/38:18-20, 218; **31/38:27,**
218; **31/38:30,** 185; **31/38:33,**
9; **31/38:34,** 9; **32/39:5,** 176;
33:22, 80; **46/26:10,** 154, 173;
46/26:20, 154; **50/27:4-5,** 207;
51/28:19, 208
Ezekiel: **1,** 5, 8, 48; **1:26-27,** 32;
8:3, 154; **8:5,** 154; **8:14,** 154;
11:16, 220; **11:24,** 220; **13:5,**
173; **16:4-7,** 202, 222; **17:8,**
230; **18:20,** 185; **20:44,** 57;

23:19, 203; **28,** 68-69, 97,
98; **28:12-14,** 97; **28:12-19,**
76; **28:13-14,** 68; **28:13-16,**
155; **28:16-18,** 100; **28:17-18,**
68-69; **30:3,** 173; **32:30,** 154;
36, 218; **36:1,** 218; **36:4-5,** 218;
36:8, 218; **36:8-9,** 218; **36:8-15,**
218; **36:12-14,** 218; **36:16-17,**
218; **36:19-22,** 218; **36:21-22,**
218; **36:24,** 220; **36:25,** 221;
36:26-32, 9; **36:27-28,** 218,
221; **36:33,** 221; **37:1-14,** 207;
37:15-19, 207; **37:23-24,** 207;
47:1-12, 157; **47:12,** 230
Daniel: **4:35,** 80; **7,** 164-65; **7:9,**
123; **7:9-14,** 78; **7:12,** 27-28;
8:10, 80; **8:17,** 27; **10,** 48; **10:13,**
71; **10:20-21,** 71, 116; **10:21,** 82;
12:1, 82, 116; **12:3,** 82-83
Hosea: **1:10,** 217; **2:23,** 217; **9:16,**
230; **11:1,** 202, 224
Joel: **2,** 55-56; **2:22,** 230; **2:28,** 9;
3:5, 140, 263; **3:17,** 57; **3:18,** 157
Amos: **2:9,** 93; **5:21,** 191
Obadiah: **15,** 174; **17,** 140, 263
Micah: **2:1,** 263; **2:12,** 140; **7:14,**
208; **7:18,** 208
Habbakuk: **2:14,** 156
Zephaniah: **2:13,** 154
Zechariah: **14:3,** 126; **14:16,** 263
Malachi: **3:1,** 138, 140; **3:11,** 230;
4:1-5, 173; **4:5-6,** 138, 140

New Testament
Matthew: **2:6,** 201; **2:20-21,** 201-2;
3:1-3, 140; **3:4,** 138; **3:7-12,**
173; **3:8,** 230; **3:10,** 230; **3:11,**

173; **3:12,** 231; **3:13-17,** 60; **5:17,** 233; **6:9-13,** 184; **6:14-15,** 184; **7:17-19,** 230; **7:19,** 231; **8:10,** 202; **8:29,** 113; **8:32,** 113; **9:33,** 202; **10:6,** 202; **10:23,** 202; **10:25,** 69, 76; **10:28,** 128; **11:7-15,** 138; **11:13-14,** 124; **12:1-12,** 238; **12:24,** 69, 76; **12:27,** 69, 76; **12:31,** 59; **13:23,** 230; **13:41,** 28; **15:11,** 247; **15:24,** 202, 215; **15:31,** 202; **16:27,** 126, 231; **17:10-13,** 138; **17:12-13,** 124; **18:17,** 250; **18:20,** 59; **18:23-35,** 184; **19:28,** 129, 202, 265; **19:30,** 175; **20:16,** 175; **20:28,** 186; **21:25,** 143; **22:30,** 83; **24:30,** 28; **25:14-30,** 231; **25:31,** 28; **25:31-46,** 161; **25:41,** 107; **26:2,** 209; **26:28,** 210; **26:57-68,** 28; **27:24-61,** 192; **27:27-44,** 180; **27:42,** 202; **28:18,** 29, 165, 186–87; **28:18-19,** 128; **28:18-20,** 108; **28:19,** 217; **28:20,** 162

Mark: **1:2-4,** 140; **1:9-11,** 60; **1:23-26,** 112–13; **2:23-28,** 238; **3:1-4,** 238; **3:22,** 69, 76; **3:23-27,** 100; **3:28-29,** 59; **3:30,** 59; **4:20,** 230; **5:7,** 68; **5:10,** 113; **5:13,** 113; **6:45-52,** 39–40; **6:48,** 40; **9:11-13,** 138; **9:13,** 124; **10:31,** 175; **10:45,** 186; **11:30,** 143; **12:25,** 83; **12:26-27,** 147; **13:25,** 80; **14:1,** 209; **14:61-63,** 28–29, 78; **16:15,** 165; **16:19,** 165

Luke: **1:11-17,** 124; **1:13-17,** 138; **1:32,** 68; **1:35,** 68; **1:76,** 68; **1:80,** 136; **2:13,** 80; **2:32-33,** 226; **3:2-6,** 140; **3:8-10,** 230; **3:21-22,** 60; **3:22,** 134; **6:1-9,** 238; **6:43,** 230; **7:29,** 143; **7:36-47,** 184; **8:15,** 230; **8:28,** 68; **8:31,** 113; **8:33,** 113; **10:1-20,** 265; **10:18,** 116–17; **11:4,** 184; **11:15,** 69, 76; **11:18,** 70; **11:18-19,** 76; **11:19,** 70; **13:9,** 230; **13:10-16,** 238; **13:30,** 175; **14:1-5,** 238; **16:25,** 175; **19:8-9,** 175; **19:12-27,** 231; **20:4,** 143; **20:37-38,** 147; **21:24,** 217; **21:27,** 28; **22:1,** 209; **22:19,** 261; **23:43,** 156; **24:50-53,** 165

John: **1:3,** 21, 25; **1:12-13,** 22; **1:12-16,** 48; **1:14,** 22, 33, 157; **1:18,** 25; **1:19-22,** 138; **1:23,** 140; **1:29,** 186, 209; **1:29-34,** 137; **1:33,** 58; **1:34,** 58; **1:36,** 209; **2,** 135; **2:19-21,** 157; **3:13,** 156; **3:16,** 25; **3:19,** 152; **4:5-6,** 140; **4:10-26,** 157; **4:19-24,** 252; **4:22,** 215, 225; **4:36,** 222; **5:1-18,** 238; **5:17,** 156, 161, 239; **5:22,** 187; **5:25-27,** 186; **5:28-29,** 187; **5:53-57,** 250; **6:70,** 216; **7:22-23,** 238; **7:37-38,** 158; **7:39,** 158; **8:19,** 17; **8:44,** 26, 27; **8:56-59,** 38; **9:4,** 161; **9:14-16,** 238; **10:17-18,** 185; **10:22-39,** 17; **10:35-36,** 77; **10:37,** 161; **12:24,** 230; **12:31,** 89, 117; **12:34,** 26; **14:6,** 252; **14:7,** 17; **14:11,** 17; **14:20,** 17; **14:30,** 117;

Subject Index

Note: Discussions of biblical and extracanonical books, along with apostles, evangelists, and prophets, are included in this subject index. References to specific chapters and verses are included in the scripture index.

A

Aaron, 182, 204n2, 256

Abel, 87, 251

Abihu and Nadab, 178, 251

Abraham: circumcision and, 256, 257; death of, 123; God's promise to, 22, 202, 225, 237–38; heir of, 224; Holy Trinity and, 31; management of sin and death, 70, 88; Word of the Lord and, 20

Acts, 89, 109

Adam: Christ as new Adam, 130, 161, 239; Garden of Eden and, 153, 155, 156; and sin and mortality, 25–26, 85, 87, 105, 190, 245; Son of Adam, 26–27

adoptionism, 14–15, 14n1

Ahab (king), 73–74, 120

Akiva (rabbi), 34, 34n8

Anakim, 94–95

Andrew of Caesarea, 82, 114, 117, 118

angelic beings: cherubim, 98, 164, 164n2, 254; in divine council, 73–74; guardian angels, 138–39; heavenly hosts, 66, 80; as holy ones, 125–26; humans, destiny of, and, 82–83, 137; John the Forerunner and, 136–37; nature of, 98, 98n3, 108–9; as patrons of churches, cities, and nations, 82, 88; reality of, 65; seraphim, 98, 120; stars and, 80–82, 99; Torah given by, 121. *See also* dark principalities and powers

angel of death, 114–15

Angel of the Lord, 15–18, 15n2, 58

Anselm of Canterbury: *Cur Deus Homo* ("Why the God-Man?"), 170

Antichrist, 26

apkallu, 91–92, 104–5

Apocalypse of Abraham, 107, 194–95

283

penalties, of the Torah, 248–50

penance, 175

Pentecost, 55–56, 205, 209–10, 218–19, 221, 222

persecution, early Christian, 38n12

Peter (apostle), 46, 56, 77, 106, 186, 241, 245

Peter, First Epistle of, 43, 44, 45–46, 122

Peter, Second Epistle of, 43, 44, 45–46, 122

Pharaoh, 211–12, 216

Pharisees, xiv, 228–29, 238, 240

Philo of Alexandria, 18, 18n3, 19, 54n1, 81–82, 169

Phinehas, 204n2

physical spaces, 246–47

Plato, 71–72, 110, 111, 149–50

Plutarch, 169

polygamy, 132–33

possession, demonic, 110–11

Presence of God, 54–55, 59, 67, 156, 175–77

priesthood. See clerical orders

prophets, 4, 119, 137, 139–40

propitiation, 177–78, 179, 181–83

Proskomedia service, 190

Protestants, 85, 131, 171, 192–93, 233–34, 236, 251, 260, 261

Q

queen mothers, 132–34

Quran, 114

R

Rabbinic Judaism: on Body of God, 30, 30n6, 34; *Merkabah*

("chariot") mysticism and, 5, 5n2; on Messiah, 134n6, 138; on Name of Yahweh, 57; origins and disjunction from Second Temple Judaism, xi–xii, 2, 36, 270–71; rejection of ancient cosmology, 75; on Satan, 116; on Word of the Lord, 23

Rehoboam (king), 205

religion of the apostles: approach to, x–xi, xiii–xv, 10, 269–71; common perceptions of, ix; evolutionary paradigm and, xiii–xiv, 13, 19, 37–38, 74–75, 86; Orthodox Christianity and, ix–x, xv, 271; Second Temple Judaism and, xi–xiii; terminology, xn1. *See also* angelic beings; atonement; Creation; dark principalities and powers; divine council; God and Godhead; Israel; Paradise; saints; salvation; Torah

repentance, 108, 173–74, 177, 192, 249–50

Rephaim, 93–94, 112

restitution, 175

Resurrection of Christ, 60, 83, 90, 100–101, 123

Revelation, 47–49, 67–68, 99, 128

righteousness, 172–73, 175–76, 228, 257

ritual, 190–92

Roman Catholicism, 251, 260

Roman Empire, 110, 111, 188

S

Sabaoth (Lord of Hosts), 66, 80

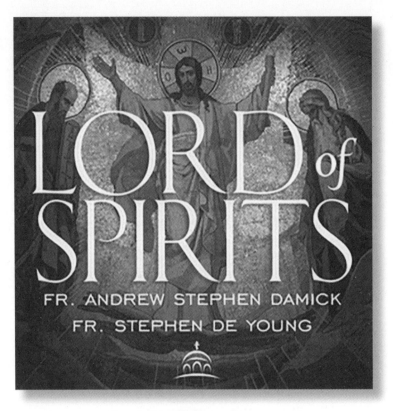

Lord of Spirits

The Seen and Unseen World in Orthodox Christian Tradition

The modern world does not acknowledge but is nevertheless
haunted by spirits—angels, demons, and saints.

Orthodox Christian priests Fr. Andrew Stephen Damick and
Fr. Stephen De Young host this live call-in show focused on
enchantment in creation, the union of the seen and unseen as
made by God and experienced by mankind throughout history.

e edition of this show airs on the second and fourth Thursdays of the
at 7:00 p.m. ET / 4:00 p.m. PT. Tune in at Ancient Faith Radio.

www.ancientfaith.com

The Whole Counsel Blog

The Scriptures in the Orthodox Church

In this blog, Fr. Stephen De Young examines
biblical subjects and themes through the lens of the
Great Tradition of the Orthodox Church.

https://blogs.ancientfaith.com/wholecounsel/

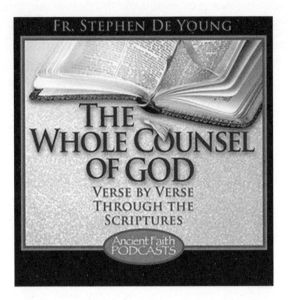

The Whole Counsel of God Podcast

Verse by Verse through the Scriptures

This podcast takes us through the Holy Scriptures in a verse-by-verse
study based on the Great Tradition of the Orthodox Church. These
studies were recorded live at Archangel Gabriel Orthodox Church in
Lafayette, Louisiana, and include questions from his audience.

https://www.ancientfaith.com/podcasts/wholecounsel

Ancient Faith Publishing hopes you have enjoyed and benefited from this book. The proceeds from the sales of our books only partially cover the costs of operating our nonprofit ministry—which includes both the work of **Ancient Faith Publishing** and the work of **Ancient Faith Radio**. Your financial support makes it possible to continue this ministry both in print and online. Donations are tax-deductible and can be made at **www.ancientfaith.com**.

To view our other publications,
please visit our website: **store.ancientfaith.com**

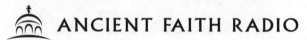

Bringing you Orthodox Christian music, readings, prayers, teaching, and podcasts 24 hours a day since 2004 at **www.ancientfaith.com**